The
Compound

THE COMPOUND

by William Gale

IN COLLABORATION WITH DETECTIVES
Ed O'Rourke and Vito Moles

RAWSON ASSOCIATES PUBLISHERS, INC.
NEW YORK, N.Y.

Library of Congress Cataloging in Publication Data
Gale, William.
    The Compound.
        1. Gangs—New York (City)   2. Violence—New York
(City)   3.   Terrorism—New York (City)   I.   O'Rourke, Ed.
joint author.   II.   Moles, Vito, joint author.
III.   Title.
HV6439.U7N44   1977   364.1'066'0974723   76–53672
ISBN 0–89256–017–7

Published simultaneously in Canada by
McClelland and Stewart, Ltd.
Manufactured in the United States of America
by The Book Press, Brattleboro, Vermont
First Edition

Dedicated to the members of the Bronx Gang Intelligence Unit, past and present—and, with gratitude, to the New York City Police Department and Bronx District Attorney Mario Merola and his staff for their help.

All of the events in this book are essentially true. Names and the sequence of certain events have been altered to protect the rights of privacy of certain individuals.

Contents

The
Compound

1.
Our Savage Youths

This book, a true story, is about what happened when youth gangs seized control of an apartment complex of five once-middle-class buildings, forced the tenants out, and turned it into a gang compound. It took place in New York City's South Bronx in 1971. It could happen today in any American city, for youth gangs—mirror reflections of the gangs in this story—have in just a few years become a national crime problem of the first magnitude. They are *the* news story of the 1970s.

The buildings were constructed in 1923, when the neighborhood was quiet and respectable. The complex was entered by walking up a broad stoop, which led into a courtyard, around which the five buildings fanned; in the center of the courtyard was a giant flower bed. On the street level, there were attractive shops and a storefront synagogue. In mild weather the tenants would sit on the benches in the tidy, triangular Hayes Square Park, directly across the street.

During the war years of the forties, the flower bed was converted to a victory garden, and practically every window of the complex displayed a small American flag. But by the 1950s the neighborhood had begun to deteriorate. The fence around the flower bed was constantly being broken—repaired, it was broken again—and the flowers were trampled or ripped out of the soil. The flower bed eventually disappeared under a layer of cement. Youth gangs formed, and there were street fights between rival gangs. By 1960 the stonefront synagogue had vacated the premises, unable to meet the rent because so many of its members were moving away. And despite the fact that the sixties saw the virtual demise of the gangs—drug addiction and army conscription had depleted their ranks—the neighborhood just didn't seem safe any more. As conditions worsened, old-timers still living in the apartment complex seldom went out after dark. By the late sixties, few drove their cars even in the daytime. Too often when you stopped for a red light, small boys with hammers would run over and threaten to smash your windshield if you didn't give them money. And soon there was talk of street gangs roaming the neighborhood again. Gangs much more violent than the earlier ones—but then our society was much more violent too.

A man who had come to repair the oil burner in one of the buildings was so intimidated by the sight of the youths lounging in the tiny park across the street that he insisted that the landlord provide him with three security men. That same week, early in 1970, the grocer, who had been doing business for years in a store on the street level of the complex, suddenly moved out. The youths hanging out in the park across the street had been making it a daily ritual to walk into the store, take what cans they wanted off the shelves, and walk out with them. One year later, now wearing gang colors, they began a systematic takeover of the five buildings across the street from the once-peaceful park they had already usurped.

The Mongols, an extremely violent gang, moved into the basement of one of the buildings. The leaders of the gang had convinced the janitor that their presence would be to his best interests. Their clubhouse on the premises would *guarantee* that he would have no trouble with the other gangs that had begun terrorizing the neighborhood. He remained silent. He knew if you were foolish enough to try to evict a gang, it was only a matter of time before the building burned. And furthermore, the tenants had no idea the gang had moved in; the entrance to the basement was not through the courtyard but through a rear alley. It wasn't long before the alley was scarred with graffiti and littered with debris.

A heated clubhouse is a status symbol, and so the membership of the Mongols began to multiply. And a little later, when a fire reduced the clubhouse of the Seven Immortals to charred rubble, this gang moved into another area of the basement. In a matter of weeks, well over a hundred gang members were living in the basement of one of the buildings in the complex on Bryant Avenue. This meant cramped quarters, but the gangs had a simple solution to the problem of overcrowding: They began terrorizing the tenants. Soon it wasn't uncommon for a tenant to come home to find the door to his apartment off its hinges and the furniture inside smashed. As the terrified tenants moved out, the gangs moved out of the basement and into the vacant apartments upstairs—rent-free. The landlord was powerless to stop them.

Not long afterward, the Savage Nomads—one of the two most powerful gangs in the Bronx—moved into another one of the buildings. And now in the evenings, with the sound of stereos and bongo drums ripping through the air, the gangs overflowed into the park across the street, which they renamed Nomad Park, painting the park house and benches with their gang colors. Tenants and shopkeepers, meanwhile, continued to move out as fires and robberies within the five buildings became more and more frequent.

The Storm Troopers and their hundred-odd members were the next to move in, and soon after them came the Latin Diplomats. Now every apartment in the five buildings was occupied. About seven hundred gang members and assorted "wives" were in residence. In less than six months, the apartment complex had become a gang fortress, the broad stoop its bridge and the courtyard its moat. No one entered without permission of the gangs there— except, of course, the police, the hated "bluecoats," who conducted periodic raids.

The buildings, once beautifully cared for, began to decay. Windowpanes were knocked out, their glass adding to the rubble that began piling up in the courtyard. Soon one window and only one window in the five buildings still had a curtain, a kitchen curtain left behind by a tenant, which fluttered like a tattered flag between the few jagged pieces of glass still sticking to the wooden frame. Before the gangs would abandon the complex, two years later, four murders, two shootings, and countless beatings would take place there.

Meanwhile, new street gangs were mushrooming all over the South Bronx during 1971. Six new ones emerged within a matter of days. And carloads of guns were finding their way into their hands. Unlike the gangs of the 1950s, with their homemade zip guns, these had automatic rifles, shotguns, and finely tooled pistols.

To deal with the fierce problem of these gangs, the city's first Gang Intelligence Unit began functioning in the borough of the Bronx on December 14, 1971. A memo headed "Formation of Youth Gang Intelligence Unit" stated that the prime duty of this new program of the New York City Police Department was to develop close rapport with gang leadership and in that way "gather all information and intelligence relative to youth gangs and their activities." The list of qualifications for a Gang Intelligence officer consisted of seventeen points, chief among them the ability to relate to youths. Ed O'Rourke and Vito Moles, who collaborated with me on this book, were two of six men handpicked to join the new unit. They became almost daily visitors to the gang compound on Bryant Avenue. Their weekly reports began containing so many references to the five buildings there that they started referring to it simply as "The Compound." The name took, and soon the gangs living there were calling it that too.

O'Rourke and Moles continue to maintain close rapport with the youth gangs in their borough, but it is certainly difficult for the rest of us to identify with these savage youths, who often seem not fully human. Yet we had better try, for their numbers are multiplying, their influence increasing. Today the "brothers" of the gangs you will read about in this book infect every major American city, cannibalizing our society. The problem is so vast, say experts in the field of crime prevention, that the police and the courts are helpless without the support of every local community. "If we don't do something now, we're going to have a cataclysmic blowup in ten years" is the way one expert put it to me. According to the findings of a federally-financed twelve-city study published in 1976 by the U.S. Department of Justice, youth gangs constitute a national problem of "the utmost severity."

For this study—the first attempt ever made to compile a national-level picture of youth-gang problems based on actual visits to gang locales—teams of investigators led by Dr. Walter B. Miller, a criminologist with the Harvard Law School, went into twelve of our largest cities: New York, Los Angeles, Philadelphia, Houston, Detroit, Baltimore, Washington, Cleveland, Chicago, San Francisco, St.

Louis, and New Orleans, whose metropolitan populations of approximately 55 million comprise about 40 per cent of the total population of all United States metropolitan areas. On the hypothesis that the larger the city, the more likely the existence of gang problems, the main criterion for selection of cities was population size. Information during the initial phase of the survey also indicated moderate-to-severe gang problems in at least fifteen other major cities, including Buffalo, Boston, Denver, Newark, Milwaukee, and Pittsburgh. And while figures on gangs and gang members in major cities are inexact, available data permit conservative estimates ranging from a minimum of 760 gangs with 28,500 members in the six cities reporting serious gang problems (New York, Los Angeles, Chicago, Philadelphia, Detroit, San Francisco) to perhaps as many as 2,700 gangs with 81,500 members. Subsequent analysis indicated that the size of the *metropolitan area* showed an even more direct relationship to gang activity than the size of the municipal city itself.

What Dr. Miller found was that the size and scope of the gang problem were "far beyond any expectations." Violence perpetuated by members of organized youth gangs was discovered to be more lethal than at any time in our history—mainly because of the extraordinary increase in the availability and use of firearms—and the gangs' impact on the crime problems in their cities was far greater than their numbers would indicate, leading Dr. Miller to conclude that the nation's youth-gang problem shows "little prospect of early abatement."

It is not an optimistic picture. While youth gangs are not new to the American scene, the gangs of the seventies are more violent and more sophisticated than any in our past. Ours is a violent society, and the fury of the youth gangs, combined with their arsenals of weapons, poses a much greater threat to the public order and greater danger to us and our children than ever before. Among the findings contained in Dr. Miller's 216-page report:

• Social characteristics of today's gang members resemble those reported for past periods. The gangs originate in low-income communities, and are composed primarily of members of those ethnic groups most heavily represented in the lower educational and occupational categories.

• These ethnic groups are, by and large, the most recently migrated groups: blacks (south to north, rural to urban, or both); Hispanic (Puerto Rico, Mexico, Cuba); Asian (Hong Kong, Philippine Islands). About four-fifths of gang members are either black or Hispanic. The rise of Hispanic gangs to over one-third of the estimated totals, and their presence in each of the six largest cities, represents a new development. The rise in numbers of Asian gangs (newly-immigrated Hong Kong Chinese, for example, and, in several cities, gangs of Filipinos, Japanese, and other Asians) represents an even more marked departure from the past.

• The bulk of youth-gang members in the largest American cities are approximately ten to twenty-one years of age, but in such cities as Chicago and Philadelphia a number of gang members are as young as eight years of age.

• While New York City is estimated to have the highest gang population (eight thousand verified members and twenty thousand alleged ones), figures adjusted for population size show the highest proportion in Philadelphia, with approximately sixty gang members per thousand male youths aged ten to nineteen.

• The use of firearms as an instrument of gang violence is perhaps the single most significant feature of today's gang activity in evaluating the seriousness of gang activity as a crime problem. The majority of guns used are at the level of high-quality police weapons.

· The incidence of property destruction by gang members also appears to be on the rise: extensive vandalism of schools, parks, and other public facilities, and the destruction of buildings through arson.

· Today's gangs are operating *within* as well as outside many of the schools in our major cities, affecting not only the education of students but the physical safety of both students and teachers. All six of the largest cities reported gangs operating in elementary, junior high, and senior high schools.

According to Dr. Miller, at the outset of his study the importance of the schools as an arena of gang activity was not clearly established. (This surprised me, because I tend to see a school with a number of youth-gang members among the student body as a derivation of The Compound —gangs under a communal roof—but the school, unlike The Compound, even provides the gangs with targets for their violence: other students, teachers, and school personnel. I can't imagine a school in a gang-problem city not being an arena of gang activity.) Before long the survey's investigators found that when a metropolitan area had serious gang problems, those problems were very much in evidence in the schools. This was not the case in the past, when schools were generally considered neutral territory by rival gangs. Schools in today's gang-problem cities reported gang assaults and shootings inside the school (cafeterias, auditoriums, and other internal locations) and outside in playgrounds and environs. The following statements were taken from respondents connected with schools that were considered major arenas for gang activity in their cities:

· New York: "The schools of this city have sold out to the gangs. A major development here is the intent by gangs to gain control of the schools, their intimidation of school personnel, and their extortion of children on a large scale. The gangs have browbeaten the school administrators. They have been bought off by being permitted to use the schools as recruiting grounds."

• Chicago: "The schools have become an arena of expression for the gangs; high schools in some districts have become houses for the gangs, and students are being victimized through extortion; gangs recruit openly in school areas."

• Los Angeles: "The gang situation in all the schools is frantic. Of the inner-city schools, *all* of them have large gang populations within the schools. Gangs have completely taken over individual classrooms, and would have taken over whole schools if police had not intervened. Once the number of gang members in a class reaches a certain level, the teacher is powerless to enforce discipline."

• Philadelphia: "The schools in this city are citadels of fear; there is gang fighting in the halls; there is no alternative but to set up safety zones where fighting will be prevented through force. There is no point in trying to exaggerate the situation; the truth by itself is devastating."

• Detroit: "The gang problem here is serious—especially around the schools; every member of these gangs is involved in all sorts of crimes, from larceny through murder. Gangs are active both inside and outside the schools. The police have been meeting continuously with school and community people, and at every meeting they come up with a new name for a new gang."

• San Francisco: "There has been fighting between black and white, and black and Chinese gangs in several high schools—thus far on a relatively small scale. But if they move ahead with plans to integrate the high schools, the gang conflict will make what is happening now look like a picnic!"

The shooting and killing of teachers by gang members was reported in Chicago and Philadelphia, and of non-gang students in Chicago and Los Angeles. One high school in Los Angeles reportedly contained ten different gangs. This city also reported the following spectacular instance of property destruction: After $1,500,000 was put into the complete modernization of a city high school in 1974, gang members broke into the school and "completely demolished everything." That same year the chairman of the County Board of Supervisors (the governing body of Los Angeles County) stated: "Gang violence in Los Angeles is close to an epidemic stage."

Seven different gangs were reported to be in attendance at one junior high school in the Germantown section of Philadelphia. And in this City of Brotherly Love several major high schools were forced to close their cafeterias because gangs had claimed the right to control access, seating, and other arrangements.

The four largest cities reported gangs collecting fees from other students for passage through hallways as well as for permission to enter and remain in school buildings. One Detroit respondent wrote: "On a scale of 10, I would rate the seriousness of gang problems in the schools at 11!"

The intimidation of teachers and other school personnel was reported for New York, Chicago, and Los Angeles. The major form of intimidation was said to be threats by gang members that the teacher would be beaten or killed if he or she reported violations of school regulations by gang members, or appeared as a witness in court proceedings against gang members.

In the final pages of the Justice Department study, 87 per cent—almost nine out of ten—of the respondents in the six largest gang-problem cities declared that they felt that gang problems in their city would *not* improve during the next several years—a chilling prospect particularly in view of the fact that the survey notes as a "definite trend" attacks by the gangs on community residents, including children; as a consequence, "the security of a wider sector of the citizenry is threatened by gangs to a greater degree than ever before."

The curve of violent, often senseless crimes by street gangs continues to rise, even as the percentage of juveniles in the general population decreases. Why? In October, 1976, the National Urban League sponsored a two-day conference in its New York City headquarters devoted to this growing problem of gang violence, and the participants —present and former gang members from California, Florida, Pennsylvania, and New York—were in total agreement that gang activities are the result of underemployment, oppression, idleness, and despair—conditions prevalent today in every large American city. And so our disadvantaged youth moves through it all like a nomad, feeling powerless, his emotions frozen, until the day he joins a gang and fits in, like a piece in a jigsaw puzzle—and suddenly all those pieces form one carnivorous ego that now demands recognition and, most important, *respect*. All at once, arrogance and violence are seamlessly joined. And as a gang member, he now maintains little connection with anyone or anything except other members of his gang, which has become his family, his social life, his identity, his whole reason for being. The world outside? It's the enemy.

Clarence M. Kelley, Director of the Federal Bureau of Investigation, stated in November, 1976, his conviction that the most desirable approach to juvenile criminality is one of prevention, and that "efforts should be made to establish and maintain positive contact with teenaged groups, particularly youth gangs." The Gang Intelligence Unit of the New York City Police Department has been doing that since December, 1971, and similar units function in most major cities throughout the country.

When Ed O'Rourke and Vito Moles joined their unit it was housed in two small rooms on the second floor of the Fortieth Precinct house in the South Bronx (where it still is). Both men already had had experience working the streets there in civilian clothes as members of the Police Department's Youth Aid Division. Now, as members of the Gang Intelligence Unit—a streamlined squad of the Division, so to speak—they would still wear civilian clothes, but they would drive their own private cars instead of unmarked police cars. And while they would carry .38-caliber revolvers, they were not to make arrests but instead were to pass on what they learned about the gangs to arresting officers.

When the new unit took to the streets, conditions in the South Bronx were deplorable—much like those in the ghettos of the key gang-problem cities of Dr. Miller's report. This area, approximately fifteen square miles, which had once been a respectable community of middle-class whites, was now being described by *The New York Times* as "a city of death," "an urban purgatory," "a small crime-ridden nation," "a huge dungeon of despair," "the real cancer of our society." Approximately 40 per cent of the families were on welfare. There was an alarming incidence of tuberculosis there; with new TB cases averaging 52.5 per cent for every 100,000 residents as compared to a city average of 32.6 per cent. The South Bronx contained 25 per cent of the reported cases of malnutrition in the city. The statistics were grim, and the omens sad. Once-pleasant streets were disfigured by burnt-out, graffiti-splattered buildings, many of which had been abandoned by their owners. Empty lots were heaped with garbage scavenged by packs of wild dogs. The sole remnants of the area's ethnic past were a synagogue, whose membership was so depleted that it could no longer muster the ten men necessary for a minyan, and an open-air marketplace located on what had become the turf of one of the most violent gangs in the city. Violence of the vilest sort had become an almost daily occurrence in the South Bronx.

Vito Moles, then in his late twenties, a dark-haired, burly man with a luxurious moustache, was readily accepted by members of the gangs, most of whom were Puerto Rican. They were slower to accept the slender, red-haired O'Rourke, but eventually he became affectionately known as "Pelo Rojo": The Redhead. In a very short time, the two young men became part of what O'Rourke calls the "moonscape" of the South Bronx. One day driving O'Rourke's car, a '65 Plymouth, and the next Moles's '70 Volkswagen, they would tour the borough, where there were already over one hundred youth gangs. From time to time they would park near a gang clubhouse. Sometimes, if they knew the gang, they would visit inside. Other times they would sit in their car and wait for the gang to approach them. They never wore uniforms, and the gang members, so wary of the "bluecoats," would come over to the car, pile into the back seat, and rap for an hour or two. Why did they talk so freely? They knew the two men were police. In fact, while working with the Youth Aid Division, O'Rourke and Moles had even arrested some of them.

O'Rourke: "They realized that getting arrested for something they did was all part of the game. They didn't hold a grudge against us. Our lines of communication stayed open. They'd bitch and moan about the bluecoats and what they'd done to them, but they didn't associate us with the bluecoats. They'd never seen us in a uniform. They just never seemed to put two and two together and figure out who was bringing them this bad luck. A member seized for murder. Weapons taken in a clubhouse raid. Most of it came from Gang Intelligence. But they never stopped talking to Vito and me. I'm still amazed they never sat down and put it all together, but they never did."

Moles: "We told them—right from the start—that we don't make arrests. That our job was to prevent gang fights. We never told them what we were really doing—keeping tabs on them."

O'Rourke: "They never knew that we were building such extensive records on them, that we were keeping photo files and records of their street names. They may be mean, but they still have the kid mentality. No matter how you cut it, most of them are only fifteen or sixteen years old. And they love for the Establishment—Vito and me—to come and sit and talk with them."

Moles: "We gave them the recognition they wanted . . ."

O'Rourke: "And we played on this. Every time there was an arrest, we used to go to a precinct and Vito would use the Polaroid camera. We'd stand right up and take the picture and they accepted this . . ."

Moles: "Because they knew they were getting recognition. Some gangs that we never even knew would let us take their pictures. They thought we were from the *Daily News.* We didn't tell them that—they assumed it. And another way we built up their confidence in us: We never lied to them. We found out you can't lie to them. If you lie, or promise them something and don't live up to your promise, they'll never tell you anything again, or even talk to you. They cut you right off."

O'Rourke: "That's right. You have to fulfill your promises to them."

Moles: "We got the reputation for being O.K. dudes— cool cops. So when a new gang would mushroom, we'd drive over and pay them a visit. We'd introduce ourselves and then invite them to check us out with the leaders of some of the heavy gangs. And invariably when we went back a couple of days later, they had checked us out and the ice was broken. The rest came easy. These kids have big egos, and having two cops come out to see them really gave them status."

The elitists—the gangs in The Compound—were no exception. Moles and Pelo Rojo were always welcome.

O'Rourke: "We'd park outside, and if we saw kids hanging around the courtyard, we'd talk to them there. Nothing heavy. Then maybe we'd see one of them hanging out a window and we'd say, 'We're coming up. We'll be up in a couple of minutes.' It was always very casual."

Moles: "We never just ran inside. We'd always stop at the stoop or in the courtyard first. Upstairs, we'd knock on the door and announce ourselves. They appreciated that touch of formality—it showed respect. Once inside, we'd squat on the floor or on a mattress and rap with the boys while the girls danced together to the Latin music that was almost always playing on the stereo."

O'Rourke: "It was a game, and we were good at it. We never asked a direct question. We'd always work around what we wanted to know. And we'd never write anything down—that would've really turned them off."

Moles: "The girls were full of information, but they didn't talk much inside The Compound. They preferred to visit with us when we were parked outside. They'd come over to the car, arms linked, and start telling us about the happiness or the trouble they were having with their 'husbands.' "

O'Rourke: "The girls loved to talk. They especially liked Vito's thick black hair. And they were always full of questions about our personal lives. Were we married? How many kids? Where did we live? Did we like being married?

And they loved to look at the snapshots of our families that we carried in our wallets. They seemed pathetically eager to know what family life was like outside the ghetto."

By the time I began researching this book, the gangs had long since deserted The Compound, leaving behind the shells of five buildings. But Ed O'Rourke and Vito Moles were still very much a part of the moonscape of the South Bronx. They had been made detectives in 1973, a few months after The Compound was abandoned—the first officers in the Gang Intelligence Unit to be promoted. Between them they had been awarded nineteen medals for meritorious service, and they had yet to fire their guns while on duty. The gangs know them and like them. And watching them at work is like watching a team of skilled actors performing. Perfect teamwork. O'Rourke, the more talkative, is always ready with a smile that crinkles his eyes. He's the MC who warms up the live audience before the television cameras start rolling. Moles is always more serious, sometimes even seeming a trifle shy. They listen to the kids and pass no judgment on what they hear. Nothing appears to shock or surprise them. They have suspended judgment. They're easily amused, and that appears to encourage the kids to keep talking. There are some, I know, they don't like, don't trust. "He's the type of guy who'd blow you away, then spit on you," says O'Rourke as Mr. Clean takes off down the street after a jovial conversation. There is no way of knowing what he thinks of O'Rourke and Moles. He may hate them, but that doesn't stop him from coming over to talk and have his ego nourished.

My collaborators, my guides through the gang-infested South Bronx, made it a point to drive me up the Bruckner Expressway, which, in the words of O'Rourke, "leads to all your elite communities north of the city. That's all those people see of the South Bronx—the tops of the burnt-out buildings. They never see the streets. The picture they get is that it's another tenement community, which is false because they don't see anybody who's living in it. If you ask them if they've heard of the South Bronx they say yes . . . they know it's terrible . . . but they really don't know what the conditions there are. Furthermore, they don't give a damn. They can stay on this elevated expressway right through the whole area until they're home in the suburbs or in their offices downtown."

But I had come to the South Bronx to prepare a book about the youths there, who, like their counterparts in cities across the country, must be the most hated and feared in our history. Kids obsessed with fantasies of power, who wear their gang colors and strut like members of Hitler Youth in the 1930s. What self-styled revolutionary wouldn't like to get his hands on them? How ripe they are for exploitation. That's a fear of law-enforcement agencies in all gang-problem cities—that the gangs may be infiltrated by terrorists who will train them and use them. And I wanted to know more about them because you and I are sharing the world with them, whether we ever get off the Bruckner Expressways of our cities or not.

So I got off the Bruckner Expressway in the Bronx, and for the next several months I saw a lot more than the tops of burnt-out buildings. In the process I filled up dozens of notebooks and scores of tapes with an assortment of facts, opinions, and arguments.

I wondered why New York's youth gangs had reemerged in the South Bronx. Harlem was wretchedly poor. So was Brooklyn's Bedford-Stuyvesant neighborhood. Why the South Bronx? The answer O'Rourke and Moles gave me could apply to any one of the other gang-problem cities in America: Gangs are always spawned in the poorest pockets of a city and then fan out to other impoverished areas. And in 1970 the Puerto Rican community in the South Bronx was totally lost. The price of oil had begun to skyrocket, and landlords began abandoning their buildings. Jobs were getting scarcer as the country began to slide into a period of recession. And who was going to hire a Puerto Rican who couldn't speak English?

As Dr. Miller's study shows, the recently migrated minority groups feel the pinch first and most severely. As Ed O'Rourke says, for the Puerto Ricans of the South Bronx "everything seems to break down when they get off the plane at La Guardia Airport." Instantly thrown into another culture, they can't cope. So they cling together, and you have a teeming neighborhood with thousands of kids between the ages of ten and twenty. And, says O'Rourke, "By the time a kid in the South Bronx reaches twelve or thirteen—he's not stupid—he knows he's going nowhere. You can't really pin it down, but you'd have to say that the spark just happened to set in the South Bronx. Extreme poverty. No father figure in many homes. Conditions in 1970 and '71 were ripe for trouble, and when it started it went like fire."

"While it's hell here, it's worse in Puerto Rico," says Moles. "We often say to them, 'Why don't you get on that plane and get back where it's warm?' They shrug their shoulders. They don't have an answer, but they're not going back. The money is here. The welfare. There are no jobs back in Puerto Rico. So they stay here, but they don't adapt to life in the city. The parents can't give their kids any direction, and so the kids turn to a gang to give them leadership, a sense of belonging."

Again and again I was struck with the apparent inability of the gang members to leave the South Bronx—even to escape to, say, Brooklyn or Manhattan when they're wanted by the police. I thought of two gang members recently picked up by the police while playing basketball in the street. They knew they'd be gotten, either by the police or by the bullets of a rival gang, but still they stayed in the neighborhood. It's as though they had psychic paralysis. O'Rourke liked that term: *psychic paralysis*. "That's a good way of putting it," he told me one day as we sat parked outside The Compound, its windows covered with sheets of tin. "Everything outside the South Bronx is foreign soil, enemy territory. The kids, like the adults, see it as an island surrounded by shark-infested waters. So they can't leave—not even when they're wanted in connection with a murder. We know that. We know that the kid'll stay clear of his gang's clubhouse but he'll stay in the neighborhood. It's not uncommon to pick a kid up in the street no more than a block away from where the murder was committed. We've sometimes asked him why he didn't run away, and all he says is 'Oh man, I can't leave the neighborhood . . .' "

I looked up at The Compound, where some seven hundred kids once lived and where four murders took place; now there wasn't so much as the sound of a leaf or a piece of paper being chased through the courtyard by the wind. Why had The Compound been so important to the gangs? Moles seemed to find the question naive.

"Security—security in numbers," he said. "There were five gangs all under one roof. Five gangs that all got along. And it was built on a slope, so from the windows up there they could see all over and see any trouble that might be heading their way. It was home. They felt secure. And if they had any fears, they could visit another clubhouse downstairs or next door and see the same things going on. They almost all had their doubts about belonging to a gang. Not the hard-core members, but the kids on the edge. Periphery members, we call them. They wouldn't start out being really bad kids, but when you get fifteen to twenty kids together and each guy tries to prove himself better than the rest—well, what they do then is unreal." Moles poked at the pair of gilded baby shoes hanging from the rear-view mirror of his car and came to this conclusion: "You might say they have the normal competition of any healthy kid, but the healthy kid acts it out on, say, the athletic field." That idea pleased him, and he grinned. "But these kids act it out within the structure of the gang. They start to compete to see who'll do the most violence . . ."

I bent my head and stole another look up at The Compound. I'd seen buildings in better condition after a bomb attack. Why, if The Compound was so important to them, had they destroyed it? Moles shrugged. He's a big man, and when he shrugs, it's an eloquent shrug. "They're like that," he said. "They destroy everything. They self-destruct. And they don't feel they're destroying their property. They're destroying the Establishment."

O'Rourke took it from there. "The Compound wasn't theirs. They took it from the Establishment . . . used it . . . destroyed it. But here's a funny thing: They never destroy what they see as their own. No gang in The Compound ever broke its stereo. They won't break their equipment. *Never*. But that building and anything that had to do with it was something else. They had electricity and gas for months without paying. They were raping Con Edison. They were ripping off *everybody*, but they weren't ripping off themselves."

"They destroyed The Compound because it wasn't theirs to begin with," Moles concluded.

And so I got to know the South Bronx and, through O'Rourke and Moles, some of the gangs seemingly intent on destroying it. I discovered, among other things, that it has some very special sounds unlike any I have ever heard anywhere else. Some are raucously happy, like those peppering a busy slice of Southern Boulevard on a Saturday night: men and women, walking out of the bodegas with the one-dollar, six-foot stalks of sugar cane balanced on their shoulders, shouting to be heard above the music blaring from the record stores and bars on both sides of the street. Some, like the sound of glass crunching beneath your shoes as you walk down a block of abandoned, burnt-out buildings, are cold and utterly lifeless. And others are eerie, like the hollow sounds of little children somewhere off in the distance, shouting and laughing amid the rubble of an empty lot. That, I think, is what Ed O'Rourke means when he refers to the moonscape of the South Bronx.

There were times when I felt compassion, and times when I found myself hating, as I did when I heard of the Black Cats gang, whose initiation rites included the mugging of a nun from the Mount Carmel parish. And so often I felt sickened by the display of so much human waste.

• A gang leader boasted of having ordered the torture death of a retarded youth who dared go to court to testify against him.

• A mother who really cared managed to move her family out of the South Bronx, only to have her madonna-faced fourteen-year-old steal back because she wanted to become pregnant by her man, a nineteen-year-old heroin addict.

• A picture in the files of Gang Intelligence showed a dead thirteen-year-old black with a large cavity in his chest. A gang had tried to gouge out his heart with a broken pop bottle, but failed when his heart got caught in his rib cage.

• A sixteen-year-old, who had spoken to me at length about wanting to help his community, punished a thirteen-year-old member of his gang by burning down his house. Six people from the same family perished in the blaze.

There were times when I felt fear at the sight of a group of small boys walking toward me with sticks in their hands.

And times when I felt my emotions numbed. When I could feel nothing at all. That's when I would take a sabbatical.

The dizzying complexities of the problem of America's youth gangs defy easy simplification. Certainly there is no easy solution. Ed O'Rourke and Vito Moles don't claim to have a solution, other than to say that it's a total community problem and the police and the courts of our cities can't solve it alone. They believe that few gang members can be rehabilitated, for by the time a boy or girl has joined a gang, the decay of youth has already begun.

I think that any effective anti-gang program will have to be a psychologically sanitizing campaign aimed at reaching the pre-teen youngster and his parents. Ideally, such a program would envelop the child, immunizing him against his environment. It would insure him a school where he would learn, feel important, and be subject to a fair amount of discipline. And it would also affect his home life, activating his parents to take a real interest in the life their youngster is leading outside the home; parents who do not speak English would be urged to learn, in order to better understand the city in which they live and take part in the way it is run. In short, such a program would help them shape a new, positive attitude compatible with survival in an urban community. For no matter how much our schools improve, unless the youngster's home life improves as well, I don't believe real progress is possible. The child who has no one at home who seems to know or care what's happening in his life feels dislocated, and will inevitably take to the street and gravitate toward the gang as a substitute for family.

While this book tells the story of The Compound and the gangs living in and around it, it is really the story of this whole subculture of violence. The gangs of the South

Bronx have their counterparts in cities throughout this nation, and never before or since The Compound has there been such a concentration of youth gangs under a communal roof. It was as though this subculture had been put under a giant microscope. So as this book takes you back inside The Compound for an in-depth, often painfully personal look at youth who "think savage," you will see in them a reflection of all the gangs now ravaging our cities.

2.
Murder in the Shooting Gallery

Christmas is practically nonexistent in the South Bronx. And so, although it was but three days after Christmas, there was nothing of the post-holiday euphoria that lay over most of the city. Still, The Compound had had a Christmas tree. It had been stolen from one of the few vendors who stocked trees and dragged upstairs into one of the clubhouses, where it promptly caught fire and was flung out the window—falling like a dive bomber shooting flames—into the courtyard below. Now it lay there on top of three feet of rubbish. That was the extent of the holiday spirit inside The Compound during Christmas of '71.

Now the sidewalk outside was teeming with gang members, and the cold night air was steamy with the threats they were spitting out against the junkies who had attacked their brothers. It was obvious to Officers O'Rourke and Moles, who sat parked across the street, that the Nellie Gomez incident of the night before was threatening to explode into a full-scale debacle. The Gang Intelligence Unit wasn't even a month old, and this was the first real confrontation with the gangs en masse. Not surprisingly, it had to do with the drug problem in the area. The gangs hated the junkies and the pushers. Leave a clubhouse unattended and sure as hell a junkie'd break in and steal anything that wasn't nailed down. Furthermore, nothing could weaken a gang faster than to have a couple of the brothers start shooting up. And Nellie Gomez was a junkie. A no-good junkie whore.

Everybody knew Nellie. She was a neighborhood girl. Some of the kids used to shoot up with her. But now she was the enemy in the gangs' on-again, off-again war on drugs, which would flare up one week and peter out the next. Right now it was *very* hot. The night before, two of the Savage Nomads had burst into a lunchroom on the corner of Westchester Avenue and Southern Boulevard, where junkies, prostitutes, and pimps were sitting elbow to elbow at the counter, and delivered an ultimatum to Nellie: "Get off the block in seventy-two hours!" Two of the dudes with her had messed them up.

Frank Magilla had exploded off his stool and landed the first punch. Then, right after him, came Nellie's man, Antonio Rivera, who attacked the other kid. The four of them tumbled out the door onto the sidewalk, where the two men began to stomp the kids, who were rolling around on the pavement, trying to stay clear of their feet. Then Nellie saw the knife in Frank's hand as it sliced through the air and down into the arm of one of the kids, just as another Nomad came running up. As Magilla and Rivera went back inside, he helped his two brothers to their feet, hailed a gypsy cab, and took them to the emergency room of Lincoln Hospital. Nellie Gomez stood up, slung the strap of her handbag over her shoulder, and, clinging unsteadily to Rivera's arm, followed Frank Magilla outside and in the direction of Aldus Street, which was only a few blocks away.

Now, exactly twenty-four hours later, the Savage Nomads wanted revenge. And the Mongols and the Seven Immortals were backing them up. The Compound—their headquarters —was empty except for some of the wives, who were leaning out the windows looking down on the crowd, which was rapidly growing denser and meaner.

O'Rourke and Moles got out of their car, went across the street, and started weaving through the crowd, talking to the kids and suggesting a meeting at the headquarters of SERA (Services, Education, Rehabilitation for Addiction), a federally-funded sleep-in drug center, a couple of blocks away. Finally the leaders disengaged themselves from the crowd and began moving down the street toward the meeting place. O'Rourke and Moles got word back to their precinct house of the impromptu meeting about to take place and then headed straight for SERA. By the time the gangs were grouping themselves in a circle in the basement there, four police officers had joined O'Rourke and Moles.

One by one the leaders present stood up and spoke: Hubert (Black Bongo) Simpson for the Savage Nomads; Joey (Lucky) Santiago for the Mongols; Jose (Skat) Vega for the Seven Immortals; Renaldo (King Cobra) Cruz for the Storm Troopers; Juan (Dice) Casilla for the Latin Diplomats. Each spoke of the trouble that the junkies were causing in the neighborhood. "I was a junkie myself once, and now it's over," said Mr. High. "But these junkies, they don't want to straighten up, and so we got to get them off the blocks. *Now!*"

Combat boots stomped the floor. Right on! The gangs weren't going to be pacified. No way. They weren't buying the idea that the police couldn't go out and lock up fuckin' junkies just because they were junkies. We don't arrest gang members, said one of the police officers, just because they're gang members. But the kids shouted him down. *Bullshit.* They demanded *action.* Yet when they were asked if they could identify the men who had attacked the two Savage Nomads the night before, they sat silent. That was gang business. It had been a loss of face for the Nomads, and they'd settle the score themselves. But now it was war on all junkies in the neighborhood, and the gangs threatened to take matters into their own hands if the cops didn't take action and lock them up.

After two hours the meeting, which had been getting more and more unruly, almost collapsed completely. The police suggested that the next day another meeting be held, with neighborhood businessmen and SERA representatives, to sit down and try to work out the problem. *Bullshit.* The gangs saw that as nothing more than a diversionary tactic. Some of the kids jumped to their feet and stormed toward the door, but when their leaders stayed as they were in the center of the circle, they came back and lounged sullenly against the wall.

One hour later, after more discussion, they delivered their ultimatum: They were giving the police seventy-two hours to clean up the junkies. Or else. Meanwhile, they pledged, they would stay cool.

But, as it turned out, while hard-core members—the leaders and their Gestapo Squads—were attending the meeting at SERA, another meeting sparked by the outrage —this one attended by some hundred and fifty other No-mads, the balance of the gang's South Bronx division—had been taking place inside The Compound. When the leaders returned from SERA, they found the others shouting for revenge. They were determined to find Nellie Gomez and her two guys and punish them. They wouldn't hear of a truce. Some of the Seven Immortals joined them, and now there was no stopping them. Of course, Black Bongo, prez of the Nomads and the most powerful leader in The Com-pound, could have, but he figured, why should he? You couldn't count on those fuckin' cops to do their job; best do it yourself. So when one of the Nomads grabbed a .32, he said nothing. A few minutes later, a mixed gang of Nomads and Immortals raced out of The Compound and into the street.

Within the hour they located a junkie who admitted having seen Magilla and Rivera attack the two Nomads. But he insisted that he didn't know where Nellie and the two guys could be found. The kids took him into a hallway near where the attack had occurred and proceeded to beat him. If he didn't talk, he was gonna get piped. And the Nomad with the .32 threatened to kill him on the spot. The junkie finally told them what they wanted to know. Nellie was over in a shooting gallery on Aldus Street, one of the scores of apartments in the South Bronx tenements where a junkie could go and shoot up.

"You gonna let me go now?"

"Shit, no. You gonna take us." And two brothers went with him to the address on Aldus Street and held him in the vestibule there, while the others raced back to The Compound for their pieces.

"We found her! We found the fuckin' junkie whore!"

Another dozen gang members scrambled to their feet and began collecting weapons: tire chains, ice picks, pipes, knives, machetes, and five rifles. Then the Savage Nomads pulled on the green army coats they had adopted as their uniform, stuffed black masks into their pockets, and, accompanied by some of the Seven Immortals, ran down the stairs, across the courtyard, down the stoop, and into the waiting small blue truck, which one of the Nomads had heisted.

The shooting gallery on Aldus Street was only two blocks from The Compound, but they couldn't risk being seen in the street carrying rifles. And they wouldn't fit under the army coats. Anyway, speeding the two blocks in the truck while pulling on the masks, and swaying as the truck turned at Aldus Street, served to heighten their excitement. They poured out of the back of the truck, raced past the two brothers guarding the junkie in the vestibule of the tenement, and ran up the stairs to the shooting gallery on the fourth floor. At least one gang member stayed behind on each floor—insurance that the tenants would stay inside their apartments, too terrified to call the police.

As luck would have it, as the gang reached the fourth floor, a dude and a chick were just going into the shooting gallery in apartment 4C. With Bad Ass in front carrying one of the rifles, the gang burst through the front door and into the apartment the police would later describe as "deplorable" and "filthy."

Dottie Judge, the black woman who had been going into the apartment with her common-law husband, Henry Smith, was pushed through the living room and into the front bedroom. Smith was held in the living room, where one of the gang began kicking him. Dottie Judge begged, "Please don't hurt me," and one of the kids replied: "We won't hurt you. All we want are the guys who were in the fight last night." Two other women were asleep on cots in the bedroom. One, Emma Williams, was the legal tenant of apartment 4C; beside her on the cot was her two-year-old son. Asleep in the other cot was Sabrina Howard, also black and, like Nellie Gomez, a prostitute and an addict.

As a couple of the Nomads took Dottie Judge out of the bedroom and back into the living room, one of the other Nomads, brandishing a rifle, poked Emma Williams awake and demanded her money. She gave him her wallet, containing four dollars. Sabrina Howard woke up, and another Nomad, holding a knife, ordered her to undress.

In the rear bedroom, Carmen Carrion, who had been sleeping beside her common-law husband, Frank Magilla, awoke suddenly when one of the gang lifted the coat that had been covering her face. Shading her eyes with her hand, she saw Antonio Rivera, Nellie's man, lying on the floor in a pool of blood. Grabbing a table leg, he had rushed one of the Immortals and been stabbed repeatedly with an ice pick. Blood was gushing up through his shirt, forming sticky red circles that were growing larger and larger. Nellie Gomez was standing, swaying, over his inert body when Carmen, raising herself up on her elbow, saw three kids start to rip Nellie's clothes off her. "No, I'll do it myself," Nellie said, and she started to undress. Then, followed by the three kids, she walked naked out of the room and into the front bedroom, where she stumbled and fell on Emma Williams's little son, who was standing, crying, alongside his mother's cot. One of the kids grabbed Nellie by the throat, pulled her to her feet, and slammed her against the door.

Sabrina Howard, standing naked between the cots, watched as the kid bent over Nellie and shouted into her ear, "Junkie whore! You put two of my boys in the hospital. Now you gonna pay." He began to punch her in the stomach and pelvis, while her eyes rolled up under her eyelids. One of the other kids ran a knife across her chest, leaving a pencil line of blood, as Nellie began a high-pitched whine. The kid who had been punching her unzipped his trousers. While two others pinned her shoulders against the door, he bent down and brought both his hands up and under her thighs, lifting her off her feet. Then, spreading her legs, he put his penis in her and began heaving himself against her. After all three of them had taken turns raping her in this position, they flung her across one of the cots. She lay there face down. "Now you—you're next," the burliest of the three said to Sabrina Howard.

Frank Magilla, sleeping beside Carmen Carrion, was shaken awake and pushed into a corner of the rear bedroom. Then four black men, all addicts who had been found in the apartment, were shoved into the room, step-

ping around and over the unconscious form of Antonio
Rivera. All the men were ordered to strip. Standing naked,
Magilla was suddenly eye to eye with a Nomad clutching
a lead pipe in his hand. "You the one we wanna kill," he
said, " 'cause two of our boys are in the hospital." Another
Nomad shouldered him out of the way, and stabbed
Magilla in the arm with an ice pick. Magilla sank to the
floor and sat slumped against the side of a bureau while
the kid with the lead pipe used it on his head. Magilla
moaned as a thin rope of saliva looped from his lips down
to his shoulder.

The Nomad with the lead pipe left the room. He was
back a few minutes later, with his trousers open, his genitals exposed, and a rifle in his hand. "That whore Nellie—
she got syphilis," he said. It was then that he and the kid
with the ice pick decided it was time to kill Frank Magilla.

At the sound of the rifle shot, gang members in the other
rooms started for the front door. One of them, Scooter,
turned around and ran back into the rear bedroom, where
he flung himself down on top of Antonio Rivera and began
stabbing him. Carmen Carrion leaped off the cot and
started toward Magilla, just as the Nomad who had stabbed
him with the ice pick reentered the room. He shoved the
naked man up against the wall with his foot, looked at the
bullet wound in his chest, from which blood was oozing,
and said disgustedly, "This one ain't dead yet." But then
came the sound of a siren from outside in the street, and
somebody in the living room shouted, "Let's go! The cops
are gonna come up here." There was a stampede toward
the front door.

Nellie Gomez stood in the middle of the room, barefoot
and wearing nothing but a skirt. One of the gang at the
door shouted, "We just blew one away—let's get outa
here!" But Bad Ass, who was carrying one of the rifles,
suddenly wheeled around and said, "I'm gonna blow this

bitch away, too." Nellie took a couple of steps backward and then bolted into the front bedroom, where Emma Williams and Sabrina Howard stood between the two cots, with the little boy lying on the floor by his mother's feet. Nellie flew past them, her long, bare arms flapping out at her sides like broken wings, and into a shallow closet. She sank down on top of a mound of dirty clothes, hunching her shoulders as though she might become smaller and perhaps, in some magic way, invisible. Cornered there, she looked up at Bad Ass and raised both hands as if to ward off a blow. He took aim and sent a bullet tearing through her shoulder, killing her instantly. Then he ran from the room and out of the apartment, leaving Nellie Gomez there on top of the mound of dirty clothes, her head sagging on her shoulder, looking like a giant and discarded rag doll.

In the street they scattered in all directions. Five of them climbed into the truck parked outside and drove to the river, where they tossed the gun that had just killed Nellie Gomez into the water. They kept the other four rifles, one of which had been used to shoot Frank Magilla. It isn't common practice for a gang to dispose of a weapon, even a murder weapon, but for some reason they wanted to get rid of the rifle that had iced Nellie—maybe because killing her hadn't been part of the plan. Whatever the reason, no sooner had the rifle hit the water than they drove back to The Compound for a victory celebration.

Police arrived at the Aldus Street address almost immediately after the gangs had fled. Soon after, advised that many of the kids had worn green army coats, they picked up two of the Savage Nomads who, after fleeing the shooting gallery, hadn't gone back to The Compound but instead had walked the streets, too excited to settle down. At nine the next morning, police went into The Compound and raided the clubhouse of the Nomads. Every member of the gang was asleep on a mattress on the floor, a wife beside him and a pile of empty wine bottles within arm's reach.

All the people found in the shooting gallery on Aldus Street were taken to the Simpson Street station house, with the exception of Frank Magilla and Antonio Rivera, who were rushed to the hospital in critical condition. Booked and photographed as material witnesses, they were then transferred to Lincoln Hospital, where they were given Thorazine to ease their withdrawal symptoms. Then they were returned to the station house, where, through a one-way mirror, they were able to identify from a lineup nine of those who had invaded the shooting gallery.

After a preliminary hearing, to which Magilla and Rivera were transported by ambulance, all nine pleaded guilty. Bad Ass of the Savage Nomads, who confessed to firing the shot that killed Nellie Gomez, was sentenced to a term of from six to eighteen years. All the others were sentenced to terms of from four to nine years, with one exception: The Reverend, one of the Seven Immortals, was put on five years probation. Two years after the murder, he would be shot dead in the street only a few blocks away from the shooting gallery, seconds after having killed a member of a rival gang.

The murder of Nellie Gomez marked the new Gang Intelligence Unit's first real involvement with the gangs in The Compound, so it seemed a natural place for me to begin researching the story of The Compound. I had yet to sit down and talk to a street-gang member, and I wondered if there was anyone involved in that case whom I might talk to. There was: Sweet Deuce, recently released from Attica prison after serving three and a half years. A gang vice-president at the time of Nellie Gomez's murder, he was out of the gang now and, according to O'Rourke

and Moles, planned to stay out. I arranged to meet Sweet
Deuce, who had just started a job as a messenger for a
printing house in midtown Manhattan.

Ed O'Rourke tried to fill me in ahead of time. "You
speak of these kids and most people see a dirty, scowling
kid who spits at you," he said. Most of them, he said, appear to be very likable. And when I met Sweet Deuce, a
tall, bronze-skinned youth with a modified Afro and quite
handsome features, I saw what he meant. Sweet Deuce
seemed cool, tentative, yet almost eager to please. But I
also knew something of his past record. He had beaten
men with pipes. Stabbed them with ice picks. Punched
old ladies who held on to their handbags when he wanted
them. But he looked me in the eye now and insisted that all
that was behind him. "I don't think savage any more" is
the way he put it. Furthermore, he was saving his money
to visit relatives in Puerto Rico just as soon as his parole
officer would permit him to travel.

We discussed the murder that had taken place in the
shooting gallery on Aldus Street almost four years ago.
Sweet Deuce said that he never saw Nellie Gomez dead.
He had been standing at the front door when he heard the
shot, but he didn't see her die. Nor did he see the giant
blowup of a photograph of her body exhibited at his pretrial hearing. But he did see the snapshots that one of his
gang took of what was happening that night in the shooting
gallery. Sweet Deuce said that among them were some of
Nellie taken during and after the gang rape, but there were
no snapshots of her after she had been shot. There hadn't
been time to take a picture of her sitting there dead in the
closet, because as soon as she was shot everybody stam-
peded for the door. Sweet Deuce had no idea of what
happened to those snaps. Maybe one of the Nomads still
had them. They were meant to be a matter of record, he

told me—proof of what happens when you mess with the Savage Nomads.

He spoke of Nellie Gomez with a kind of detached affection. He remembered her as the neighborhood girl he knew back in 1970, when he was sixteen and on heroin and they used to shoot together. He particularly remembered the Oriental slant to her eyes, which he had thought interesting because one of her best friends was a Chinese girl. When I asked him if he thought that he could be involved in a violent crime again, he shook his head slowly and replied: "Violence—I gave it up. Nobody who knows me today can believe it, but I used to go wild. I used to pipe dudes just for some recognition." And evidently often, because "Everybody used to look up to me."

Sweet Deuce told me that he joined the Savage Nomads when he was fourteen. It was no big deal. "I just kinda drifted into it. It was, y'know, the thing to do." At the same time, he boxed at boys' clubs around the Bronx, with the hope of eventually making it in the Golden Gloves. "I lost only five out of my twenty fights," he told me as he cracked his knuckles. "I got a lotta trophies." But at sixteen he got hooked on drugs, and that's when he began to "think savage." Ironically, at the time of Nellie Gomez's murder, he had just come clean, having voluntarily joined a drug rehabilitation program. "I was doin' real well," he recalled.

Then came the murder in the shooting gallery and three and a half years in Attica, the last of them working in the bakery for twenty-five cents an hour. By the time he was released, Sweet Deuce, who had gone only as far as the tenth grade, had earned his high-school-equivalency diploma via a correspondence course. Now, he said, "I got a job and I'm doin' real well again." As for the street gangs, he had no intention of ever joining one again. When he ran into any of his former brothers, "It's strictly hello and good-bye. Today I don't socialize. When a man's in a gang, he's an outlaw." For the time being, he said, he was living at home with his parents and his younger brothers and sisters. His father was disabled, and the family received welfare payments. Neither parent spoke much English. Sweet Deuce was proud of the fact that his mother and father had never had any trouble with the law.

As Ed O'Rourke seemed to expect, I found Sweet Deuce very likable, and he appeared to trust me. We both agreed to meet again.

After that first meeting, I asked O'Rourke and Vito Moles if they thought Sweet Deuce could be rehabilitated and, in his words, stay clean. "Sweet Deuce is one of the smarter kids," Moles said. "He's got a head on his shoulders. He might make it." But both officers said they thought he would stand a far better chance if he lived someplace other than the South Bronx, where every day for a kid like Sweet Deuce was a potentially explosive one.

I met Sweet Deuce several times after that. I visited the printing house where he worked, and from what I observed, he was doing a good job and his employers regarded him highly. One night, over hamburgers in a restaurant near his job, he told me that he was taking a sociology course three nights a week at a local college. He said he liked the course fine but was having trouble understanding some of the words used in class. I bought him a paperback dictionary, and the next time we met I noticed that he had it with him and it looked well-thumbed.

Then, some three months after our first meeting, it appeared that Sweet Deuce might be in trouble again. Just one block away from the tenement on Aldus Street where Nellie Gomez had been shot and killed, there were two more killings in the street. Big Zap, a member of the Reapers, was shot and killed by The Reverend, prez of the

Brothers and Sisters of the Revolution, who was then shot in the back of the head and killed instantly by an unknown assailant. A police informer had suggested that Sweet Deuce's younger brother, Jesus, fired the shot that killed The Reverend. There were plenty of witnesses. In fact, one was shot in the leg by a stray bullet, but he disappeared into the crowd. All in all, there were—as one youth put it —"some fifty to sixty dudes there . . . not countin' chicks." Except for that one unidentified informer, no one was talking, but whispers around the neighborhood suggested that it was Sweet Deuce and not Jesus who fired the fatal shot. Now the question seemed to be, who was going to get Sweet Deuce and/or Jesus first—The Reverend's brothers or the police?

The Reverend, then a member of the Seven Immortals, was one of the gang that had stormed into the shooting gallery on Aldus Street in search of Nellie Gomez and her two men that evening nearly four years before. Like Sweet Deuce and seven of the others, he had been identified and indicted and had pleaded guilty. But, unlike them, he was the only one to have been put on probation, and in some quarters it was being whispered now that that was because he had turned police informer.

Big Zap was, in a manner of speaking, related to Sweet Deuce. His sister, Maria, had lived with Big Zap and borne him a son, making them sort of outlaw in-laws. At the time he was shot and killed in the street, Big Zap was preparing to go to trial on a charge of having beaten the month-old infant to death in a fit of rage earlier in the year. It had taken several months for him to be charged with the murder, because there hadn't been any witnesses. Only Maria had been in the apartment when the baby died, and she had told the police very little. She said she had been asleep. She remained loyal to Big Zap, but when he started threatening her with a gun she left him and moved back with her parents. "He used to break everything—the walls, everything." And now, she said, some people were blaming her for his death, saying that because she had refused to go back to him, he had gone loco. Maria said she heard that he was on dope.

Now, a few days after learning of Sweet Deuce's new troubles, I sit with O'Rourke and Moles in their car, parked outside the abandoned apartment complex that was once The Compound. All the windows are tinned, and it looks like a wartime building that went through a blitz attack. Sweet Deuce said he wanted to come and talk to us today, but we've been waiting for more than an hour with no sign of him. Maria has come by, however. She stands alongside the car and chats animatedly with us. She lived in The Compound off and on in the days when she was vice-president of the girls' division of one of the gangs. She is wearing tight dungarees, wedgies, a red kerchief knotted around her neck, and large hoop earrings. She's an extremely vivacious girl, very much aware of her attractiveness.

She doesn't mind talking about Big Zap's murder or the killing of The Reverend, which is causing her brothers Sweet Deuce and Jesus so much trouble. She says she wasn't in the crowd that night. But at about five o'clock the next morning, she says, she woke up very nervous. Still, she knew nothing of what had happened until later, when she found everyone in her family crying and was told, "They killed Big Zap." But, Maria says, "I couldn't believe it till I go to the funeral."

Ed and Vito also attended the funeral of Big Zap, who used to come and sit in their car and rap with them. Big Zap, a twenty-one-year-old black Puerto Rican, says Ed, had hands twice the size of most men's, and he was mean. The police who saw the body of Maria's baby said the

sight of it made them sick to their stomachs. Now Big Zap
is buried in a grave alongside that baby's in St. Raymond's
Cemetery.

His funeral had not been what Ed O'Rourke calls "a big
gang thing," because of the possibility of violence. The
gangs stayed clear of the church, where masses were being
said for Big Zap and The Reverend within an hour of each
other. Street talk was that their two gangs were heading for
a shootout and it might take place inside the church at one
of the masses—or maybe at St. Raymond's, where both were
being buried. So there were only fifteen cars in Big Zap's
funeral cortege—a pitifully small number by gang stan-
dards—and five of them were police cars.

Maria attended his mass and then went to the cemetery,
where she stood behind Big Zap's father, who, she swears,
was too drunk to recognize her, for which she was grateful.
"He screamed, he cried, and he was laughing at the end.
That's how he always was." Big Zap's mother collapsed on
entering the church for her son's funeral mass and was
deposited back in the Cadillac, where she remained until the
service was over. But Maria, her brother Jesus, and her
mother and father were together at the mass, and at the
cemetery, too. Sweet Deuce decided to go to his job instead.
According to Maria, five of Big Zap's girl friends were
standing, crying, at the graveside. One was a whitey with
red hair. Speaking of Big Zap, whom she first met in high
school, and of his relationship with her family, Maria says:
"We all got along with him. We had pity for him." Obviously what's past is past. One gets the impression that Maria
doesn't hate Big Zap for killing her baby. In fact, it's just
possible that she has never completely accepted the idea
that he was responsible for the death. Big Zap had a bad
temper. He went loco sometimes.

"They say around they gonna catch one of my family.

They get blown away. But I go out. I don't like people tellin' me. I used to say to Big Zap: 'Hit me but *don't* tell me!' "

Vito talks of the killing and the missing witness who got shot in the leg. It's clear to me that Maria knows that she's being encouraged to talk. She laughs. "I don't know. Really, I don't know. I heard it was three people got shot." She bends to rub her knee. "I think it was me. I got a bad leg."

Vito takes the cue and drops the subject. Maria suggests that maybe she'd like to become a registered nurse. But first, of course, she'd have to go back and finish high school. The prospect of being a twenty-year-old "widow" in high school doesn't exactly grab her, however. Vito says that perhaps she can get some help from the Crime Victims Compensation Board. After all, her baby was murdered. And so was Big Zap. Maria looks interested, and Vito says he will try to arrange an interview for her with a member of the board. They just might be able to help her get a job, and then she could finish high school in the evening.

Maria positively beams, revealing a dazzling toothpaste-ad smile, and she's still smiling when she leaves, a few minutes later. The clop of her wedgies can be heard all the way to the corner, where she turns and waves back before darting across the street.

Still no sign of Sweet Deuce. But later in the afternoon, his brother Jesus comes by. It's four o'clock, and he's just gotten out of bed. A month shy of his seventeenth birthday, he looks perhaps fourteen or fifteen. Unlike his brother, Jesus is small—barely five foot four, and small-boned. But he's very wiry and animated and, in the opinion of Ed and Vito, more cunning and streetwise than Sweet Deuce. Jesus has already had some minor skirmishes with the law, and although he no longer belongs to a street gang, he was once, like his brother, a member of the Savage Nomads.

Jesus stands by the car, hands in his pockets, rocking

back and forth on his toes and heels. He wears a ring in his left ear. He says he pierced his own ear and put the ring there when he was ten years old. And he made a promise— to himself—and he obviously is going to keep it a secret. Which reminds him that he should check the calendar; it must be about time to remove the earring. It looks like a tiny gold crucifix, but it isn't. "It's like a Maltese cross, not a holy cross, man. I don't believe in that 'heaven or hell.' We're in hell now."

As for the night The Reverend was shot and killed, Jesus says he was at home watching the fights televised from Mexico City. Yeah, he heard that The Reverend's brothers had planned to invade the Ortiz Funeral Home and overturn Big Zap's casket, but shit, they changed their minds when they heard that some twenty of the mourners were carrying guns. And yeah, he's sure that the Gestapo Squad of the Brothers and Sisters of the Revolution is planning to come for him and Sweet Deuce.

Jesus grins and shrugs his slender shoulders. "When you die, you die," he says. "When I die, all I want is a white box. That's all. I wanna dress all in white so's inside the box with all that white silk, with my Afro, I'll look like a bee in a cup of milk. That's the way I want it."

Vito tells Jesus that if he's still alive next summer, "We can get you a job in the precinct house. Seventy dollars a week. You file cards. You sweep. Five days a week, eight to four."

Jesus grins and returns to the topic of death. "I don't mind dying," he says, "but if they mess with my mother and father, there'll be blood all over."

Jesus moves on, and still no sign of Sweet Deuce. Jesus says he hasn't seen him in a couple of days. Soon a friend of theirs stops by, squats down, and peers inside the car. It's O.D. He's twenty-seven, tall and burly, and he also has the nickname of "Mr. Clean," since he looks not unlike the sketch of the giant on the label of the all-purpose cleaner. He has slanting eyes, a thick neck, and a closely cropped bullet-shaped head. He's wearing a green army coat, like those the Savage Nomads wore when they went looking for Nellie Gomez. And why not? O.D. is one of the original members of the Savage Nomads. His full name is unknown, and O.D. intends to keep it that way. He has earned a reputation for acting crazy. Most recently, he's said to have stolen a priest's cassock from the rectory, put it on, wrapped a wide white bandage around his neck, and gone drinking in all the neighborhood bars. And then, still posing as a priest, he held up a store. O.D., a very fair-complexioned Puerto Rican, appears to be very jovial, but when he leaves Ed O'Rourke tells me, "He's the type of guy who'd blow you away, then spit on you."

Referring to the killings of Big Zap and The Reverend, O.D., who speaks with a slight lisp, calls them senseless. "I hate to see that kind of shit." Evidently aware that I'm gathering material on the Nellie Gomez case, he looks straight at me and says that there was, after all, a purpose behind the killing of Nellie Gomez. But this stuff is senseless.

Vito asks him if he was in the shooting gallery the night Nellie was shot. O.D. shrugs eloquently. Then he laughs, and Vito laughs too. Well, then did he by any chance see Big Zap get killed? O.D. grins. "I bleed very bad when I get shot," he replies, obliquely referring to the rumors about a wounded witness, and takes a puff of his small black cigar.

Yet a few minutes later O.D. is giving an eyewitness account. "It was like in one of those Chinese flicks," he says, proceeding to act it all out. "Big Zap's stripped to the waist. He gets shot, but he keeps comin' at The Reverend. *Stupid.* After he got shot once he could've run off. But he kept comin' toward the gun." At this point O.D. is facing Vito, and, pretending to be Big Zap, he begins to sway forward with both hands about to fall on Vito's shoulders. "Then *boom!* The Reverend gets it in the back of the head and he falls dead." O.D. straightens up, turns around, and grins. "But no gun was found." He repeats himself. "I hate to see this shit."

He takes another puff of his cigar, although he claims he's worried about his throat and that he wakes up every morning and vomits first thing. He says he may give up smoking altogether, but he doesn't sound convincing. "There oughta be a movie about all this," he says, pointing over the roof of the car to the deserted Compound.

Two weeks later, there have been dramatic changes. O.D., for instance, has been hospitalized with thirty-eight stitches in his cheek, several stab wounds in his left arm, and a deep gash between his thumb and index finger that is going to require plastic surgery. According to him, he was attempting to collect some money that was owed him when the two dudes jumped him and one of them tried to stab him in the heart. He says he grabbed the knife and held it away from his heart, and then one of the dudes held his arm while the other ground the knife into the skin between his thumb and index finger. They left him on the sidewalk "bleeding like a stuffed pig." O.D. hasn't pressed charges. He vows he'll kill the dude himself when his hand gets better.

Ed and Vito see Maria in a neighborhood laundromat, and her eyes are swollen from crying. She says Sweet Deuce and Jesus are now blaming her for their troubles. They say that if she hadn't left Big Zap, he—and The Reverend—would be alive today and they wouldn't be hounded by the law and threatened by The Reverend's brothers. Maria has moved out of her parents' apartment and is staying temporarily with her aunt several blocks away. She feels miserable.

A few nights later, it finally happens: Sweet Deuce and Jesus are arrested for the murder of The Reverend. Two detectives from the Eighth Homicide Division sit in their double-parked car and watch the two youths playing basketball in the street. When the game is over, they get out and make the arrest. Maria is there at the time, and as Sweet Deuce is hustled into the squad car he turns toward her and says, "Thanks, Maria." She looks him squarely in the eye and says, with a shrug, "Don't mention it."

A week later, she moves into a three-room apartment in the neighborhood. Welfare has promised her a telephone, and Ed O'Rourke says he has some paint he can give her. Except for a couple of kitchen chairs left behind by the previous tenant, she has no furniture. She wants furniture, and then she wants a big stuffed bear to put on her bed.

Sitting in the living room of her new apartment, Maria appears tired but exhilarated. She smiles at me and apologizes for looking "so rotten." She's forgotten to pencil in her eyebrows, and this gives her face a peculiarly blank look. She has a new boy friend, who she says has a temper like Big Zap's but he's quiet. She was dancing the night before in a social club frequented by "a lot of whiteys." On the way home—in the early hours of the morning—she was "happy but starving," so she stole some apples and oranges from a fruit market. Now that she's happy again, she says, she's always hungry. She ate twenty-five hamburgers in the White Castle at one sitting, but she allows that they were skinny ones—skinny like pancakes. Still, she can't button the top of her corduroy shorts—a fact that doesn't appear to really disturb her, however.

Maria opens her wallet, thick with snapshots. Her brother Jesus in cap and gown when he graduated from grade school. Her sister Cookie and her two children. Her eleven-year-old sister, Irma, who she says is a terrible gossip. And finally a color snapshot of herself with her baby and Big

Zap's mother, taken the day they came home from the hospital. The five-day-old baby boy lies on the bed between the two women, wrapped in a pale blue blanket.

"His picture was on the front page of *El Diario*," she says. "And he was on Spanish-speaking TV, too." Why? "Because he was born on Christmas Day. The only baby born that day in Lincoln Hospital. He weighed eight and a half pounds. A big baby. I had him in cold blood. I had nothin' to put me to sleep. I saw it all. The head kept goin' in and out, an' they had to use forceps. I had forty-eight stitches."

Maria says she'd like to have this snapshot of the baby enlarged, but first she'd scissor Big Zap's mother out of the picture.

She appears to want to talk about the baby, whose name was Felipe. Maria says the night he died she was "feelin' pain," still weak from the ordeal of giving birth to such a big baby. She had been to the doctor that day and he'd given her some medicine, and when she got home "it was like seein' three babies on the bed." She told Big Zap she was going to sleep and he was to wake her at eleven, when it was time to feed the baby. Maria figures she had slept for maybe fifteen minutes when he woke her up. The baby had a black mark on his face, and she remembers that he was "makin' big noises for a baby." She told Big Zap to call the police, but "he was afraid to call the cops . . . I don't know why. He told me he'd dropped the baby and it hit its head." So Maria called the police, and they came and took the baby to the hospital, where it died of a fractured skull and a collapsed chest.

She says that she'll probably stay in the South Bronx until her parents move. Now that Sweet Deuce and Jesus have been arrested, she says, her mother definitely wants to move. Oh, maybe in two years. Maria says she feels confident that if her brothers are innocent they'll be set free. She says she still likes all cops. "All cops are fine," she says, patting Pelo

Rojo on the shoulder. "They do their job. If somebody does something—includin' my brothers—an' the cops catch 'em, it's right. If they're innocent, they come out. If they don't ... y'know ..."

A couple of weeks later, Jesus was indicted for the murder of The Reverend. There wasn't enough evidence to indict Sweet Deuce, but he was sentenced to seventeen months in prison for violation of his parole.

Soon afterward, their parents moved from the apartment they had occupied for a decade. They had no choice but to move: The building had been destroyed by a fire that—like so many of the fires in the South Bronx—was, in the words of the Fire Department, "of a suspicious nature." But they stayed on in the South Bronx. And so did Maria. She was pregnant and alone again. Her boy friend was serving time in the same prison as Sweet Deuce. Vito Moles had already made her a gift of the bassinet his little daughter had outgrown. Maria hoped her baby would be a girl; Ed O'Rourke had promised her that if it was, he would paint her bedroom pink.

Maria's baby was a girl, and her bedroom is pink. Jesus is still in prison. Sweet Deuce is free again, but unemployed and unhappy. Ed O'Rourke and Vito Moles believe he is acting as the ringleader for a gang of little boys who rob. I haven't seen Sweet Deuce since he got out of jail.

I find that I learned a lot about life in a high-crime ghetto from investigating the shooting-gallery murder and from Sweet Deuce and his family. How it dehumanizes, for instance ...

Sweet Deuce talks of the dead Nellie Gomez with no sign of sorrow or guilt. She was just a neighborhood girl he once knew. His brother Jesus has no fear of dying at the hands of another street gang, and if he puts so little value on his

own life, how much value do you suppose he puts on anyone else's? And Maria shows her murdered baby's snapshot
with no more emotion than if it had been the child of a
distant relative who moved away and sent her the snapshot
along with the family's new address. But, terrible as they
say life is in the South Bronx, they choose to stay. They
can't bring themselves to leave, to exchange the familiar for
the unfamiliar. They can't escape the trap of their environment. So they stay, and they become both victim and vic-
timizer. And if you wish to think, as I do, that perhaps there
is hope for them and that the human spirit can survive in
so harsh an environment, then you must also believe in
miracles.

3.
Love in the Compound

Amelia first ran away from home at thirteen. She moved in with a girl friend's family in Spanish Harlem and joined an all-girl gang. But she was back home in the South Bronx after two months; back home in her mother's apartment, with its five tiny shrines to the Blessed Mother; back in her own bedroom, with its bed full of stuffed animals. She had expected (in fact, she had hoped) that her mother would punish her, even hit her. But she only made her strip naked and examined her; when she was satisfied that Amelia was still a virgin, that was that. She never learned that Amelia had run with a gang. The next day she brought her to school and told the principal Lord knows what, because Amelia was not only accepted back in class but even graduated the following June.

Amelia was completing her first year at Junior High 133 when she met Slick. He was eighteen and living with the Storm Troopers in The Compound. He hadn't seen his family since he moved in. He had been on heroin at thirteen, cocaine at fifteen, but now he was clean. Slick was sitting on a car parked outside the school when Amelia caught his eye. Her skin was the color of a caramel, and so before he

slid off the car to go and speak to her, he had already nick-
named her Candy. That same afternoon he took Amelia to
The Compound, and she didn't go home until almost midnight, but he didn't so much as touch her. She had told him
she was a virgin.

The next day the Storm Troopers were attacked by a rival
gang, and, twenty-four hours later, Slick was one of four
youths who invaded the Ortiz Funeral Home and overturned
the casket of one of the attackers, kicking the gray-lipped
corpse across the room until it rested at the feet of the
grieving mother. A couple of days later, Slick was shot in
the leg by members of this rival gang. He was carried back
inside The Compound, where somebody dug the bullet out,
poured iodine in the hole, wrapped a bandage around his
leg, and arranged for him to hide out in a nearby apartment.

While his leg was healing, Slick wrote one love letter each
day to Amelia, "my little girl," signing it "Daddy." When he
was able to hop around without the cane, he had the cane
delivered to her, and she promptly fastened it to the
wall of her bedroom, where it hung, like a trophy, surrounded by his love letters. Her mother chose to ignore all
of this, afraid that if she complained Amelia would run
away again.

When he was fully recovered, Slick came to pick up
Amelia and take her to live with him in The Compound.
They would be married that evening, he said. He had gotten
the permission of his prez, who would perform the ceremony.

For someone who had lived alone with her mother since
the age of three, which was when her father had abandoned
them, the crush of people in The Compound was both over-
powering and comforting. It was like being part of an
enormous family. When she arrived there, the members of
the girls' division of Slick's gang were busy decorating the
five-room clubhouse for the wedding, hanging long coils of

brightly colored paper, while some of the brothers sat listening to the stereo, or slept on the mattresses scattered about the floor. The wedding was the main event of the day, and everyone was looking forward to it, even other gangs in The Compound whose members had been invited to the ceremony. Everyone in Slick's gang had donated two dollars, so there would be plenty of wine and beer and, of course, the big vanilla wedding cake, which was traditional for what the gangs called an "outlaw-style wedding."

Slick presented his bride with a plastic orchid, and Bricktop, a husky, redheaded Hispanic girl, wrapped around Amelia's head the white towel which was to the outlaw-style wedding what the white veil is to a traditional wedding. "You're the first bride we have who wears a white towel," said Bricktop. "White's for virgins, and we never had one before." When Amelia was ready for the ceremony—the plastic orchid pinned to the red satin blouse her mother had given her for Christmas, her dungarees stuffed down inside her boots, and the white towel securely draped around her head—she took her lipstick out of her shoulder bag. "That's against the rules," said Bricktop, snatching it away from her. "No makeup allowed in this club."

Nowhere was there a mirror long enough for Amelia to see how she looked as a bride. Until now she had always thought she would be wearing a white dress, like her Holy Communion dress—only to the floor, of course—with a white veil that dragged on the floor. But she wasn't disappointed, really. She felt excited and a little frightened— the way she figured a bride should feel. And she was a June bride. She liked that.

"You take Slick to be your husband?" King Cobra, the prez, said to Amelia. The crowded room had become very quiet, and although she answered in a small voice, everyone heard her response. Then he turned to Slick. "You take Candy to be your wife?" Slick's reply was unexpectedly soft and gentle. Then Slick took Amelia's hand in his, and together they moved a few steps closer to the prez. Although Bricktop had told her of this all-important part of the ceremony, Amelia was still scared, and she shut her eyes as the prez took her hand and moved to cut the fleshy part of her thumb with the machete. "It'll only be a little cut," Bricktop had assured her. "Sometimes, like with the Savage Skulls, it's a big cut—twelve inches maybe—on the arm. You never gonna lose that. You always got a big scar. You go to the hospital for stitches right after the weddin'. But we do only a little cut."

Amelia felt the cut of the blade, after which she had to open her eyes in order to squeeze the cut and make the blood pop so that she and Slick could let their blood intermingle. When they did that, King Cobra, who was short and husky and not much taller than Amelia, climbed up on a chair, held a can of beer aloft, and proceeded to pour it over their heads. Suddenly the room exploded with noise. Everyone crowded around then, the stereo began to play, and bottles of fruit wine started passing from hand to hand. "Kiss!" the prez commanded, and Slick kissed her hard on the lips, after which King Cobra threw the first piece of vanilla cake straight into Slick's face—the sign that he was now a husband. It was *official*.

Some eight hours later, King Cobra announced that it was time for the honeymoon to start. Amelia and Slick were led to the bedroom and locked in. This was the only time the bedroom would be exclusively theirs. All the mattresses but one had been dragged from the room. In one corner there was a large cardboard box full of sandwiches, potato chips, and beer. In the opposite corner there was an empty paint can, since they wouldn't be allowed out of the bedroom—even to relieve themselves—for the next twenty-four hours. Meanwhile, the celebration outside continued well into the following afternoon.

While Amelia didn't exactly drop out of Junior High 133 after her wedding, she now attended infrequently, preferring to remain inside The Compound. Anyway, the school term had only a few weeks to go before summer vacation. The Storm Troopers liked to break the night—stay up until dawn and sleep until late afternoon—and she quickly adjusted to that, waking up in time to weave her way between the mattresses and turn on the television set and, with Bricktop, Crazy Anna, and some of the other girls, watch the soap operas. She also helped clean the clubhouse, which usually meant picking up whatever was on the floor and tossing it out the window, "airmailing" it into the courtyard below. Then she and some of the other girls would go out for cigarettes, wine, and beer for the brothers, who woke up an hour or two later. Sometimes on the way back to The Compound they would go down into the subway and have their pictures taken in the photo booth there. Each girl would have a string of five snapshots of herself, and once or twice Amelia thought of maybe putting one of her pictures in an envelope and mailing it to her mother just to show her that she was alive and well, but she never did. Not once did she consider visiting her mother, who had been too ashamed to go to Junior High 133 and tell them that her fourteen-year-old daughter had run away again, or to the local precinct and ask the police to help her find her daughter.

Somewhere in Amelia's memory she recalled her mother's mother in San Juan saying, *"El hombre es de la calle y la mujer es de la casa"* (The man belongs in the streets and the woman belongs in the home). She believed that, and so she was perfectly content to remain inside The Compound for days at a stretch. She also approved of the list of club rules, which applied to every girl. Among them was one that read: "No fucking around with more than one guy. You are to have only one boy friend and to stay with him." And when King Cobra ordered all girls to wear one earring in the shape of a cross "in the left ear only," she was quick to comply. She knew the consequences if a girl didn't obey. ANYONE DISOBEYING THIS ORDER WILL GET SEVEN LASHES FROM EACH MEMBER, read the notice nailed to the inside of the apartment door. She had seen the whip once, when Apache, leader of the girls' division, took it out of the closet and stood in the center of the room, cracking the air with it. Amelia figured the whip had to be at least five feet long.

No pressure was put on Amelia to become a member of the gang. And she had no idea if a wife would have to go through the same initiation rite a single girl did: sexual intercourse with several of the brothers. Wild Child, a fifteen-year-old runaway, was the newest recruit. On the night of her initiation, Amelia sat with her back to the room and watched television while Apache, Bricktop, and several of the other girls stood in a circle and watched the initiation. Amelia didn't know and didn't ask if Slick was one of the brothers who had sex with Wild Child. The next day, a man came into the courtyard of The Compound asking if anybody had seen a girl about so high with blond streaks in her hair. Nobody gave him any satisfaction, and he left. Wild Child, who had been watching from a window, said that he was her father. "Your old man's a fool," Bricktop told her. "He should know better than come messin' around The Compound like that. He lucky he didn't get himself iced."

Some days were dull, and then Amelia would sleep a lot. But then, suddenly, there might be unexpected action.

The day a newspaperman and a photographer came to interview some of the gang presidents was like a fiesta. Everybody turned out. Black Bongo and Big Mama of the Savage Nomads took charge, and they wouldn't permit the newsmen inside The Compound, so the interviewing and picture-taking took place in the courtyard. The leaders, their wives and Gestapo Squads stood in the center while the regular gang members either hung out of their windows and watched, or stood at a respectful distance around the perimeter of the courtyard. Eventually Bongo wearied of the reporter's questions and, wine bottle clutched in his fist, wandered off into the crowd. It was then that King Cobra stepped forward, pulling Apache and Bricktop with him, and posed for the photographer. "The Compound," he said to the reporter, "is our home. We all live together, and we love each other like brothers. We're not criminals like they say. We're just a group of guys working together to help out the people." The dudes standing close enough to hear what he said raised their fists and cheered.

The week the newspaper article appeared, King Cobra was contacted by a professor from a university in upstate New York, who invited him and some members of his gang to come to the university for a weekend and speak to him and his associates. About what? asked Apache. Sex, replied King Cobra. And Bricktop laughed so hard, her eyes teared. "You shittin' us?" But as the prez explained—and Amelia found it difficult to comprehend—they would go up to the university and sit around with those professors and tell them "what we do for sex." In return for the information, King Cobra said, "We gonna get rooms on the campus . . . get fed . . . and get bus fare up an' back." Apache said she was fuckin' sure there was a catch someplace, but no one paid any attention. The big question now was who King Cobra would tap for the trip. He finally chose Apache, Bricktop, Wild Child, Slick, and Amelia. Then he sat and stared for maybe a good five minutes before deciding on brothers Mooch and Mister Freeze.

Since it was important that Black Bongo and Big Mama not know about the weekend trip—otherwise, they'd grab it for themselves and the Nomads—the eight travelers did not leave The Compound together but instead met at the bus terminal. Amelia and Slick were the last to leave; like the others, they carried nothing with them that might suggest they were going anywhere but out for a walk. Except for King Cobra, who had served time in Elmira Reformatory, none of them had ever been this far away from the South Bronx, and the trees and grass flashing past the bus windows made them uneasy. They spoke very little, and after a couple of hours they were fast asleep.

At the university, Amelia found it a weird experience to sit in the center of the enormous room, surrounded by these men staring down at them, asking questions and writing down what they said. At first only King Cobra showed any bravado; the others remained silent and suspicious. "Hey, what kinda room is this?" he shouted, and one of the professors who was sitting up on the third tier answered: "A rotunda." That set Mooch and Mister Freeze to snickering, until King Cobra silenced them with a snap of his fingers.

For two mornings, they met the professors in the rotunda and answered their questions. By the second morning they were more relaxed; only Apache seemed to remain suspicious. King Cobra, in fact, got to the point where he stood up and walked around while he talked of such things as "finessing" and "plucking a chicken." "Finessing?" echoed one of the professors. "It's the same as fuckin'," said King Cobra. "Just another word for fuckin', that's all. And pluckin' a chicken's the same."

Bricktop told in detail of her trips to the *botanica* for the little bitter-tasting pills the girls take "when they gotta get rid of the baby."

Amelia sat, tight-lipped, her hands folded in her lap, as Slick, catching a little of King Cobra's showmanship, stood up to describe their wedding ceremony. When one of the professors directed a question to her, she shook her head from side to side without speaking. She wasn't even certain that she had heard the question, but she was fairly certain it had something to do with birth control.

"Are there lesbians—gay women—in your gang?" That question brought Apache to her feet, boiling mad. "What kinda question is that?" she shouted. The professor repeated the question in a patient, even tone of voice, and that made Apache even madder. She knocked over her chair, raised her leg, and sent the heel of her combat boot slamming down on the table top. "No—we don't have no queers in our gang," she said, one fist planted on her knee and the other punching the air. "Understand? *No queers!*" Then she picked up the chair, sat down, folded her arms across her chest, and glared up at the motherfucker.

"Once we had a dyke in the gang," King Cobra said. "When we found out she was queer, we gang-banged her and threw her out."

On Sunday, when they had completed the two discussion periods, the professor in charge presented them with four shopping bags containing condoms, foam contraceptives, birth-control pills, and intrauterine devices. Back in The Compound the next day, Mooch and Mister Freeze spent an hour pelting their brothers with the boxes of condoms, and before the day was over they were using the cans of foam to cover all four walls of the living room with rapidly disintegrating graffiti.

Amelia disliked having missed a Sunday in The Compound. She especially liked waking up to the sounds of the caged roosters crowing on the fire escapes nearby. On Sundays, when the elevated subway ran less frequently, you could hear them, and it reminded her of when she was very little and her mother took her to visit her grandmother in Puerto Rico. There the cockfights were a good thing; here they were illegal. But any Sunday afternoon all Amelia had to do was look out the window and see a group of men carrying shopping bags, and she knew that in those bags were some of the roosters she'd woken up to in the morning. Within the hour they'd be fighting in a pit in a basement somewhere nearby.

Amelia liked Sunday afternoons best of all, for it was then that the gangs threw their doors open and really mingled—outside in the courtyard, across the street in Nomad Park, and inside as they moved from floor to floor, clubhouse to clubhouse. Like visiting royalty, Black Bongo and Big Mama, the leaders of the Savage Nomads, would tour The Compound with Bongo's two German shepherds, Savage and Nomad, lumbering up the stairs behind them. Even Apache, who could handle a snake whip as though it were a yo-yo, was in awe of Big Mama. Everything about her said POWER: her mahogany-colored hair that frizzed out on both sides of her broad face; the mole on her chin that she made look even bigger and blacker by covering it with Magic Marker; her combat boots with the built-up heels that added another three inches to her height. But as far as Amelia was concerned, the high point of any Sunday was when she and Slick could go to the beach.

The first really hot day of the season, Bricktop took her and Wild Child "shopping" at Korvettes on Bruckner Boulevard. Each of them came out with a couple of bikinis and a bottle of suntan lotion tucked under her clothes. "Now we're really into jitterbuggin' summer," said Bricktop.

Sometimes they went to Orchard Beach on a Saturday, slept overnight on the beach, and spent all day Sunday there. Other times they broke the night in The Compound and went to the beach Sunday morning without ever sleeping.

Either way, they'd take the subway to the last stop and hop a bus. Then, when they got off the bus, they'd walk four blocks up the half-moon-shaped beach to Section One, carrying the six-packs or jugs of wine. Sometimes there would be a crowd of them—Mister Freeze, Crazy Anna, Mooch, Bricktop, Angel, and Wild Child—and sometimes it would be just the two of them. Of course, beach or no beach, they were leaving their turf, and so they went prepared for possible trouble. The girls carried the knives and revolvers in their clothes, and when they stripped to their bikinis they piled their clothes on top of the weapons and took turns standing guard over them. But Amelia never did see trouble at Orchard Beach.

She would lie there on the sand beside Slick, and as the beach got more crowded, he'd almost always suggest they go for a walk in the woods behind the beach, and there they'd make love. It would be so quiet. Nobody else in sight. Amelia guessed that was what it must be like when a man and his woman had their own place and didn't have to share with anybody else but each other. It was so peaceful in the woods that sometimes they'd fall asleep there.

She liked Saturday nights in The Compound least of all. Well, not *all* of Saturday night. The part she hated came early, when King Cobra passed out the weapons and the brothers cleaned them. It was a weekly ritual. Amelia would sit and watch Slick clean a gun twice with a soft towel until its stack glistened and the black barrel had a bluish highlight. For some reason—she didn't know why—she always expected that one of the brothers would finish his cleaning, hold up the shiny gun, and shoot it right then and there.

One Sunday morning at about five—she had just fallen asleep with her head on Slick's chest, having learned by now not to be distracted by the sounds of the moaning and panting coming from the other mattresses—Amelia was awakened by a voice from the courtyard: *"Hey, Angel! Hey,*

Angel!" Then she was vaguely aware of a tall, naked figure walking around their mattress and going over to the window, which was open from the top, the paper shade flapping against the frame. Then, suddenly, there was the roar of gunshot and the shattering of glass, and the tall, naked figure toppled back into the room, the head hitting the floor only inches from the mattress. In a moment, a light was lit and she saw Angel lying there on his back, blood oozing out of a hole in his chest.

She couldn't remember exactly what happened after that, but sometime later she found herself sitting in the living room with a sheet wrapped around her. Most of the doors in the apartment had long since been broken from their hinges or were missing altogether, so it was impossible to lose sight of Angel's body on the floor in the bedroom. That room was empty now except for Angel and Wild Child, with whom he had been sleeping. Naked, dazed, she crouched on a mattress in the corner. And soon there were police racing through the courtyard downstairs, and then two detectives were squatting beside Wild Child and talking soothingly to her, while a third covered her nakedness with a towel he had found in the bathroom. It was an extremely dirty towel, and the sight of Wild Child looking small and numb with the towel around her started Amelia crying. And after Angel's body had been taken out of the apartment and the detectives had left, she went into the bathroom, where she sat on the edge of the tub and cried until her throat ached. Then she went into the bedroom, dragged out her mattress, and went to sleep in the living room.

When she awoke, she was alone in the room. Sitting up and looking around, she discovered that the apartment was deserted except for her and Wild Child, who sat huddled against the wall in the bedroom, the dirty towel still wrapped around her. She looked out at Amelia and smiled the crooked smile of a small child. Amelia went into the bedroom, knelt down, and cradled her in her arms. Wild Child didn't make a sound, and after a moment Amelia saw that she was asleep.

Angel lay in state at the Ortiz Funeral Home for one night. He wore a navy blue suit, white shirt, and black tie; his gang jacket was draped over the lid of the sugar-white casket. Wild Child had wanted to come see him, but since she was a runaway with a father ready to grab her on sight, Apache decreed that she couldn't go. When the others, wearing their colors, left for the funeral home, Wild Child was sitting alone in front of the television set, watching a rerun of *The Untouchables*.

Slick, Mooch, and Mister Freeze were already there, serving as an honor guard to prevent anyone from busting in and overturning Angel's casket. His mother, father, and two kid brothers sat facing the casket, his mother fingering her rosary, while the gang, two by two, filed by for a last look at Angel. King Cobra had a camera, and he took a color picture of Angel lying there on the satin pillow, with the holy picture stiff and shiny between his hands. The pop of the flash cube angered Angel's father, but he kept his head bowed and said nothing. He and his wife were relieved when none of the gang turned up for the funeral the next morning. Just as the casket was about to be closed preparatory to the drive to the church, Angel's father snatched the gang jacket off the lid, took it out into the alley behind the Ortiz Funeral Home, and burned it.

A few weeks later, Bricktop went down to the *botanica*, the store that, besides selling candles, incense, and religious statues, also sold other things less devout, and came back to The Compound with some pills for Wild Child. She took them as she was instructed to do, and within twenty-four hours she had aborted. For the next several days she remained inside The Compound, lying on her mattress, looking pale and miserable.

When Amelia missed her period, she just naturally assumed that she was pregnant. She had never taken the Pill, because, like most of the other girls in The Compound, she worried that it might cause cancer. And Slick, like most of the brothers in The Compound, didn't like to use protection, because "with a scum bag on, you don't feel nothin'." The thought of a baby seemed unreal, however. She didn't have any brothers or sisters, or even little cousins. She had never held a baby. Now she was curious to see a baby up close, to touch it, maybe even hold it. She remembered once—or was it twice?—seeing a girl with a baby in her lap, sitting on a bench in Nomad Park. So she sat by the window with the glass left shattered by the bullets that had killed Angel, and waited for several days in hopes of seeing her again. When she finally did, she promptly went downstairs and across the street to the park, where she sat on a bench next to the bench where the girl sat, holding the baby in her arms.

It wasn't noon yet, and the pie-shaped little park was empty except for them. The girl regarded Amelia with suspicion. "You live over there?" she finally said, nodding in the direction of The Compound.

"Yes . . ."

"Why you starin' at my baby?"

Amelia shrugged. "I wasn't starin'," she said. "I just think it's a pretty baby, that's all."

The girl's expression softened. "It's a she. You got a baby of your own?" Amelia shook her head. "That's no place for a baby," the girl said. "I used to live there with one of the Mongols. I live home with my mother now, and the rats there are so big that last week they chased a German shepherd down the stairs and out into the street. That's the truth. And night before last, I heard an awful noise comin' from the bathroom, and I went in, and there was this big rat with its throat bit open, dyin' right there in the tub. But bad as it is, it's safer there for my baby. I don't trust those kids," she said, pointing across the street to some of the Baby Nomads standing on the stoop of The Compound. "They throw a dog off the roof, they just as likely throw a baby."

She looked hard at Amelia. "You pregnant?" Amelia shook her head, no. "Well, don't get pregnant—not while you livin' in there. The guys fuck an' fuck, and then when they get you pregnant, they act like it was all your fault. They always leave it up to you to protect yourself. Sometimes the guy you fuck with, he'll punch you in the stomach to make you lose the baby. I seen 'em do it. They like knowin' they can make a baby, but they don't *want* a baby. You get what I mean? So when I know I'm pregnant, I split. I want the baby so's I don't go down to the *botanica* for a pill. I go home to my mother . . . but I come back like this now and then, and sometimes I go upstairs and visit, 'cause in some ways The Compound is more like home. But I wouldn't live there with my baby—no way."

Amelia wanted to hold the baby, but somehow she couldn't get up the courage to ask.

The next day she went to the clinic at Lincoln Hospital and waited for four hours before her number was called. The doctor told her that she was about seven weeks along and that she was slightly anemic. On the way back to The Compound she saw that Nomad Park was empty, and she went and sat on a bench and put her feet up. After a few minutes she heard someone call, "Candy! Candy!" She turned around and saw Bricktop and four or five of the girls standing across the street beside the detectives' car

—the two who were often parked outside The Compound. Bricktop waved her over.

"This here is our virgin bride," she said, putting her arm around Amelia's shoulders. "Name's Candy. She's Slick's wife." The detective whose hair was even redder than Bricktop's smiled at her. "Show her your snapshots," Bricktop said, and he handed them to Amelia. They were snapshots of two children, a boy and a girl. "Pelo Rojo's got beautiful kids," said Bricktop. "An' there's a third one, a baby." Then she bent down and reached across Pelo Rojo to poke the other detective, sitting behind the wheel. "This here is Vito, and he got no kids. Whatsa matter, Vito, you shootin' blanks?" The dark-haired man with the full moustache laughed, and Bricktop and the girls laughed even louder. But just then Wild Child came walking across the courtyard of The Compound, and Bricktop stopped laughing. She leaned back against the car, her eyes following Wild Child, and said to Amelia, "You stay away from that one, y'hear? She's headin' for big trouble."

The next day Amelia looked out the window and saw the detectives' car parked outside The Compound again. She came down and spoke to them. Lately her ankles had started to swell, so she asked if they would mind if she sat in the back seat for a minute. Not only didn't they mind, Pelo Rojo even got out and opened the door for her.

Amelia couldn't figure how they did it—or even *if* they did it—but she found herself wanting to talk to them. To tell them that she was pregnant, for instance, and that she was getting scared. But she held her tongue and simply asked Pelo Rojo if he would show her his kids' picture again. He took the snapshot out of his wallet, and she studied it and asked their names. Then he reached into his wallet again and handed her a snapshot of his wife, a pretty woman with light brown hair and a nice smile. "You got a picture of your wife?" she asked the one called Vito. He did, and he handed it to her. It was a wedding picture: he wearing a tuxedo and his wife, a tall brunette, in a beautiful white dress and long veil, holding a bouquet that must have at least two dozen flowers in it. "She's pretty. You oughta have babies—they'd be beautiful babies," Amelia said, handing back the snapshots. Then, because she could think of nothing else to say, she got out of the car, waved good-bye, and walked back inside The Compound.

The next afternoon she came downstairs again and got into the car and talked to the two detectives. This time she told them her mother's name and address, and said that one day when they had time, she'd appreciate it a lot if they could stop by her mother's place and tell her that her daughter Amelia was O.K. and had been thinking about her. "Don't tell her you know where I live," she cautioned them. "Just say you met me—y'know, around—and I got talkin' and I asked you to do me that favor. Tell her I looked good, O.K.?"

By the time she got back upstairs, the trouble had started. She was no sooner inside the clubhouse than Bricktop pointed a finger at her. "I told you to stay away from that little cunt, right? That Wild Child cunt, right? Now you gonna see what good advice I give you . . ."

Just then the front door flew open with a kick from Apache's boot, and Wild Child, barefoot, came hurtling across the room. Bricktop grabbed her before she could fall and held her by the elbows as Apache ran across and punched her in the stomach. Then, grabbing Wild Child by the hair, she kicked her into the bedroom where Angel had been shot and locked the door. "Good thing we got them doors fixed," Bricktop muttered. "Pencil! Pen!" Apache demanded, snapping her fingers. Bricktop started rushing around, lifting up chairs and mattresses, kicking the curls of dust, searching for something Apache could write with. She returned with a stubby pencil and a piece of paper and handed them to Apache, who squatted down on the floor and wrote WHIPPING TIME in large letters across the top of the paper. "What d'you think that douche bag was doin'? She was upstairs fuckin' two of the Mongols, that's what!" She began writing furiously again, then stopped. "The night we go to Ortiz to pay our respects to Angel and we leave her alone, where'd she go? Next door, to screw with the Diplomats!" She finished writing, scrambled to her feet, and thrust the paper at Bricktop. "You get this nailed up on the wall and see to it that everybody's here tonight to see the punishment." Then she bolted out of the apartment and down the stairs, taking them two at a time.

"Y'see?" said Bricktop, holding the paper in her hand. Amelia came closer and read: WHIPPING TIME—WILD CHILD—FOR SLEEPING WITH OUTSIDERS.

At ten o'clock that evening Wild Child was escorted from the bedroom that had become her prison into the living room, where Apache stood in the center of a circle formed by the solemn-faced members of the girls' division. The brothers stood outside the circle, leaning against the walls. Amelia, the only nonmember among the girls, stood beside Slick, holding on to his arm with both hands.

As Bricktop and Crazy Anna stripped Wild Child naked, Apache slowly, ceremoniously removed her large loop earrings—the signal that she was about to attack. She then raised one leg high off the floor and sent her foot crashing down. Wild Child cringed and backed away from her, only to be shoved back into the center of the circle, where she stood, head bowed and shoulders hunched. Apache advanced toward her, and suddenly brought her right knee up and into Wild Child's soft belly. The girl's head snapped back, and from her throat came a piercing cry of pain.

Amelia turned away, leaning her head against Slick's arm. The circle widened, giving Apache more room. She swung her arm and gave Wild Child a karate chop, cutting off the cry that was still filling all corners of the room. Then a series of fast blows to the face and body sent the girl crumpling to the floor, where Apache began to stomp her. Wild Child tried to roll away, and Apache pinned her to the floor by bringing the full weight of her knee down on her. Then she stopped beating her and stood there, hands on hips, breathing heavily.

Now the circle around Apache and Wild Child broke as the girls formed a line that extended the length of the room. Once in position, with Bricktop at the head, each girl spread her legs wide as King Cobra passed down the line, handing out wooden slats, belts, and electric cords. When Crazy Anna, who was last in line, had wrapped the belt around her fist, Apache dragged Wild Child by the hair over to where Bricktop stood. She twisted her around until Wild Child faced Bricktop, and then she forced her down on her hands and knees. Stepping back, she took aim and kicked Wild Child in the buttocks. As if she'd been set in motion by some sort of key or spring, Wild Child began crawling between Bricktop's legs, and as she did Bricktop bent over and sent the electric cord flying, its socket cutting into the flesh of her buttocks. Wild Child crawled faster and faster as each girl in turn attacked her naked flesh. By the time Crazy Anna had struck her, the skin had been cut open and the flesh was flecked with blood. Passing between Crazy Anna's legs, Wild Child collapsed at the feet of King Cobra, who stood there waiting for her, the snake whip coiled around his forearm. The girls melted into the background then, joining the men—and Amelia—at the perimeter of the room. Now even Apache moved away from the center, although she took care to stop short of the others, so that she was still obviously second in command of the punishment.

Suddenly King Cobra started running backward down the middle of the room. Midway, he stopped and spun his arm in the air so that the whip uncoiled and its tip slapped the floor. As it did, Wild Child raised herself on her elbows and looked up at him. Pressing her hand to her mouth, Amelia stepped back, but whoever was standing behind her shoved her forward. She tried to cover her eyes, but Slick reached over and pulled her hands down. No one turned away when the prez meted out punishment.

King Cobra swung the whip, and it coiled around Wild Child, toppling her over on her side. The whip snapped free and he swung again, and this time it cut across her chest and Wild Child's skinny arms flew up as though trying to catch it. Again and again the whip lashed her, and it began to resemble some kind of gruesome game: The whip struck and the skinny arms automatically grabbed at the air.

Then King Cobra allowed Wild Child to lay hold of the whip. She held on to it with both hands, and he started to pull it, at first very slowly and then faster and faster, around and around, until her naked body was bumping the floor. And still she clung to the whip. Finally he dropped the whip and once again started running backward down the middle of the room. He stopped midway, and then he started running back toward Wild Child, who lay there, gasping for air and still holding on to the tip of the whip. When he was about three feet from her, King Cobra leaped in the air and came crashing down on her with both boots. Amelia felt the blood draining from her face, and she doubled over, folding both arms across her stomach. But no one, not even Slick, took notice of her, for now everyone in the room was moving toward the center, where King Cobra stood, pulling the whip free from Wild Child's grip.

Amelia fainted. When she regained consciousness, she was on a mattress in the bedroom where Wild Child had been imprisoned earlier. The door was closed, but from the room outside she heard the sounds of the stereo and bongo drums, and for a moment she thought that maybe she had had a bad dream. She struggled to her feet, went over to the door, and leaned against it. She was afraid to open it. She didn't know why she was afraid, but she was. Just then she heard voices and the sound of running from the courtyard below, and she went over to the window and looked down. Cops were hurrying through the doors directly below her, and she recognized Pelo Rojo and Vito running up the stoop. Amelia went back to the door, opened it, and stepped into the living room. Bricktop and Crazy Anna danced by her, and across the room she saw Slick and several of the brothers squatting on the floor, playing the bongo drums. Before she could start across the room to tell Slick that the police were coming, there was pounding on the door. Apache looked around the room and, with palms up, gestured for them all to increase the action. As she opened the door, the stereo was turned louder, the brothers pounded the drums harder, and the girls danced faster. *See? We're just havin' a party, that's all. Why you cops hasslin' us for?*

The police were no sooner inside than they shut the stereo off and ordered the brothers to stop playing the bongo drums. The girls stopped dancing and stood watching while the police searched the apartment. One of them opened the door of a closet to find a pile of dirty sheets and towels at least five feet high. He began poking at it with his night stick, and heard the sound of moaning from somewhere inside the closet. The officer began tearing away at the pile. In a moment, half of the sheets and towels lay at his feet and Wild Child was visible there on the floor.

"Jesus!" Amelia heard one of the cops exclaim at the sight of the battered girl.

Amelia moved toward Slick, but he caught her eye and nodded for her to stay where she was, so she stood and watched while the cops ordered the brothers to their feet and herded them down the stairs, en route to the station house. Then the ambulance arrived and they took Wild Child away, after which detectives questioned each of the girls separately. When it was Amelia's turn, she was shaking so much that she folded her hands together and pressed them between her knees. She told the detectives that she knew nothing about what had happened to Wild Child. Where had she been? Asleep. Asleep? She began to sob. When she was finally able to talk, she said, "I'm gonna have a baby. So I sleep a lot. That's good for the baby."

Apache was taken down to the station house too. Then, when some of the girls turned the stereo back on and began dancing, Pelo Rojo came over to where Amelia was standing alone by the window and told her that he had seen her mother and given her the message. "Your mother said she worries about you and prays for you every night," he told her. He patted her shoulder, and then he and Vito Moles left. They were no sooner gone than Bricktop came over to her and told her to be careful of what she said to the law. What happened to Wild Child, she said, could happen again. Lying on her mattress, just before falling asleep, Amelia said a prayer in Spanish that she hadn't said or even thought of since she was a little girl.

When she awoke a few hours later, Slick was sleeping beside her. He and all the brothers, except King Cobra, had been released. Apache was still being held for questioning. Amelia got up, walking lightly around the other mattresses and out into the living room, where Bricktop and Crazy Anna lay snoring on the bare floor. She went into the kitchen, turned on the faucet, and splashed cold water on her face. She wanted to comb her hair, but her comb was inside a pack of tissues tucked beneath the mattress, and she didn't want to go back into the bedroom for fear of waking Slick. She crossed the room, opened the door very slowly, and then ran toward the stairs. Out in the courtyard, she almost tripped over a broken bicycle wheel abandoned among a tangle of rusty plumbing fixtures. It was deathly quiet, as it always was early in the morning. She made it down the stoop and onto the sidewalk, and then for a moment she didn't know which way to run. She had almost forgotten the way back to her mother's apartment. Just then Pelo Rojo and Vito drove around the corner. They stopped beside Nomad Park, and Vito got out and waved to her. She ran across the street to the car and got in, and without saying a word to her, the two detectives drove her directly to her mother's.

Amelia's son is almost four years old now, and she lives with him in a tenement not far from her mother's. She is on welfare, and most days, weather permitting, she sits on the stoop and does embroidery. Some summer afternoons she sits with her little boy, Ramon, in what was once Nomad Park, opposite the buildings that once comprised The Compound. Amelia still refers to it as Nomad Park—a habit—and the bench she sits on is still splattered with the gangs' colors, although they're considerably faded now.

"Slick? He's upstate doin' time for manslaughter. I never saw him again. He never tried to see me or anything. Leavin' the way I did must've cost him loss of face. I was real scared he'd want revenge. I was so scared that when my time came for the baby, my mother got enough money together to send me down to my grandmother in San Juan. There's where Ramon was born. He's a real Puerto Rican.

"Me and Slick are still married. To get a divorce, a wife

has to go see the prez, but if the husband don't want a divorce too, they gotta stay married. If he agrees to the divorce, then the prez takes the machete and makes a cut again on the thumb—same place like before—only this time they don't mix blood but just pour red wine on the cut." Amelia holds out her left thumb and shows the small scar. "But why bother? I figure Slick will be dead before long. There's no such thing as an old gang member. They don't live long. Drugs, police, or somebody get them.

"I don't know what to do with my life. What gets me sometimes is how much my life is like my mother's now. Me all alone with my child. No man around. Just the two of us, like it was with my mother and me when I was little. Only difference between me and my mother when she was my age is I want to get away from here. I don't want my son to grow up and be part of a gang. I want him to have everything I didn't have." Amelia smiles at that. "Y'see, just like my mother. She always wanted me to have the best, and even though she was on welfare, she worked hard to give it to me. She washed clothes on the side to add to her income, and she did it by hand, too, because we didn't have no washing machine. She also used to make gloves and do embroidery to make extra money. I learned this embroidery I do from her. I always looked nice when I was little. My mother gave me a big Communion."

4.
School Days, Dear Olde Savage School Days

Most of the gang members living in The Compound attended—after a fashion—Junior High School 133. Not surprisingly, it had the reputation of being the most dangerous school in the Bronx, if not the entire city. "A pure jungle" is the way Vito Moles remembers it. When it opened in 1963, in an already deteriorating neighborhood, the handsome, modern building was ready to receive 1,400 students, ages twelve to fourteen. Its principal, a capable, tough-minded woman, was accustomed to dealing with difficult children. "They're all God's children," she often said. By June, 1976, when JHS 133 ceased to exist, it had an enrollment of fewer than 400 boys and girls—some as old as sixteen and seventeen—who walked to school along blocks of abandoned and burnt-out buildings. The South Bronx was fast becoming an urban ghost town. A population of over 650,000 in 1971 had, by 1976, declined to approximately 390,000—a loss of more than a quarter of a million people.

"Things that happened in the community were very harmful to us" is the way a former assistant principal explains the decline of the school. And The Compound was certainly one of those ruinous happenings.

Not that JHS 133 had ever been a model school. Long before The Compound, students there were terrorizing other students—and teachers. In the late sixties a substitute teacher, a short, balding man the kids called "Porky Pig," was assaulted in the classroom by a fifteen-year-old girl, and the assistant principal remembers, "I could have almost cried at the sight of his face—blood all over it." Another teacher was paying a strapping youth twenty-five cents a day to, as the boy bragged, "keep the class cool." Even the assistant principal, a husky man who had once coached high-school football, was attacked outside the school by a fourteen-year-old wielding steel handlebars he had ripped off a bicycle. Still, there were no organized street gangs, and the violence was sporadic.

But by the early seventies, when the gangs emerged flaunting their colors, JHS 133 had an enrollment of 2,250, and classes had overflowed into the school cafeteria, gymnasium, and auditorium. By this time violence was almost an everyday occurrence. The new principal never walked the halls alone. And the gangs of The Compound, chronic truants, began using the school to recruit new members.

They would emerge from The Compound wearing their colors, twenty or thirty strong, and take a finger-snapping stroll down to the school, where they would station themselves outside, highly visible to the students inside. At dismissal time they acted like a magnet for the younger boys eager to be taken over to Prospect Avenue and shown how easy it was to rip off an old lady and get away with her cash. The next day, with the easy money in his jeans, the kid might repay his benefactor by stealing food for him from the school cafeteria. Then, a night or two later—just as they said they would—the gang would break into the school, urinate and defecate on the floor, and spray their street names on the walls. Before the week was out, the twelve-year-old would be walking and talking like his idol, Chocolate Chip or Mister Dung, and wearing his jacket inside out so's the fuckin' teachers wouldn't see his new gang colors. But shit, man, the first day he wore his colors under cover, his gang—wearing their colors for everybody to see—bust into the school and raced through and out the back, on the way knocking a couple of teachers on their asses. Cool. Real cool.

Girl students, meanwhile, were vying for invitations to The Compound. Often after attending a party there, the girl stayed on as a wife and dropped out of school.

The situation worsened to the point where some students threatened by gang members were being chauffered to and from school by teachers. (Few parents in the South Bronx own cars.) In retaliation, some teachers' cars were vandalized and others set on fire. One teacher had a daily ritual: He tied his car via a ten-foot linked chain to a traffic stanchion, then put locks on both the part of the chain wrapped around the stanchion and the part wrapped around his car's axle. One day he came out of class to find both his car and the ten-foot chain missing. Gangs from The Compound had used an acetylene torch to cut off the two locks.

Assaults on teachers increased, and most victims were too terrified to press charges. It became so difficult to recruit teachers to JHS 133 that for an entire semester there were six classes unattended and staff teachers had to take turns covering these classes as best they could.

The school was constantly being broken into at night. Its architecture made entering relatively easy: It was built on a slope, with each of its four floors at some point accessible on the ground level. A safe containing bus passes was rifled. Musical instruments belonging to the school band were stolen and peddled around the neighborhood; the going price for a trumpet was ten dollars. Finally, after fifteen members of a Compound gang, armed with a .22-caliber rifle and assorted pipes and clubs, invaded the school one afternoon and fired a shot through the door of the administration office, all exit doors—in violation of the fire laws—were locked and chained from the inside.

The assistant principal began suffering dizzy spells. He went to his family physician, who took his blood pressure. The doctor was so alarmed by the high reading that he refused to tell him exactly how high it was, except that it was over 200. The man promptly applied for a transfer to another school, and left JHS 133 within six months.

About this time Miguel Delgado, a mathematics teacher, became very vocal on the subject of how he thought the school was failing to meet its students' needs. A documentary-film crew visited the South Bronx and accompanied Delgado, a tall, rather ascetic-looking young man, as he walked the streets and discussed the problem as he saw it. "Schools have helped create the problem by giving courses that mean nothing," he said, as kids pounded his back or slapped his palm in passing. "Reading? *Talk* is the means of communication. The kids will talk all day long. A guy with a good rap is respected. But they're in schools where talking is forbidden . . . is criminal. Talk—the ability to rap —equals manhood."

Most of the other teachers at JHS 133 didn't believe that the curriculum was at fault. Some of them regarded Miguel Delgado as an opportunist, "a professional Puerto Rican" now that it would do him some good, gain him some recognition. They remembered that when he first came to the school he was wearing a Brooks Brothers suit, a shirt and tie, and short hair. Now he wore jeans and a work shirt, and his hair hung in a long braid. Furthermore, they said, his classroom was more like a math circus than a math class, with a bulletin board that was a riot of hot Latin colors.

The only son of a fair-skinned, blue-eyed Puerto Rican mother and a Venezuelan father, whose own father had been a governor of Caracas, Miguel Delgado had come to JHS 133 in 1968. It was his first real exposure to a truly Hispanic environment. Despite his name and the fact that he had been raised in New York City, he had grown up far removed from the ethnic community of the South Bronx. In college he had belonged to a WASP fraternity.

"He didn't look Hispanic . . . or act Hispanic," recalls Sylvia Freedman, who came to the school as a history teacher one year after Miguel Delgado. "Miguel was so square, so pure. A beautiful, pure person. He always wore a shirt and tie, and his hair was so short it looked like it was growing in, not out. The first time I saw him, I thought he was about forty. He was actually only twenty-eight."

Sylvia Freedman was thirty-five at the time, a mother of two children, and recently divorced from an Orthodox rabbi who headed a congregation of Sephardic Jews in New Jersey. It was in her husband's temple that she had her first exposure to what she calls Latin-type personalities. And Miguel Delgado definitely did not appear to her to be a Latin-type personality.

"He asked me out, and we ended up downtown at my apartment in the West Village. It was always filled with crazy, wonderful Village people. And that evening a friend introduced himself to Miguel and added, 'I'm a dealer.' 'What do you deal in?' asked Miguel. 'Drugs,' answered the man, and Miguel was so shocked. He told me he'd never come back if a man like that was going to be there. He was afraid a contact like that could jeopardize his job at the school."

Sylvia Freedman and Miguel Delgado were married the

following year, 1969, and a year later they became acutely aware of the reemergence of the South Bronx street gangs. "One day a big crowd of kids tumbled out of the school and into the street," Sylvia recalls. "A boy had made a pass at a girl belonging to a member of the Savage Nomads and so there was going to be a rumble."

The gangs intrigued Sylvia and Miguel. She says now, "I dug them—like theater." And Delgado regarded them as probably the brightest kids in the school, the ones with the most energy, the most potential—provided, of course, that someone could motivate them to stay in class and apply themselves. He was convinced he could. He approached the principal with a plan, and he received permission to go ahead with his experiment.

Books were rarely opened in his math class. To activate his students to want to deal with numbers, he would start them out measuring their own bodies. How many inches from your elbow to your wrist? How many inches from your knee to your ankle?

Then the principal gave Delgado permission to move his class to one of the classrooms in the one-story, aluminum mini-school situated in the schoolyard. The smaller school, built to relieve the incredible congestion in the main building, seemed more appropriate for what Miguel Delgado said he was most concerned with: establishing a friendly, family-type environment conducive to learning. His street kids weren't into books; to them everything was rapping. And Miguel was good at that. For instance, he would squat down on the floor of the classroom and play jacks with some of the girls. The dudes would laugh and kid him about that, and he would take that opportunity to start rapping with them about what masculinity really means. He thought he was making genuine progress. Other teachers didn't think so, claiming that his students were practically dismantling the mini-school—stripping the copper tubing from the air-conditioning units, driving stolen cars into the schoolyard at night, parking them behind the mini-school, stripping them, and setting what was left of them on fire.

By then Sylvia and Miguel Delgado had become what they thought of as surrogate parents to some of the gang members and their girls. They were living in a duplex apartment on Manhattan's West Side, and the gangs would turn up there at all hours of the night, to be fed and sometimes to sleep. "It was a very expensive program we were running —without a grant," Sylvia says. "Sometimes the kids would rip us off. Ripping you off and loving you at the same time. That was all part of it. We were creating a kind of empire— an environment—for people to meet and contact."

To some of the other teachers at Junior High School 133, it was a doomed empire, with Miguel Delgado playing Maximilian and Sylvia his Carlotta.

They introduced some of the gang members to the off-Broadway theater. "These kids, who couldn't sit still in a classroom, sat quietly, fascinated, in a theater." Delgado also arranged for some of the gang members to speak at universities. Black Bongo, for instance, addressed a class at Columbia University.

"Bongo," says Sylvia, "was a father for his gang. A god. Really a very special person." He and Big Mama spent many nights in their home.

The special rapport that Sylvia and Miguel Delgado had established with the gangs in The Compound gained them attention from the media. They received numerous offers to appear on television. Miguel appeared with a group of gang members to discuss the New York City school system. One dude said: "When you talk, they tell you 'Don't talk.' When you touch, they tell you 'Don't touch.' It's *bullshit!*"

About that time, she says, they began to "feel danger." She thinks many people began to expect them to inform on the gangs or to somehow control them. "That's the last thing Miguel would want to do to anybody—*control* them."

The following semester he approached the principal with a new plan for another special class; surprisingly, he was given approval. This class, however, would be in the regular school building. "But then," says Sylvia, "they began to chop away at it. Miguel wanted to take the kids out of the school on field trips. At first they said yes, and then they decided no. Imagine, twenty-five kids like that kept in one room." In the mini-school, apart from the main building and the rest of the faculty, they had wandered in and out of the classroom freely; in the big school they would be expected to stay put. Miguel's critics among the other teachers would be watching, eager to complain of his unorthodox methods.

But neither he nor his students were intimidated by the move back to the main building. They wandered in and out of the classroom at will, and some began arriving via the window instead of the door. Miguel Delgado continued to eschew a conventional curriculum. Homing pigeons are popular in the South Bronx, so he built a pigeon coop and kept a pigeon in the classroom. One day someone let it out of the coop and it flew down the hall and in and out of several other classrooms, with Miguel's students in hot pursuit. Convinced that most of his students suffered an identity problem—scarcely a week went by that they didn't go down into the subway and get a string of snapshots from one of the instant photo booths on the station, as though to reassure themselves of their own existence—he took the large mirror that hung in the teachers' cloakroom and put it on the wall of his classroom, so that at any time of the day a student could look in the mirror and see himself or herself reflected.

Then Delgado, the math teacher, decided to give a lecture on sex education. He felt that it was essential that these kids know something about birth control. On the day of the lecture he was standing outside the classroom with four of his students, holding a large condom in his hands. The assistant principal, an elderly lady, was passing by at the time, and she asked him: "What kind of class is this, Mr. Delgado?" "Sex education!" he replied, and, turning to his students, he said: "O.K., now let's go inside and demonstrate."

About this time Sylvia Delgado, who had transferred from JHS 133 to a high school in Brooklyn, had become seriously ill, and she thinks Miguel was "feeling squeezed." In any event, soon after his lecture on sex education, he was suspended by the Board of Education, which had compiled a list of some 164 charges against him. Among them: On an occasion when his class had become "totally unruly" he made no attempt to quiet them, and when the principal, together with nine other school officials, attempted to enter the classroom, his students barricaded the door with their bodies and he made no attempt to control them; he permitted the presence in his classroom of a boy who was not a student at Junior High School 133 and who had been warned numerous times not to enter the premises; permitted his students to smoke in his classroom during school hours; permitted a student to stand on the windowsill of his classroom; permitted four boys from his class to gamble by pitching pennies against the back door of the classroom; permitted students to play handball in the classroom; permitted two students to dance together in the classroom to the music of a record player during the time set aside for academic instruction; permitted students from his class to run around freely in the second-floor halls; during the lunch period, permitted students to throw chairs in the corridor outside of his classroom; permitted his students to explode firecrackers in his classroom.

When he was given a written report of these charges, Delgado called it "garbage" and, according to the Board of Education, "accused one of the authors of the report—in street language—of grossly immoral tendencies without offering any supporting facts."

Barred from the premises of the school, Delgado had copies made of the charges, and, stationing himself across the street, he distributed them to students while a line of pickets recruited from his class chanted, "Free Delgado!"

He planned to fight for reinstatement and, with the assistance of the Civil Liberties Union, make a test case of his suspension. Then one afternoon, Sylvia Delgado says, a young, black Puerto Rican came to the door of their apartment and asked to see Miguel. He told Sylvia's son that he was Miguel's brother. The boy shut the door at once and told Sylvia and Miguel that the man had a blanket spread over his arm and something stiff was under the blanket. The next morning Miguel Delgado left the apartment, and it was several weeks before Sylvia learned that he had fled to Los Angeles. He cut his hair and went into hiding. When he finally contacted her, he told her, "They were out for my mind—now they want my life." Why were they? One can only guess, for Miguel never explained.

He left Los Angeles after a few months, settling in a Midwestern city, where he got a job in a hardware store. The last time she saw him, Sylvia says, he had lost thirty pounds and was practicing yoga three times a day. "Miguel's working at staying alive. All he wants now is to live in peace and forget his experience in the South Bronx." The only person of that period with whom he has kept contact is Black Bongo, who, Sylvia says, is the only one Miguel Delgado feels he can wholly trust.

When her husband fled to the West Coast, Sylvia says, she felt that she would die without him. "I didn't think I could survive alone." For a time Big Mama came to stay with her. Now, although she says Miguel is still very special to her, Sylvia has decided she can't live with those anxieties any more, and now she's fallen in love again and moved away. "I think I'm going to live," she says. She too wants to forget the South Bronx, although she regards the experience as a special period of discovery. But it still rankles her to think of the charge that Miguel Delgado couldn't control his students.

"That was the whole thing—*control behavior*," she says. "They said he had no control over the kids, but what they probably feared was that he'd have ultimate control. That he could establish an army."

Paul Steimaszyk, one-time dean in charge of discipline at JHS 133, disagrees most emphatically. He says that to this day former students of 133 come to him and say of Miguel Delgado: "That guy really screwed us up!" Steimaszyk contends that Delgado was so permissive that he encouraged them to misbehave.

Joseph Imperial, the assistant principal who asked to be transferred out of JHS 133, feels that he has never been made a principal because he has been such a good disciplinarian: "Now I can't document that, but I have an outstanding record as an educator—my record speaks for itself—but one of the facets of my behavior as an assistant principal that I think my superiors have held against me is that I've been a good disciplinarian. A good disciplinarian but never brutal to the children."

Soon after Junior High School 133 closed prior to reopening as an annex to a local high school, Imperial attended a reunion of teachers who once taught there. A lot, he said, were saddened to see it go. But it's unlikely that Miguel Delgado is. No doubt he is still convinced that, had he been permitted to continue teaching his class in his own way, he would have succeeded where more conventional teachers failed. Ed O'Rourke and Vito Moles question his sincerity, suspecting that he and the gangs were using each other for the same purpose: to gain power in the school. I suspect that so far as the gangs were concerned, he was primarily a symbol of the Establishment. Sure, he reached them. He touched them briefly. But man, you don't trust the Establishment no matter how sweet the sounds it makes.

The gangs did to Delgado what they did to JHS 133— and what they would ultimately do to their own headquarters. Given the chance, you use what the man gives you, or what you can take; use it up, then destroy it.

5.
Brother Sunshine, He Died for Peace

Carlton Williams was a phenomenon. A vice-president and warlord of the Latin Diplomats, one of the five predominantly Puerto Rican gangs in The Compound, he was a black who preached nonviolence. But what made him even more extraordinary was the fact that he was sincere and, furthermore, highly respected by every one of the gangs. Brother Sunshine, they called him. He could wander into any clubhouse anywhere in the South Bronx and, without fear, fraternize with the gang there. Big Mama, the sullen queen of The Compound, was actually known to smile at the sight of Sunshine blithely making his way up the stoop. He was living proof that a peace-loving dude could not only survive, but could actually go around urging the gangs to cool it, to sit down and try to settle their differences without resorting to violence.

Ed O'Rourke and Vito Moles were fascinated by Brother Sunshine and the power he wielded among the gangs, but they didn't pretend to fully understand what made a soft-spoken, easygoing black able to function as a bona fide peacemaker in a gang world that was predominantly His-

panic. Furthermore, Sunshine was a New York–born black
—a real foreigner.

It didn't take a lot to make him happy. Some pot. Some
wine. Some girls. At twenty-five, Brother Sunshine was
about nine years older than the average gang member. A
father figure? "No way," says Vito Moles. "Sunshine was a
cool dude with that real jive talk." There was no doubt that
his ability to talk easily and persuasively made him a Big
Man, but Ed O'Rourke thinks the fact that he was a Vietnam veteran and a rehabilitated junkie also helped him earn
his very special niche as a kind of folk hero. Vietnam gave
any dude a certain glamor. He'd gone there and come back
—alive—with stories to tell to kids most of whom were too
young to have served in Vietnam and furthermore had never
even been outside the Bronx.

Brother Sunshine's reputation as a peacemaker had won
his gang media recognition—not wholly deserved—as a
group that specialized in keeping the hot tempers of the
South Bronx street gangs cool; this had gotten them a rent-
free clubhouse courtesy of the city's Youth Services Agency.
But one night, while sitting in the back of the car driven by
O'Rourke and Moles, Brother Sunshine confided that it
was sure getting tougher and tougher to convince his brothers to stay cool. "They're startin' to think savage," he said.
"They want a big arsenal. They wanna take the dues money
and buy weapons." It was the first time the two officers had
ever seen him look down-in-the-mouth. "No way I gonna
hand them guns and say, 'O.K., go get revenge. Go shoot
somebody.' No way."

A few weeks later, shortly before the Thanksgiving holiday, they saw him again. This time it was at a factory loft
his gang had rented for a Sunday-night dance. Wearing an
Aussie bush hat and flashing his pearly smile, Brother Sunshine was sitting behind a desk at the door, collecting the

dollar entrance fee from the brothers and sisters. He had no time for conversation; and anyway, the record player in the big room beyond was so clangorous that pantomime was the only sure means of communication. So, seeing O'Rourke and Moles, he just reached out to slap palms and mouth the words "Stay cool!"

Late the following afternoon, his mother stopped by The Compound. She could usually find Sunshine there at that time of day, lazing around and rapping with his brothers. But a kid named Fish told her, "You just missed him, Mama Sunshine. He's gone over to One Thirty-three to break up a rumble. But nothin' to worry about," he assured her. "Sunshine's just doin' his thing." She smiled, and before she left she told Fish to remember to be sure to have a nice Thanksgiving.

About that time, Brother Sunshine was approaching the schoolyard of Junior High School 133 with Biscuit, a fifteen-year-old Diplomat, at his heels. It was Biscuit who had burst into the clubhouse five minutes earlier to report that some Black Spades—about fifteen of them—and some of the Seven Immortals had come into the schoolyard and grabbed Yogi, a brother, ripped off his colors, then blindfolded him and knocked him unconscious with a baseball bat. The cops had just come and taken him to Lincoln Hospital.

Now the schoolyard was deserted, and Sunshine and Biscuit walked around the block looking for some signs of life. The school was built on a slope, and now, standing on the top of a long flight of steps leading down to a pie-shaped slice of pavement behind the school, they saw some thirty-five dudes milling around. The dudes, all wearing their colors, watched as Sunshine started down the steps toward them, confident, as always, that he'd be able to rap with them. But Biscuit hesitated, his eyes panning over the crowd. He saw some pipes, some chains, and—Jesus, a *gun*.

He wanted to turn and run then, but he saw Sunshine, near-
ing the bottom step, raise his hand and make the peace sign,
and so he followed as if by rote.

Sunshine stopped on the last step and lifted his leather
jacket to show that he wasn't carrying any concealed weapons. Then he stepped down, and the dudes began moving
in around him as he began talking in his slow, easy way.
He said that he just wanted to know why anybody would
beat up on one of his brothers. No sweat, understand? He
felt sure that there was some sort of misunderstanding. The
dudes eyed him, and the ones in front, standing directly
opposite Sunshine, looked at one another. They said nothing; they simply looked at one another and then back again
at Sunshine. Biscuit was standing behind him on the bottom
step, and despite the cold, sweat was trickling down his
back. He was scared, man. The sound of Sunshine's voice
had given him a measure of reassurance, but now nobody
was talking, not even Sunshine, and the silence was ominous. Just then Biscuit saw one of the dudes start smacking
his palm with a pipe wrapped with black tape, and he
panicked. He pulled his combat belt from around his waist
and started swinging it. He stood there whipping the air
with the belt, until he felt the urine stinging his thigh. Then
he turned around and started running back up the stairs as
fast as he could.

When Sunshine started talking again, trying to assure
the dudes that everything was still cool, it wasn't. They
were pressing in on him. One of them suddenly reached out
and gave him a punch in the stomach. In a matter of seconds, six of them were up on the steps directly behind him,
and one of them had an eighteen-inch pipe in his fist.

The first blow hit Brother Sunshine on the back of his
head. He rocked on his heels but fought to stay upright.
"Get him!" he heard somebody shout. He opened his mouth
to say something, and then he felt two more blows behind

his right ear. In the instant before he lost consciousness and fell, he must actually have felt the back of his head cave in and the warm blood start to stream down the back of his neck.

The attack had lasted exactly thirty seconds. When the squad car arrived, Brother Sunshine lay dying on the pavement, a sunburst of sticky blood like a halo around his head and blood bubbling out of his mouth. He died in the back seat of the squad car as it sped down Bruckner Boulevard to Lincoln Hospital. As Vito Moles describes it, "Sunshine was beaten on the head with an eighteen-inch pipe until his brains were hanging out."

Within the hour word of Brother Sunshine's murder swept through The Compound, and there was a mass exodus as members of the Mongols, the Storm Troopers, the Savage Nomads, and his own brothers, the Latin Diplomats, streamed across the courtyard and down the stoop, heading for the scene of the crime. Detectives O'Rourke and Moles followed them, driving slowly, taking care to keep a respectful distance, for they knew how tense a situation this was. Not only had Brother Sunshine, the peacemaker, been iced, but the rumor was that some of the Seven Immortals, a Compound gang, were involved. It was unheard of for one Compound gang to attack another. After all, they were family. Not surprisingly, there wasn't a single member of that gang in the crowd that was so dense that it filled the sidewalks, picking up momentum as it moved and forcing pedestrians to jump up on stoops or into the gutter in order to get out of the way. And when it came to street crossings, it crossed—red light or no red light—and the traffic stopped for it.

The detectives parked across the street and watched as the gangs swarmed around some of the Latin Diplomats who were standing on the pie-shaped pavement where Sunshine had fallen. Then all of them encircled the police officers stationed there. O'Rourke and Moles couldn't hear any of the dialogue, since so many were shouting at once. Then some of the gang members started moving away from the center of the crowd and stood, crying, with their arms around one another's shoulders. About a half-hour later the crowd broke up, and the gangs, now less emotional, slowly started back toward The Compound independently of one another.

The last to leave were the Latin Diplomats. Dice, the prez, spied the detectives' car, disengaged himself, and came across the street. He looked stricken. Leaning on the door of the car and waving his hand back in the direction of where he had just been, he said, "Sunshine died for peace. They killed a saint, man. That's what they done. Sunshine was a martyr for peace. Everybody loved him. He was The Man." Then, almost apologetically: "If somethin's not done, all hell's gonna break loose."

"How about a ride back to the clubhouse?" Moles asked him.

Dice shook his head. "No, I gotta stay with my brothers. We gotta do Sunshine's work now." He straightened up, slapped palms, and returned across the street, to lead his brothers back to their storefront headquarters.

The next day, as Dice was leaving The Compound, a car pulled up to the curb and someone inside called his name. It was Zip, prez of the Ugly Orphans. Dice walked over to the car, and Zip told him, "We got three of the mother-fuckers who iced Sunshine. Get in." Dice got into the back seat, where two of the Orphans made room for him, and they drove to the gang's basement clubhouse several blocks away. There he found one of the Seven Immortals and two of the Black Spades kneeling, their hands and feet tied. "Here," said Zip, handing him a .32-caliber revolver, "avenge Sunshine."

The three dudes started pleading with him not to shoot

as Zip left the room, closing the door behind him. "Dice, don't do it!" "You know me, Dice. It was a mistake. We loved Sunshine." "I swear it wasn't me, Dice. I swear!"

The gun felt good in his hand. He put its nozzle to the temple of one of the Spades, and the dude started to blubber so hard that spit was bubbling out of his mouth. Then Dice moved on to the other Spade and pressed the gun against his head, and the dude bit his lip, squeezed his eyes shut, and stayed motionless. Then he went over to the third one, the Immortal, and shoved the nozzle of the gun against his temple and began slowly turning it around, while the dude stared up at him, beads of perspiration on his face. Then Dice pulled back and cocked the gun, and the three of them started bellowing. He stood there like that for almost a full minute. The urge to kill the motherfuckers was so great that he thought that if he didn't pull the trigger at least once, he was going to get sick to his stomach. Then he heard the door open behind him, and for some crazy reason the sound of the door snapped him out of it. This was no way to do honor to Sunshine. Dice turned around, handed the gun back to Zip, and walked out of the clubhouse.

Brother Sunshine's funeral was a community event. His body lay in state inside the Thessalonia Baptist Church, which was located only yards from the spot where he had been attacked. Wearing purple bands around their left arms and heads, the Latin Diplomats stood guard over his silver casket until one in the morning. On the day of his burial the gangs inside The Compound—including the Seven Immortals—hung sheets out their windows bearing messages of mourning written with Magic Markers. GOODBY SUNSHINE. REST IN PEACE, PEACEMAKER. THERE'S A NEW SAINT IN HEAVEN. When the time came for the church service, there wasn't a single gang member left inside The Compound. Everyone went to the church to pay respect to the memory of Brother Sunshine.

Protocol was observed. The gangs entered the church separately, with each prez leading his group up the steps. Then, standing by the casket, he draped his gang's colors over the lid of the casket. When the lid became so heavy with gang colors that it appeared some might fall into the casket, the gangs arriving last were respectfully asked to place their colors over the back of the pew in the last row.

Standing in the pulpit, surrounded on all sides by floral wreaths, the preacher eulogizing "God's child, Carlton Williams" compared him to Christ in his spirit of self-sacrifice. "He that loses his life for others shall save his life," he said, at which point one of Sunshine's wives broke down, sobbing uncontrollably.

Five of the Latin Diplomats served as pallbearers. Just behind the silver casket and Sunshine's grief-stricken relatives, the rest of the 250-member gang—male and female—filed out of the church, eyes downcast, each one carrying a floral tribute—anything from a wreath to a single flower—which was ceremoniously deposited into one of the three limousines specially reserved for floral tributes.

Ed O'Rourke and Vito Moles attended the church service, as did many members of law-enforcement agencies, various community leaders, and representatives of Mayor Lindsay's Task Force. The Commissioner of the Youth Services Agency, who said he feared that "mass havoc" might follow the murder of the peacemaker, climbed into his official limousine and joined the procession to the cemetery, which was led by the Latin Diplomats, marching four abreast before the hearse. The funeral cortege, photographed by cameramen from all the leading metropolitan newspapers and television stations, had a police escort, and the sidewalks along the route were lined with spectators, many of whom doffed their hats and dabbed at their eyes as the hearse drove slowly by.

The South Bronx was ominously quiet for the next two weeks. A pall seemed to settle over The Compound. The courtyard, always so full of activity, was deserted now except for an occasional Baby Nomad riding a bicycle around and over the piles of garbage airmailed there from the windows upstairs. Yogi, the gang member whose attack outside JHS 133 had brought Brother Sunshine there on the run, was still listed as being in only fair condition at Lincoln Hospital. In hopes of piecing together a more coherent story of Brother Sunshine's murder, the Forty-first Precinct had set up temporary headquarters inside the school. Shortly afterward, an eighteen-year-old member of the Black Spades and a fifteen-year-old member of the Seven Immortals were arrested and charged with the murder of Carlton (Brother Sunshine) Williams. Meanwhile, Dice, the prez of the Diplomats, assumed a philosophical attitude.

"Figure it this way," he said to O'Rourke and Moles one day. "Sunshine's got no more troubles. He's never hot, he's never cold. He's resting. That's better than us."

Mama Sunshine pleaded with Dice, "No revenge. Carlton lived for peace." Still, gangs are wired to one another by rumor, and rumor on the gang grapevine had it that the Latin Diplomats had decided to avenge Brother Sunshine's murder.

Then the ominous quiet broke. Dice put out a call for peace. It was time, he said, to stop the rumors that threatened a bloodbath. He asked the leaders and members of twenty gangs from all over the Bronx to gather in the gymnasium of the Boys' Club of America chapter on Hoe Avenue—neutral territory. It was to be a peace meeting—a peace conference, for the purpose of drawing up a peace treaty in honor of Brother Sunshine. And to guarantee that it would be nonviolent, Dice had arranged for a member of the Turbans gang to take position, with a rifle, on a rooftop across the street from the Boys' Club on the day of the meeting.

When that day came, television crews and news reporters with their cameramen stood outside the Boys' Club, waiting to be admitted, as the gangs filed in to attend what was the largest meeting of street gangs in the city's history. First to enter was the all-black gang called the Black Pearls, wearing their huge, soft-brimmed purple-and-white hats. Next were the Savage Skulls, wearing their sleeveless denim jackets with the skull and crossbones on the back. Then the Turbans, with their black-and-gold jackets and black caps with gold pompoms. Now the Young Sinners, Javelins, Dutchmen, Magnificent Seven, Dirty Dozen, Liberated Panthers, Peacemakers, and others. Finally, four of the five gangs from The Compound arrived en masse. The Seven Immortals came later and alone. Last of all came the Black Spades, the other gang in disrepute, since, like the Seven Immortals, they had a member under arrest for Brother Sunshine's murder. The backs of their jackets were decorated with a huge black spade pierced in dead center by a pair of crossed knives.

Inside, the power structure was much in evidence. Presidents, vice-presidents, and warlords sat on folding chairs in a circle in the middle of the club's gymnasium. Gang members took seats in the bleachers, while wives were made to wait outside the building in the cold. Only two females were permitted inside—the presidents of the all-girl gangs, the Alley Cats and the Savage Sisters—and their folding chairs were placed in the last row, behind those of the warlords.

Although the gangs had come ostensibly to talk peace, the atmosphere in the gymnasium was electric. Old wounds heal slowly, and there were still plenty of open cuts. Dice spoke first, paying tribute to the memory of Brother Sunshine, "a member of the family," drawing a parallel between his death and the assassinations of Malcolm X and Robert Kennedy. "Brother Sunshine had dedicated himself to his people." In conclusion, Dice raised both hands high above his head and shouted: "All police operatives must leave the meeting—or we got nothin' to say!" Ed O'Rourke and Vito Moles walked out, along with other plainsclothesmen who had been standing in the rear of the gymnasium. When the gang leaders were satisfied that only approved representatives of the media remained, the meeting was continued.

Poncho of the Savage Skulls stood up to speak feelingly of Brother Sunshine, and then wistfully of peace. Suddenly his voice grew louder, and he wheeled around, pointed a finger at one of the Seven Immortals sitting in the bleachers, and charged him with being one of the dudes who had stomped Sunshine. The accused stood up, his shaved head with pigtail glistening under the big overhead lights, to answer his accuser: "I wasn't there, man. I was in court that day. I can prove it."

One of the Turbans jumped up then and shouted, "You fuckin' Immortals. You invade our turf. You stab one of our brothers. An' you here to talk peace? You full of shit. *You got no chance against us!"*

Perhaps feeling some kinship with the Seven Immortals, since both gangs were said to be involved in the murder of Brother Sunshine, the prez of the Black Spades walked to the center of the gym, spread his legs wide apart, and took the heat off the Immortals by accusing the Savage Skulls of having used shotguns against his brothers. Snake, prez of the Skulls, ran to the center and placed himself squarely in front of the Black Spade and retaliated by charging the Spades with having shot at a couple of his boys. Members of his gang sitting in the bleachers got up as though about to move down toward the floor. Dice took over then, silencing them all with a clap of his hands.

"Listen, brothers, we're here to talk peace," he reminded them. "You understand that word, peace?" That got the meeting back to its purpose. Poncho of the Savage Skulls stood up to speak again. He spoke quietly now, and the brothers in the bleachers leaned forward, straining to hear what he said.

"Why we all right?" he asked. "Because we're just one big Oreo cookie, y'know? We all Puerto Ricans and blacks." He paused to finger the tiny pearl set into his earlobe. "Now if we don't make peace, brothers—whitey will come in and stomp us."

Pleasure blazed through the crowd. Gang leaders leaped up, shouting for peace, while their brothers in the bleachers whistled and cheered, Poncho grinned. The politicians, he said, resuming after the spontaneous ovation, were letting down the people in the ghetto. "We're gettin' nothin'. We hassled by the police, by the people, by everybody." He said he lived on Fox Street and "that street is *dirty,* man. It's always been dirty. The Sanitation Department says we mess it up. I say it's never been clean in the first place!"

There was scattered applause. "An' the fucked-up houses. An' the fucked-up schools. We gotta make it better." He stopped, seeming to wait for more applause; when it didn't come, he returned to the purpose of the meeting: peace. "When I heard about Sunshine dyin', I told Dice that I would take a life for Brother Sunshine. But Dice told me no, so I won't. If the Diplomats want peace, then there'll be peace."

A tall, husky black youth, a member of the Young Sinners, got to his feet and said he thought a lot of their troubles was due to the police. "If you're walkin' on the street with a bunch of guys and they see you, man, they jump out of cars an' put you up against the wall an' search you. Right on the street in front of everybody, man. Can they do that?"

Right on! Right on! shouted the gangs in the bleachers, fists raised in the Black Power salute. He continued: "I was walkin' down the hallway once when I was still in high school, an' we were changin' classes and the hall was crowded. I bumped into this cop. I didn't even know it, man. He told me I bumped him deliberately. I said I didn't an' I was sorry. He began bad-mouthin' me. He called me a wise guy. There was some shovin' and pushin', and he arrested me on assault. It was thrown out of court the next day."

From somewhere in the bleachers: "Yeah, the minute we put on our colors we get hit by the cops. We don't wanna break the law, but we gotta feel free to do our thing." *Right on! Right on!*

"It ain't the cops," a Black Spade said. "It's them junkies." He came down out of the bleachers. He made his way to the circle in the center of the gym, put both hands on his hips, cocked his head to one side and began whining:

"Hey, baby, you wanna deuce?[1] You wanna tres?[2] *Tengo, la tengo* . . . you name it. Pito, pito?[3] Maybe you wanna belsita?[4] I know where you can get it . . . I got bams,[5] baby. Whatchoo lookin' for, baby? You want it . . . I got it . . ."

The gymnasium exploded with whistles, cheers, and the sound of boots stomping the floor. The Black Spade held up his hand for silence. "We wanna get rid of the junkies and stop kids eleven and twelve and thirteen from shootin' up drugs," he said. Again came the wild response. The

---

[1] A two-dollar bag of heroin.
[2] A three-dollar bag of heroin.
[3] Reefers.
[4] A little bag.
[5] A kind of liquid stimulant, occasionally taken with heroin.

flashbulbs of the press photographers' cameras popped on all sides. And it was then that a prez got up, walked over to the door, opened it, and invited the wives, who were shivering in the cold outside, to come in and join their men. The girls filed in, walked directly over to their men, and slipped their arms through theirs. Again there was the pop of flashbulbs, which the couples pretended not to notice.

Now one of the Latin Diplomats stepped into the center circle. The South Bronx, he said, was a hell hole. He said he had first experimented with heroin when he was nine. "An' I been cut in the face twice," he added, turning slowly around while pointing to the two scars extending from cheekbone to chin on one side of his face. "I been arrested three times since I was sixteen—an' I'm just past seventeen now. The Bronx is evil, man—*evil*. The dude you may be shakin' hands with today may be the dude who'll cut your throat tomorrow. When my kid grows up, I want him t'say that I did somethin' for the community, y'know."

The meeting was losing focus again, so Dice reclaimed the floor and reminded the brothers that they had come to draw up a treaty. A peace treaty in honor of Brother Sunshine. A treaty that every dude present would respect—or else.

Else what? a warlord wanted to know. Dice was ready with an answer. "If a brother breaks any of the rules of the peace treaty—say, he invades another gang's turf—his brothers will be duty-bound to take him back into the middle of that turf and leave him there. Abandon him, get it? Like a dog, get it? An' it'd be up to that brother to get out of that turf without gettin' a beatin' or a bullet."

There was a moment of silence and then, suddenly, thunderous applause. Boots started stomping the floor in rhythm to the hand clapping. Dice grinned and held both his hands high in the air with fingers spread wide. "Now," he said, loud and clear, "we start drawin' up that treaty."

Over the next hour he and the other leaders sitting on the floor of the gymnasium hammered out a five-point treaty, while gang members in the bleachers sat in respectful silence. Finally Dice stood up and read each point aloud from a paper he held in his hand. Then the rotund young divinity student who ran the Boys' Club stepped forward to ask that the leaders form a circle, join hands, and take the pledge for peace. Each prez, vice-prez, and warlord rose and joined hands—with the exception of the two girl gang leaders, who remained seated; it would have been considered unseemly for them to have joined the circle. Then Dice disengaged himself from the circle to make a final announcement. He said that there would be more meetings for peace —"away from the eyes and ears of the intruders"—and, with a majestic wave of his arm, he took in all the newsmen and cameramen, who at that moment were busy jockeying for position, each anxious to record the final words, the final bit of action.

Peace reigned in the South Bronx for exactly four weeks. Although the peace effort failed, it wasn't for lack of support from some community leaders. One week after the meeting in the Boys' Club, Dice was picked up by military police for being AWOL for eighteen months from the Marine Corps. He was charged with having jumped off the train that was taking him to Camp Lejeune for training. On learning that Dice was in the Brooklyn Navy Yard brig and about to be shipped out to the Marine base at Parris Island, South Carolina, for a court-martial, Bronx Congressman Herman Badillo interceded with the Marine commandant's office to prevent the transfer. "He needs to be close by should trouble break out among the gangs which only he could resolve," explained Badillo. Dice was eventually freed, and he promptly returned to the Latin Diplomats' clubhouse in The Compound. He still talked of peace, but it was too late. Five South Bronx gang members had been slain in a five-week period.

The Latin Diplomats have disbanded. Now, four years after the peace meeting in the Boys' Club, Dice is working for a city social service agency, and teaches karate to ghetto youngsters in the evenings. He is the father of two sons, and man, he wouldn't want them to join a street gang. At twenty-seven, Dice, like Brother Sunshine, preaches non-violence. For one thing, he believes that television glamor-izes violence. He thinks people aren't just naturally disposed toward violence, they've got to be helped along. And Dice feels television violence helps a lot.

"Bang, bang, you're dead. That's all. They show just the violence. No real pain. No funeral. No plot of earth. No sign of what happens to the wife and kids after that guy gets killed."

He says he tries to keep his five-year-old "away from things like *The Untouchables*. That's not what's happening. If he watches, then he should watch it as an education."

Dice even avoids newscasts. "I find them depressing. If things are messed up, all the newscast tells you is they're really *more* messed up! When kids see lootin' and burnin' on a newscast, the grownups should tell them that those are some of the effects when people are not in control. Like, 'Hey, now watch and see how many are goin' t'get hurt!' Or when a store burns, tell him, 'Imagine whose business that was. How is that guy gonna feed his family now?' "

When he talks of Brother Sunshine, Dice still refers to him fondly as a member of the family, and he likes to re-call how they first met.

"I was walkin' down Trinity with my two brothers when this black dude comes alongside and starts rappin'. He's full of smiles an' jive. An' he starts tellin' us about his good friend Dice. 'Do you know him?' What a great guy this Dice is. My brothers start laughin', and finally I say to the dude, 'Do you know who I am?' Well, he says, you're a brother. I say, 'Yeah, that's right, but I'm also Dice.' He don't get embarrassed. He just gives us that big, happy grin of his . . . slaps palms . . . and that's how he joined up with us."

Lately Dice has been thinking that maybe Sunshine may have actually been "a secret Youth Services street worker," and that that chance meeting was planned. The city's Youth Services Agency at that time had several gang members on its payroll in the hope that they might help funnel their gangs' energies away from violence and toward more peaceful endeavors, and the agency's records showed that Carlton (Brother Sunshine) Williams had been scheduled to start to work as a gang street worker with YSA the week after his murder. (Dice doesn't know, and it doesn't matter now anyway.) Had the Diplomats survived, he says, he planned to raise enough money for a monument for Sunshine's grave. "Something fitting, like an angel praying."

Chester Jones, a member of the Black Spades, pleaded guilty to manslaughter in the killing of Brother Sunshine and was sentenced to serve three years in the Elmira Reformatory. The member of the Seven Immortals arrested at the same time was subsequently released for lack of evidence.

6.
The Insult

The worst that can happen to a street gang—short of annihilation—is a loss of face. A gang doesn't forgive or forget an insult. So when the gangs in The Compound refused space to the Satan's Angels—an act tantamount to slamming the door in their face—the South Bronx expected a bloodbath. Residents of the area began taking detours of several blocks to avoid going anywhere near The Compound.

The Angels was a peanut-sized gang, with only thirty-seven members. But they had guns, lots of guns. And a prez called Sex Machine, or simply S.M., an ex-Marine who was so gun-crazy that he gave every gun a pet name. "Peanuts" was a .45 automatic named for his son. A .38 Smith & Wesson was "Bonnie," the baby's mother. And a .38 Enfield traditionally bore the name of whoever happened to be the current favorite in his harem.

Gangs both in and out of The Compound considered him loco. He wore a pith helmet constantly, indoors and out. He wore it walking around the clubhouse stark naked. He even wore it when he was having sex. And Sex Machine had sex whenever and wherever he felt the urge. Standing in the shower. On the floor of the clubhouse during a meeting. In the alley next to the clubhouse. Loco. *Real* crazy. And didn't he once strangle a cat and nail it to the door? And when the carcass stank, he took it down . . . strangled another cat . . . and nailed that one up? *Real* crazy. Too crazy to live in The Compound.

Ed O'Rourke and Vito Moles considered him a pathological killer with an almost hypnotic control of his gang. He was to them what Charles Manson was to his "family": a deity. They appeared to have no will of their own. Not one would hesitate to do whatever he commanded.

One icy night soon after the gang was barred from The Compound, S.M., reeling drunk, sent one of the Angels dangling from the roof of a five-story tenement, a rope around his waist and a can of white paint in his hand, with the order to put the gang's name on the side of the building in letters three feet high—big enough to be seen from The Compound. And he said he'd do the same on *every* corner building on *every* block of their turf, so every time those motherfuckers looked out a window they'd see SATAN'S ANGELS. But the next day, sober, he forgot all about it. You don't get revenge with a paint brush.

Although the Angels' exclusion from The Compound had been the joint decision of all the gangs there, he held the Savage Nomads, the dominant gang, wholly responsible. And Black Bongo, the Nomads' prez, personally responsible. The Gang Intelligence Unit figured it was only a matter of time before the two gangs were at war. Still, months went by without trouble of any kind.

Should a full-scale war break out between gangs whose arsenals include high-powered rifles, revolvers, even machine guns—sophisticated weapons sometimes introduced to gangs by Vietnam veterans—it would make the rumbles of the zip-gun era look like child's play. And it was inconceivable to O'Rourke and Moles that a gang as violent as Satan's Angels would let the year end without getting revenge.

And the Angels didn't intend to. Sex Machine planned to make the Christmas of '72 one the gangs in The Compound would never forget. Every weapon in the gang's arsenal was clean, loaded, and ready to be used. But first S.M. wanted to deliver an insult. Something that would make Bongo look like an asshole. He had it! He sent Pee Wee out into the street for a dog. The mangiest, sickest-looking mutt he could find. A black one. And back Pee Wee came with a half-starved mongrel. S.M. promptly named it "Black Bongo." Using a Magic Marker, he printed the name on a slice of cardboard, hung it around the dog's neck, and ordered Pee Wee to take the dog over to The Compound and dump it. Despite the fact that just being sighted walking up the stoop might cost him his life, Pee Wee went without hesitation. He sprinted up the stoop, dropped the dog on the top step, and managed to get away before any of the kids milling around the courtyard could stop him. Within the hour, the dead mongrel, its throat cut, was tossed into the alley next to the Angels' clubhouse.

S.M. had already planned his next move. The Angels would snatch both of Bongo's German shepherds. Man, how he liked to strut around with those fuckin' mutts at his heels! Bongo's fierce-looking dogs were as essential to his image as pith helmet and guns were to S.M.'s. And S.M. knew it. So he'd grab the dogs, gouge out their eyes, slit their tongues, and dump them back at The Compound.

He had no sooner outlined his plan than Ratso came bursting in with both his eyes practically closed and his mouth cut and bleeding. Three Nomads had ambushed him. S.M. leaped to his feet, cords standing out in his neck, and for a moment Ratso thought S.M. was going to hit him. "Whatever Nomads we see from now on, we ice," he said. Finally. A declaration of war.

That evening the Angels decided to celebrate. They stocked up on wine and beer and swept out the Smoke Room—set aside for members intent on getting high—and then some walked down to the Club 130, a social club that became a discotheque on Saturday nights. Its owner steadfastly refused to grant membership rights to gang members, which took a very special sort of courage, but he wasn't so foolhardy as to refuse to sell them a one-dollar admission ticket. He asked only that they not wear their colors inside.

Chita, Mouse, and Honey Bear, three of the seven girl members of the gang, arrived at the club arm in arm. Chita had really gotten herself dressed up. A pair of rhinestone earrings hung down to her shoulders. She was in a party mood, figuring that the time had come to cool it with Cowboy. With a war coming up, the chances were that he'd be dead soon, anyway. He was so fuckin' tall, he'd probably be the first Angel to get himself iced. That's what had caught her eye in the first place: his height. How often do you see a six-foot Puerto Rican? Most of the time Chita found herself dancing with a dude whose head came up to her shoulder. Like right now, who was making his way toward her? Pee Wee, that's who.

He walked past Mouse without even looking at her. Mouse, who stood four feet ten, thought she knew why Pee Wee wanted to dance with Chita. He was on eye level with her tits.

Honey Bear, as usual, was heading for trouble. She had honey-colored hair and dimples, and she could get just about any dude she wanted, but she evidently didn't want the one in the long overcoat with the swastika on the sleeve, because he'd just punched her in the neck. Mouse guessed she probably didn't even feel it, because if Honey Bear's heart condition didn't kill her one of these days, heroin probably would.

Just then Ratso came over and asked Mouse to dance. They pushed their way out onto the dance floor, and she began dancing with her eyes closed. She knew that if she didn't keep them closed, she was going to heave. That's how disgusting Ratso's swollen lips looked. When Mouse was starting to really move, she was bumped and practically knocked off her feet. She opened her eyes, and damn if it wasn't Fish plowing across the floor after some dude, smashing his fist into his palm and hollering so loud that he could be heard over the din of the jukebox, "Your ass is grabbed! Your ass is grabbed, motherfucker!"

Chita swung around so fast, so as not to lose sight of Fish, that one of her earrings struck her in the cheek. Now who was Fish fuckin' with, anyway? Then the dude he was hassling turned around to face him, and Chita recognized him. A tall kid with a round baby face. A Savage Nomad. "Name's Big H," muttered Pee Wee.

With his Fu Manchu moustache, Fish could look real mean when he got worked up, and he sure was worked up now. Mouse knew it, and she grabbed Honey Bear and steered her over to Chita. Then the three of them stood together in the center of the dance floor, bathed in a purple light, and watched Big H shove his way through the crowd and run down the stairs with Fish after him. It didn't look good.

Gummy, who had come to the Club 130 with Big H, caught up with him, and together they took the stairs two at a time. "I think my time's comin'," said Big H when they made it to the sidewalk. Then, suddenly, Fish was there behind them, a beer can in one hand, with the other reaching out for Big H's overcoat collar. Gummy didn't know what had caused the static, but he'd never seen Big H look so scared.

"Fish, you know me for a long time," Big H said, trying to placate him. "You know how I am. I just come home

from jail. I don't know what's happenin' with the Nomads."
He was pleading now. "I don't want no static."

Fish got even madder. "Shut up!" he yelled, smashing
his fist into his palm again. Mouse had just come downstairs. She wanted to get out of there and back to the
clubhouse fast, but then, without taking his eyes off Big H,
Fish handed her the can of beer, and then he was taking
off his overcoat and handing that to her, too. Mouse began
trembling all over. Maybe Fish was going to ice Big H
here and now. He began moving in on him, with Big H
backing away. Mouse felt as though her heart was going
to explode. She couldn't stand it. She started to run, with
the beer can in one hand and Fish's overcoat hanging over
her arm, and the coat tripped her and she fell. *Shit*. She
scrambled to her feet, jumped over the coat, and took
off again.

"I ain't jivin', man," said Big H, still backing away from
Fish. Then he stopped, turned, and ran. Mouse heard the
sounds of feet pounding the pavement behind her, and she
tossed the beer can into the gutter, as though that would
free her to run faster. She kept running until she got to
the clubhouse, without ever once looking back.

She collapsed, wheezing, into the nearest chair. Several
Angels were in the room, dancing, and the door to the
Smoke Room was closed. Nobody paid any attention to
her. When she got her breath back she looked around for
Sex Machine, and when she spotted him coming out of the
kitchen, she went over and told him that Fish and a Nomad
were fighting outside the Club 130. He didn't say anything,
just pushed past her and disappeared into one of the back
rooms. In a minute he was out again, shoving a gun down
inside his coat pocket. At the front door he stopped and
tossed another gun at Cowboy, who caught it, and they
ran out into the street together.

When they got to the Club 130, there was a small crowd

on the sidewalk but no sign of Fish. Nobody knew where he'd gone. They raced upstairs just as Chita and Honey Bear were putting on their coats to leave. Sex Machine ordered them back inside to look for Fish. Chita was explaining that she'd seen Fish leave and he hadn't come back when Sex Machine slapped her hard across the face. She and Honey Bear did as they were told and went back inside the club.

Back on the sidewalk, there was still no sign of Fish. Chita and Honey Bear came down and stood there, waiting to be told what to do next. It was starting to rain, and Honey Bear's coat was thin; she began shivering. Suddenly they heard the honking of a horn. It was Fish leaning out the window of a battered-looking Chevy. "I've got one!" he hollered. "I've got a Nomad! Everybody to the clubhouse."

Sex Machine and Cowboy ran after the car, leaving Chita and Honey Bear behind. The cold rain had made the sidewalks slippery, and as they walked carefully on their clogs, Chita took off her rhinestone earrings and dropped them into the pocket of her coat. She didn't feel in a party mood any more.

Mouse was back in the chair again when the front door flew open. Everybody in the room froze at the sight of Big H standing there with his arm pinned behind his back. He was blubbering, pleading with Fish to let him go. But Fish kept on shoving him, until he finally got him into the Smoke Room and slammed the door shut.

The next moment came the sounds of Big H being beaten. No one outside made a move or said a word. They stopped dancing and stared at the closed door behind which Big H was doing a lot of crying and begging. Mouse put both hands over her ears and kept them there. Then the door to the Smoke Room opened, and she saw Big H in his shirt sleeves, leaning up against the wall, and he was bleeding from his nose, mouth, and both ears. It looked to her as though Fish was going to bring him out of the room, when the front door flew open again. It was Sex Machine and Cowboy with their guns drawn, and Pee Wee behind them. They headed straight for Big H.

At the sight of them coming toward him, he sank to his knees. His nose and eardrums had been busted, and now he began choking on his own blood. Never in her life had Mouse heard a sound like that. Fish jumped in front of Big H and said, "Don't shoot. You don't have to shoot." But S.M. shoved him aside and took aim. And, although only semiconscious, Big H still knew fear. He pulled his knees up to his chest, wrapped both arms around them, and buried his chin in his chest. He was in that fetal position when S.M. began emptying his gun into him. With the impact of each bullet Big H's body shook convulsively, but he never let go of his knees. When the third bullet ripped into his chest, Pee Wee started shooting. Then, when neither of them had any bullets left, S.M. turned around to Cowboy and demanded, "What're you gonna do? You gonna shoot him or what?" Cowboy took aim and shot Big H twice in the leg. He felt sure Big H was dead, but how come he didn't topple over? He just stayed there crouched on the floor, still hugging his knees as the blood gurgled up through his shirt and trousers.

Sex Machine tossed his gun on the floor, grabbed Big H by the hair, and started dragging him across the room toward the door. At the threshold he let go of him, bent down, and lifted him up under the armpits. "Take his legs," he ordered Fish. But first Fish pulled the shoes off Big H and threw them across to where Big H's overcoat lay on the floor. Then he took his legs, and together they carried the body out of the Smoke Room.

Chita and Honey Bear were approaching the clubhouse when they heard the shots. When the door opened from the inside, they saw Big H being dragged and heard S.M.

saying to nobody in particular, "This is what's gonna happen to all the Savage Nomads." Suddenly, as they were hoisting the body over the threshold, one of the Angels leaped forward. He had a knife, and he lunged toward the body to stab it. "Forget it. He's already dead," said S.M. Then he and Fish were out on the sidewalk, and when Honey Bear saw Big H's face with the blood pouring out of his busted nose, she started to retch. As S.M. and Fish disappeared around the corner of the building, with the body sagging between them, Chita and Honey Bear rushed inside.

As they made their way down the alley in the rain, a man on the third floor of the building across the way—a gypsy cabbie checking out the weather—was looking out his kitchen window. At first he thought the two men down below were carrying a tire. When he looked again, he saw that what they had was a body. So he rushed to his telephone and dialed the emergency number, 911. He was telling the police what he had just seen when S.M. and Fish dumped Big H down the wooden steps that led into the side entrance of the very building from which the man was telephoning.

When the squad car arrived on the scene, the blood from Big H's nose had frozen, forming a ludicrous Groucho-type moustache on his upper lip. There were twenty-seven bullet holes in his body; one of the bullets had pierced his brain.

Meanwhile, the party in the clubhouse had resumed. Pee Wee was clumping around in Big H's shoes, and Fish made it known that Big H's long brown overcoat was his now. Exhilarated, Sex Machine felt like celebrating. Christmas was coming, he said, and he already had presents for everybody. Emptying a gun, he started moving around the room, passing out shells. "Souvenirs from Big H," he said, grinning.

Mouse took her shell home and put it on her dresser. A couple of hours later she woke up, got out of bed, and threw it out the window. It was bothering her too much.

Chita threw her shell away before she started up the stairs to the third-floor apartment she shared with her mother in the only building on the block that was still inhabited. She had disposed of it in the empty lot next door, after which she dug down into her coat pocket for the rhinestone earrings and put them on. Maybe they'd act like good-luck pieces and she wouldn't have bad dreams.

Honey Bear kept her shell, falling asleep with it clenched in her fist.

Ed O'Rourke and Vito Moles parked outside The Compound every day of the following week. The usually-busy courtyard was deserted. Gang members darted in and out of the buildings, their heads down. Visiting the various clubhouses, the detectives found no one willing to discuss Big H's murder. Sitting outside in their car, they'd occasionally hear a bongo drum being pounded somewhere inside The Compound, but it had a forlorn sound. Word on the street was that the Satan's Angels had allied with the Dirty Dozen gang and together they were out to kill all the Nomads. There was no sign of Black Bongo or Big Mama. Then, three weeks before Christmas, Black Bongo was rushed to Lincoln Hospital with a bullet in his chest. He said he had no idea who shot him.

When he was discharged from the hospital shortly after the first of the new year, Black Bongo—with the two German shepherds at his heels, a bottle of wine in his fist, and the other arm wrapped around Big Mama—squatted down on the top step of the stoop of The Compound. Fuck the cold! He'd spent the fuckin' Christmas in a hospital, and now he was back home where he belonged. And if the Angels wanted to start the new year with a war, they'd get a war. He had an army. An army of hundreds. The whole fuckin' Compound would take on the Satan's Angels and wipe 'em out! But then the stitches in his chest started to sting, and he was thinking of going back inside when a car drove by, a gun poked out of the window, and he heard somebody say: "This is for you, Bongo"—and the stoop was sprayed with bullets. Big Mama threw herself across him, pushing him out of range just as a bullet ripped into her leg.

While Big Mama was recuperating in the hospital, Cowboy, Pee Wee, and two other members of the Satan's Angels were arrested and booked in connection with the murder of Big H. Warrants were out for Sex Machine and Fish, who was also wanted for questioning in connection with the recent death of his fifteen-month-old son. The baby had been picked up by his feet and slammed repeatedly against a wall until his skull cracked open.

Now the Savage Nomads were eager to talk to O'Rourke and Moles about the Angels, but none of them had any idea where S.M. and Fish might be hiding. Acting on a tip that the former had a plane ticket for Puerto Rico, plainclothesmen staked out the departure gates at Kennedy Airport without success. It wasn't until March—three months after the murder of Big H—that Sex Machine was picked up by a patrolman working with the Auto Recovery Unit of the Forty-first Precinct. The patrolman spotted the stolen '64 Chevy first and then, from a mug shot posted in the anti-crime office at the station house, he recognized the youth in the pith helmet sitting beside the driver of the stolen car. The man behind the wheel, a forty-year-old unemployed mechanic named Jose, was taken to the station house along with S.M. and charged with grand larceny. Sex Machine was charged with the murder of Big H. Then both men were sent to Rikers Island to await trial.

Although he insisted that the car thievery was only a hobby with him ("I don't make no money from it"), Jose, who had a long record of car thefts, was anxious to make a deal with the police. He said he and Sex Machine were very good friends. "Every time he kills somebody he tells me," he boasted. And although Jose insisted that he knew nothing about Big H's murder, he said he'd spent Christmas morning at the Satan's Angels' clubhouse and S.M. had handed him a Smith & Wesson and told him, "It's hot. Save it for me." Jose took the gun and buried it beneath a floorboard in a shack situated in the rear of a junkyard. He was sure he could find it.

Jose rode to the junkyard with a detective and retrieved the gun from where he had buried it three months earlier. According to Jose, there were three other guns that he knew Sex Machine wanted to get rid of, but he didn't know where they were. He was sure he could find out, however. So it was arranged for him to sit beside S.M. in the prison mess hall. S.M. told his friend that as soon as he was released from prison, he wanted him to dispose of three guns he had hidden. Jose assured him that he would and S.M. gave him a phone number to commit to memory. "Call it as soon as you're sprung," he told him.

It was arranged for Jose to make the call, after which he drove to a Catholic church on the corner of Tiffany Street and Southern Boulevard, with detectives following in another car. There he met two youths, who promptly disappeared around the side of the church, returning in a few minutes with a dirt-encrusted black bag, which they deposited under the back seat of his car. The bag was opened at the station house; inside, wrapped in rags, were three guns and about two hundred rounds of ammunition. Tests showed that three of the four guns collected by Jose had been used in the killing of Big H.

Sex Machine was indicted for murder, and one week later Fish was apprehended. Early in the fall, together with Cowboy, Pee Wee, and two other members of the gang, they went on trial in the Supreme Court of Bronx County. Mouse, Chita, and Honey Bear were taken into protective custody as material witnesses and moved to a hotel, the name of which was unknown even to their families.

Mouse was pregnant but refused to be examined by a doctor, insisting that her baby wasn't due for many months yet. She also refused to name the father, except to say that he was fifteen and—with pride in her voice—he wasn't a member of any gang. Chita, who worried about both Mouse and Honey Bear, nevertheless told the assistant district attorney, a young woman who had become the girls' confidante, that she didn't much enjoy being holed up with a couple of "sickies." Honey Bear's heart was giving her pain, and each week she was taken to Montefiore Hospital for an examination. Chita was also much concerned about Cowboy, and said that if he had to go to prison, she sure as hell was going to wait for him.

On the first day of the trial, the Satan's Angels marched into the courthouse wearing their colors. They sat the whole day, staring menacingly in the direction of the jury box. It was the first time any of them had ever seen Sex Machine without his pith helmet. He sat hunched forward, with both hands up to his head. He was growing bald.

On the second day, in the detention pen during luncheon recess, S.M. attacked a prisoner involved in another trial, whom he suspected of being a stool pigeon. He stomped the youth so badly that he had to be hospitalized.

The Satan's Angels didn't return to the courtroom after the first day, but S.M. assumed the role of intimidator, staring fixedly at both jurors and prosecution witnesses.

The trial was in its third week when Mouse, Chita, and Honey Bear, still in protective custody and waiting to be called to testify, began growing extremely restless. In an attempt to keep them occupied and in good humor, the assistant district attorney encouraged Chita and Honey

Bear to practice reading and writing. Chita and Honey Bear weren't interested. Mouse had never learned to read or write. Chita occupied her time by trying out the new makeup supplied her at her request. But when she grew bored with the collection of lipsticks and eyeshadows, she became depressed and cried because she said she missed her mother and worried about her living alone on the almost-deserted block.

"It's the only house not burned out. There's no running water. My mother, she's got to go down in the street now all by herself with the pan and get the water from the hydrant. Even to flush the toilet, you gotta go down to the hydrant. Maybe somebody'll jump her." By "somebody" Chita meant a mugger, a wino. That was always a possibility. You had to cope with that every day. And, like most of the people in the South Bronx ghetto, her attention was riveted on surviving day to day. That her mother might be harmed by the Satan's Angels in retaliation for her daughter's cooperation with the law simply hadn't occurred to her. That was somewhere outside the frame of day-to-day survival. Had she considered the possibilty, it is unlikely that she would have agreed to testify in court.

Honey Bear, meanwhile, was spending hours before a mirror, experimenting with new hair styles. When she tired of that, she tried keeping a diary. Then she abandoned that in favor of writing personal notes. Her first was directed to the female assistant district attorney:

Hi. Just a fine lines to you and your mind. People like you. Your Big, Blonde and very nice and you know you got all the guys before your eyes. You think your a lover, but deep you know you ain't got, what you really want, you sweet, kind, very nice. But you better comb your hair every night. Blonde DA like you I would like to have, cause when ever I get in trouble,

I would always look you up in the yellow pages. When your in the office you look very nice. But Sweetie you better think twice if your hair looks right. I like you and hope not to forget you.

One of the detectives working on the case also caught Honey Bear's fancy, and she wrote to him, too.

To Big Groovy Bear—
Blueyes they call you the lover from under the cover and there will be no other like Blueyes the lover. Your eyes are Big and Blue. Your face is white and flat, But Only you are getting kind of *fat*. I call you Bear cause you're fat and juicy. But you know your kind of groovy.

You Big Groovy Bear, I love you.

News of what was happening in the courtroom alternately intrigued and bored the three girls. They were fascinated, however—especially Chita—to learn that Cowboy had agreed to testify for the prosecution. The assistant district attorney had offered him a deal: parole for the time already served if he would plead guilty and tell everything he knew about the murder of Big H.

Although he was in prison, Sex Machine was still his prez. And so through the prison grapevine—cell block to cell block, prisoner to prisoner—Cowboy passed on word of the D.A.'s offer to him. Then S.M. passed his order along to Cowboy: Agree . . . get paroled . . . stay out of trouble . . . and then come to trial "and change the whole story around. Say you lied to get free."

From force of habit, Cowboy did as he was told, concocting a story full of halftruths, which the assistant district attorney told him she didn't believe. She gave him exactly twenty-four hours to tell the truth. Unless, of course, he wanted to go on being dominated. Now it was up to him. And before the deadline was up, Cowboy was back, and this time telling the truth to a court stenographer, after which he was put into protective custody in a motel far from the courthouse and the Satan's Angels, who were still fiercely loyal to their leader.

The assistant district attorney, who was working seven days a week on the case, was awakened by the phone early one morning to be told that Mouse was having labor pains. She rushed to the hotel and found the girl in bed, clutching a stuffed panda in her arms. No one had seen the panda before; evidently Mouse had stashed it away, saving it for just this terrifying moment. But at the sight of the assistant district attorney standing at the foot of her bed, she pushed the panda under the covers and insisted that she was not having labor pains. "Only a bellyache. I ate pizza with too many peppers. That's all. The baby won't come for a long time yet. Honest." But a few minutes later Mouse pulled the stuffed animal out from under the covers, pressed it against her only slightly swollen belly, and started to scream. She was rushed to the hospital in a squad car, and three hours later she gave birth to a three-pound girl. Hearing of the birth, Chita insisted that she be given a holy candle to light, while Honey Bear immediately set about composing a note "To the Little Mama."

Two weeks after the birth of her baby, Mouse was brought to court to testify. As she entered the courtroom Sex Machine turned around and looked her squarely in the face, and the frightened girl promptly fainted. She was carried from the room and revived, and she returned to testify in a voice that was little more than a whisper. She took special pains not to look in the direction of the defendants.

Next it was Chita's turn. Chita burst into tears during her testimony, saying that although Big H wasn't a friend, "they didn't have to kill him." Finally Honey Bear took the witness stand.

Defense attorneys asked each girl if she took drugs. Mouse admitted having taken heroin at one time, but she swore that she wasn't taking drugs any more, nor had she been under the influence of any drug at the time of the murder. Chita admitted that she had a drug arrest for heroin, but insisted that she hadn't taken any on the day of the shooting. Furthermore, she added with considerable pride, she was now an ex-member of the Satan's Angels. Honey Bear, her hair freshly washed and set, appeared to enjoy her moment in the spotlight. She said she joined her first street gang at the age of twelve, and she readily admitted that she had used heroin on the day Big H was murdered. So what? Then she stole a glance in the direction of Sex Machine, blanched, and temporarily lost her cool.

In his summation the chief defense attorney asked that the jurors "Look at these poor broken-down, without-hope-of-anything little girls that testified here." Honey Bear looked over at the assistant district attorney and flashed her a dimpled smile. Mouse simply sat there looking nervous and miserable, shielding her eyes from Sex Machine, who, leaning forward in his chair, was trying to will her to turn around and look at him. Chita, her hair elaborately coifed and her face expertly made up, glowered at the counsel. She resented being thought of as a poor broken-down little girl —a poor broken-down anything.

Sex Machine was found guilty of first-degree murder and sentenced to twenty-five years to life. Smiling for the first time since the trial began, he congratulated the assistant district attorney on the way she had handled her case against him, assuring her that there were no hard feelings as far as he was concerned. Fish was sentenced to a term of eight-and-a-third to twenty-five years, and in a subsequent trial for the murder of his infant son he drew a term of twenty-five years to life. Pee Wee and the other two defendants pleaded guilty to varying degrees of manslaughter and were sentenced.

The assistant district attorney has continued to maintain contact with Mouse, Chita, and Honey Bear. Mouse, she says, is an extremely good mother, and her baby has grown plump and pretty. Chita, who still lives with her mother in the same apartment, did not resume her relationship with Cowboy, who disappeared from the South Bronx immediately after the trial ended. Honey Bear is, at this writing, pregnant and worried because her heart is still giving her trouble. She has finally gotten around to keeping a daily diary, and it is her most prized possession. She swears that after her baby is born she's going to move away from the South Bronx. She says it's no place for a kid to grow up.

Not surprisingly, with the sentencing of Sex Machine the Satan's Angels gang ceased to exist. And, ironically, the gang's exclusion from The Compound—the insult that had started the gang war—also marked the start of the demise of The Compound. For Sex Machine had dared to challenge the leadership of The Compound. He had stormed the fortress and lost—but, by having dared, he had caused the gangs within that fortress to lose face.

7.
Welcome Home, Big Mama

She was an original. There had never been a girl gang
leader like Big Mama. In the gang subculture, where the
female—even the head of a girls' division—is a second-
class citizen existing primarily to serve the needs of the
males, she had as much power as any prez in The Compound, with only one exception: her husband, Black Bongo,
supreme leader of the Savage Nomads. Even the other
leaders in The Compound feared him, and with good
reason. Still, it wasn't Bongo who had made her prez of
the female Nomads. Big Mama had made herself prez. But
he had made her his wife not because she was the best-
looking or the sexiest, but because she was the only other
Nomad as mean and tough as he was.

Big Mama and Black Bongo were inseparable. They
were, in a sense, the Ma and Pa of The Compound. The
wide stoop was their front porch, their own private slice of
turf. Other gangs in The Compound walked its steps, but
no one sat there except at their invitation. No gang lived
in The Compound without the express permission of Big
Mama and Bongo. No outside gangs dared visit without
their permission. And the sight of the two of them sitting

side by side on the stoop, flanked by Bongo's two massive German shepherds, Savage and Nomad, were as much a part of the landscape as a paper shade flapping out a cracked window and the debris piling up in the courtyard behind them.

Big Mama, as taciturn as Bongo was talkative, had no intimates other than him. And although still a teenager, she was an authority figure, a kind of short-tempered step-mother to the girls she ruled. And while Bongo had plenty of other girls both in and out of The Compound who were prettier, Big Mama—a chunky, thick-featured Puerto Rican who wore her mahogany-colored hair frizzed over her ears like a pair of electrified ear muffs—was his only wife. And when he was shot during the fracas with the Angels, she, like a good wife, visited him in Lincoln Hospital every day without fail. And when he was out of the hospital and sitting on the stoop again and a car drove by and sprayed the steps with bullets, it was, as we already know, Big Mama who pushed him out of range and caught a bullet in her leg.

Chiclet, a Baby Nomad who had been riding his bicycle around the courtyard at the time, raced upstairs to the clubhouse of the Seven Immortals, where Ed O'Rourke and Vito Moles were visiting, and banged on the door, shouting, "Big Mama's been hit!" The officers ran downstairs and across the courtyard to where she lay, clutching her leg and moaning, with Bongo standing there looking down at her, a firm grip on an ear of each of his dogs. The detectives picked up Big Mama, carried her down the stoop to their car, and rushed her to Lincoln Hospital.

Her arrival at the dilapidated old institution (it was once a nursing home for runaway slaves, and was super-seded in 1976 by a new Lincoln Hospital) had the staff there preparing for the worst. The chief of surgery had only recently told the press that his staff had to work "literally barricaded behind locked doors because street gangs roam the corridor at will, terrorizing staff members and patients." Now, with Big Mama a patient, nurses and doctors at Lincoln lost no time in petitioning for city policemen to reinforce the hospital's security, as well as round-the-clock patrol cars to cruise nearby streets. Two surgeons, in fact, refused duty until they could be assured of adequate protection from physical assault on the night shift.

Ed O'Rourke and Vito Moles visited Big Mama the day after she was shot. Bongo was there, and while she lay in bed looking sullen and bored, he told them that he knew who had shot her—and him—and, man, we'll get those motherfuckers ourselves. We don't need no help.

Through street tipsters the Gang Intelligence Unit learned about the alliance between the Satan's Angels and the Dirty Dozen gang. The Unit was directed to an apartment some six blocks from The Compound. Wearing bullet-proof vests, police surrounded the building and burst into a three-and-a-half-room ground-floor apartment, where they confiscated five rifles, two sawed-off shotguns, two automatic carbines, and 1,025 rounds of ammunition. There were no gang members present, only a frightened woman tending her four-year-old child. Police characterized her as a "dupe" of the gangs.

The next afternoon some fifty Nomads, along with members of the Savage Skulls—with whom Bongo, in anticipation of an all-out war, had made a hasty alliance—swarmed into Lincoln Hospital and went thundering down the corridors in search of Satan's Angels, who, they claimed, were planning to murder Big Mama in her bed. Doors to patients' rooms flew open and gang members burst in, rummaging through closets and then dropping to their knees to check under beds. Nurses raced down the corridors to bring wheelchair patients to the relative safety of the public waiting rooms, while terrified aides barricaded themselves in linen closets. As a dozen Nomads armed with pipes and chains headed for the operating room, police and hospital security guards intercepted them and managed to hold them back until police reinforcements arrived. One Nomad was arrested, and a twenty-four-hour police guard was assigned to Big Mama's room.

At dawn she was transferred downtown to Bellevue Hospital, and no one, including Black Bongo, knew where she had gone. A corps of Nomads kept Lincoln Hospital under constant surveillance, but no further attempts at a raid were made. It was while Big Mama was recuperating at Bellevue that four of the Angels were arrested and charged with the murder of Big H. After that, tension lessened in the neighborhood. Then, on the day of Big Mama's discharge from Bellevue, Bongo, who only then knew of her whereabouts, turned up at the hospital with a loaded .38-caliber revolver tucked inside a bouquet. When the gun was confiscated, he flew into a murderous rage. *That fuckin' gun's for protection—mine and Big Mama's. Don't you blue-eyed motherfuckers know that the prez of the Angels is still out there somewhere?*

Big Mama's return home that day was the first big social event of 1973. She was received with all the hoopla befitting her position as queen of The Compound. Sheets, stiff from the January cold, hung from windows with WELCOME HOME BIG MAMA scrawled on them by the gangs' graffiti experts. Two of the Nomads joined hands and carried her up the stoop, across the courtyard, and upstairs to the clubhouse, while members of the Mongols, Seven Immortals, Latin Diplomats, and Storm Troopers leaned out their windows and joined the Nomads in a round of cheers.

Preparations for the welcome-home party had taken several days. Not only had the Nomads' clubhouse, which hadn't been swept in months, been swept clean, but the walls had been scrubbed down as well. And since it was going to be an open house for all the gangs in The Compound, an incredible amount of beer, wine, and grass had been rounded up. Days in advance of Big Mama's return, Baby Nomads were sent into the street to fleece kids of their pocket money and charge housewives a dollar to shop at the local supermarket, while the gang's Gestapo Squad visited local merchants and "solicited" donations for the Welcome Home Big Mama fund.

When she was carried over the threshold of the clubhouse, Big Mama entered a purple den pulsating with Latin rhythm and reeking of incense. All the white bulbs had been replaced with purple ones; the brothers were pounding the bongos, competing with the stereo that was playing full blast; and the perfume of the incense bought at the *botanica* was heavy enough to mask the sweet scent of the grass— just in case the cops paid an unexpected visit. As Big Mama, clutching her cane, was set down on her throne (a bench ripped out of Nomad Park especially for the occasion), her honor guard joined the other members of the Gestapo Squad who were in the kitchen cleaning their guns . . .

Everybody comin' to the party is gonna get frisked. This is gonna be a peaceful party. An' the first motherfucker who steps outa line is gonna get iced. By order of Black Bongo, prez and supreme leader of the Savage Nomads.

Early on Bongo had announced that there would be "no chicken pluckin' " except in the Sex Room, where the walls had been plastered with pornography and sprayed with fluorescent paint. Now, after uncorking a bottle of Swiss Up wine with his teeth, he had another announcement: "No more'n six couples in the Sex Room at one time. Understand? Six—no more." And it went without saying, but he'd say it anyway: "Kitchen's off limits to chicks. Kitchen's where the leaders sit and rap when they got somethin' important to talk about. A chick or anybody else less than a warlord come in the kitchen, they get their ass kicked."

By ten that evening, The Compound was ringing with noise. Every gang member was either at the party or on his way to the party. Everybody, that is, but fourteen-year-old Buckwheat, a Nomad, who was half asleep on a bench in Nomad Park. He had escaped from the Inwood House drug center downtown two days before, and he hadn't had anything to eat since, except one chocolate bar and a bag of potato chips. Even if he had a dime—which he didn't—he couldn't call home. They'd just ship him right back to Inwood. Man, how he'd like to go upstairs to the party. He was exhausted, but still his foot was keeping time to the rhythm of the drums. But he couldn't go upstairs. No way. Some of the Nomads had beat on him just before Christmas, and he was in disgrace. They'd called him a no-good junkie. Still, The Compound was like home, and so he had come as close to it as he dared. And now, despite the noise and the cold, he was about to fall asleep.

As the two transvestites approached The Compound, one of them, Joey the fag, thought she recognized Buckwheat. For a moment she considered running across the street to the park, shaking him awake, handing him a buck, and telling him to take off. On a night like this, Nomad Park was no place to be. Especially without an overcoat. Like as not, some of those dudes upstairs would come down and see him sleeping on that bench and they'd cap his ass. But Jocelyn, who kept insisting that she was freezing *her* ass off, was nudging her up the stoop, and so Joey kept moving and didn't even have a chance for a second look to see if it really was Buckwheat or not. It sure as hell looked like him. Anyway, whoever it was, he was going to freeze to death lying there asleep like that.

By the time they had climbed the four flights to the party,

Joey the fag and Jocelyn were breathing hard, what with the stairs (Jocelyn was thirty-one, after all) and the laughing. This promised to be one of the best nights ever, said Jocelyn, still hugging the chubby fur jacket around herself. "And from where I'm standin' now," she said, rolling her eyes as one of the Gestapo Squad patted her down for weapons, "it's gonna be one hell of a year." Then Joey got herself patted down, and she rolled her eyes and cooed. Tall and twenty-one, she and Jocelyn, who fancied she looked like Diana Ross, were considered jive niggers— right guys—by the gangs in The Compound, and nobody minded their drag. Neither did the prostitutes who, like them, worked the truckers who rode cross country to the Hunts Point produce market, parked, and waited in line for the gates to open at dawn. There was enough action for everybody, the prossies and the gays. There was an unwritten law: The prossies checked out at three and the gays came on, looking just as foxy as the girls in their wigs, tight skirts, three-inch-high clogs, and padded bras. The elderly watchman, who kept the fire going in a fifty-five-gallon drum, was just as gabby with the gays as he was with the girls. As for the truckers, they either didn't know the difference or didn't care, reaching down to help Joey or Jocelyn up into the back of the truck, willing to believe . . . *Well, honey, I got the rag on an' all I can do tonight is give you a blow job . . .*

The Gestapo dude had no sooner finished frisking Joey than around the bend of the stairs came the Savage Skulls, led by Snake, their prez and his wife, Savage Rose, her face half hidden by a giant pair of dark glasses. Joey and Jocelyn paused at the door to see if the Skulls were going to submit to the weapons search. Of course, the Gestapo dude didn't lay a finger on Savage Rose, but Snake and his brothers took turns being patted down, and that, said Joey, was a good sign. *This gonna be a re-fine party.*

Oh yeah? said Jocelyn, stepping over the puddles of wine staining the floor inside, to which more was being added each time a dude opened a new bottle or can and spilled the first drop as tribute to missing brothers—absentees due to either the long arm of the law or the knife or gun of a rival gang. "If Big Mama had real class, she'd make 'em kick this tribal crap," Jocelyn said, accepting a paper cup of fruit wine from a Nomad who looked like he was maybe sixteen. Just maybe. "They all gettin' younger and younger." Watching the Skulls file into the room, she decided, "They sure do make an entrance." But she was talking to herself, for Joey had gotten hold of a joint and was wiggling to the music. Jocelyn watched as Snake and Savage Rose made straight for Big Mama. He patted her shoulder, and Savage Rose slapped palms with her. But Big Mama had still to crack her first smile of the evening.

"You see in the *News* this week that they say the Skulls are the meanest?" Jocelyn asked. Joey shook her head and kept right on wiggling in place. "They say they pushed junkies off the roof—and they supposed to have a rape squad." That last bit flagged Joey's attention, and she moved closer. "Seems when a girl wants to get into the gang, or if she acts up and refuses to have sex, they put the rape squad on her." Joey took another squeeze on her joint and pondered that one. "I don't believe it," she said and started wiggling again. "Me neither," said Jocelyn, only seconds before a dude she never laid eyes on before came over and asked her to dance.

Meanwhile, Buckwheat was awake now on the bench downstairs in Nomad Park, and his fingers and toes were so numb that he thought for sure they were going to break off. He hadn't meant to fall asleep out in the cold like that. He had sat down to rest and think. Where, he wondered, were Ramon and Freddie? They'd run away from Inwood the same time he did, and they all came uptown together, but somehow they'd got separated. It seemed to Buckwheat that he always ended up alone. If there were still three of them hanging out together, they could manage.

Fully awake now, he became aware of the sweat that was pouring down his back. And his gut hurt, and it wasn't just from hunger, either. If he didn't get a fix pretty soon, he'd be plenty sick. So he got to his feet and walked as fast as he could out of the park and down toward Tiffany Street.

Upstairs in The Compound, Savage Rose and her girls had taken the spotlight. And while Big Mama, surrounded by her girls, sat on her special Nomad bench and watched, the female Skulls lined up and delivered a rousing rendition of their new club song. Savage Rose, still half hidden behind dark glasses, sang it straight, but the line of girls behind her accompanied the lyrics with plenty of arm flapping, hip rolling, and pelvis snapping . . .

> "Hey, hey, whatdya say?
> Savage Skulls are on their way
> Lookin' good, lookin' fine,
> Pluckin' that chicken all the time.
> Lookin' fine, lookin' good,
> We belong in Hollywood,
> We belong in Hol—ly—wood!"

Buckwheat wandered around for the next half-hour, darting in and out of vestibules in an attempt to escape the cold. Several times he saw somebody he thought he could take off, but each time he decided against it. He was feeling too fuckin' weak. With Ramon and Freddie along, it would've been a cinch. But alone it was something else.

He crouched in the corner of a vestibule in a burnt-out building on Tiffany Street. He must have fallen asleep, because when he opened his eyes there were three dogs on the top step of the stoop, staring in at him. There hadn't been any dogs there before. They sure were mangy and mean-looking. Wild ones, Buckwheat guessed, and he'd no sooner thought that than one of the dogs, the middle one, with his snout pressing against the cracked glass of the door, curled his lip and growled. Buckwheat didn't move a muscle, but just stared back at the dog, who was obviously the leader of the pack, and soon the three dogs turned and left.

Back at The Compound, Stay High was living up to his street name. Swiss Up was trickling down the side of his mouth, and the joint between his fingers was searing the skin, but still he managed to get up off the floor, where he'd been squatting, and go over and make a grab for Sugar, who had just finished performing "We Belong in Hollywood." Stay High wanted to take her into the Sex Room, but Sugar squirmed free of him. *Later, O.K.? No, it ain't O.K., bitch!* And he smacked her with the flat of his hand. Ordinarily Sugar would have gone with him to avoid trouble, but tonight she had an advantage and she wasn't about to give in. After all, Snake and Savage Rose had both said that *all* the Skulls were to take care and cause no static. We gotta show the Nomads we're cool. And Stay High wasn't cool. So she turned away from him and headed for Savage Rose, with Stay High stumbling after her.

"You—*freeze!*" Savage Rose commanded, stepping between them. But Stay High couldn't freeze even if he wanted to, and he stumbled against her and she fell back against the wall. "Jibaro!" she screamed. "You no-good, fuckin' hick. You belong in a tree. Jibaro!" Savage Rose had a high-pitched voice, and now it cut through the party noise, snapping hold of everyone's attention. Two of the Skulls' Gestapo streaked across the room and knocked Stay High to the floor. Then Snake started kicking him, rolling him over and over across the floor until he bumped into the mattress where Joey and Jocelyn were sitting. They jumped up as Snake whipped off his belt and began to beat Stay High with it. When he stopped, the Gestapo dragged Stay High out by his feet, down the stairs, with his head and shoulders bumping each step, and out into the courtyard, where they proceeded to kick his ass. Snake had shown leadership and so had Savage Rose, and now, as Sugar made for the Sex Room with one of the Storm Troopers, Big Mama and Bongo nodded approval.

Buckwheat had dozed off again. And this time he knew it, because when he woke up he remembered dreaming of Annie. If only he could get through to Annie. She'd help him. She was his girl, the first he'd ever laid with. She'd bring him some change, some food. But he'd phoned her twice yesterday. The first time somebody hung up as soon as he spoke, and the next time it was "Go 'way. Leave Annie alone, she's only a kid. Go 'way."

Then, suddenly, out of the blue—*Wing*. Why in hell hadn't he thought of him before now? He struggled to his feet and gasped when the cold air first bit him. Then he slipped his hands into his sleeves, ducked his head, and headed for Wing's restaurant.

He stayed close to the buildings and kept his jaws locked tight so his teeth wouldn't chatter. The wind was at his back now and he was making time. 'Cause now was the time, as the kids would say, to go "get your wings clipped." Show up on the block with a ten-dollar bill, or a cool new shirt, and everybody took it for granted that you'd been to see Wing and got your wings clipped.

The restaurant was closed. Nobody in the South Bronx eats chicken chow mein at two in the morning. But Buckwheat kept twisting the doorknob and rapping on the glass, even though inside everything was dark. It was at times like this that Buckwheat counted on a miracle. Had to have a miracle. And sure enough, he got one. Wing came out from the little room in the back, snapped on the light, saw him at the door, and came shuffling between the linoleum-covered tables toward him.

When he unlocked the door, Buckwheat stumbled inside. By now he was looking really sick, and Wing, although short and slight, somehow managed to support him until he got him into the back room, where Buckwheat fell down on the rumpled cot. He lay there with his eyes closed, and felt the sweat on the back of his neck sticking to the pillow. Wing went to the sink in the corner, soaked a paper towel with cold water, and came back and placed it on his forehead. "I need help," he was finally able to say. "I need help bad."

"How much do you want?" asked Wing.

"Twenty."

Wing looked down at Buckwheat, who was the only one of the kids he was never afraid of, and he wished he hadn't stayed behind in the restaurant tonight. Because now he was afraid of Buckwheat too. Afraid that he might die there on his cot. Mistaking his silence, Buckwheat opened his eyes and said, "I don't expect the twenty for nothin'," and began fumbling with his trousers. Without sitting up or looking at what he was doing, he succeeded in unzipping his fly.

Wing went to a box hidden behind a pile of newspapers, came back, and pressed two ten-dollar bills into his hand. "Better you go now," he said, and helped him to his feet. And then together they went shuffling back across the restaurant toward the front door, Buckwheat leaning heavily on Wing. Once outside, hearing the door being locked behind him, he suddenly felt very, very scared.

Still, he made it over to Aldus Street and up four steep flights to the shooting gallery. He knocked on the door of apartment 4C, and on the other side Emma Williams peered through the peephole, recognized him, and opened up. "What's the matter, you don't know of my troubles?" she said, standing in the doorway. "This is no place to be. Police have been hasslin' me ever since the gangs shot Nellie here last year." But Buckwheat pushed past her and into the living room. She followed him and kept right on protesting, even after he had slipped her the two bills. ". . . an' they chased her into the bedroom over there an' into the closet an' they shot her dead. They stabbed Frank with an ice pick an' . . ."

Buckwheat put both hands over his ears and held them there. "Please," he said, "help me." And he kept his hands over his ears until Emma Williams stopped talking and disappeared into the kitchen. Then he heard the familiar sounds that meant she was going to give him the fix after all. "Buckwheat—you come in here." He rolled up his sleeve and ran into the kitchen, holding out his bare forearm with the telltale track marks.

"Hey, Charlie!" Bongo shouted, and everybody in the room turned toward the door, where the whiteys stood, the guy in a dark suit and tie, his arm around a chick whose hair was the color of butter. The brothers and sisters stepped back, making way for Bongo as he led the whiteys over to Big Mama, his head tilted back as he drained the last drop from the wine bottle.

"I seen her some place," Joey whispered to Jocelyn. "I think I seen her in the movies or on the television."

"Not me," replied Jocelyn, meanwhile taking in the chick's long fur coat, which she was taking off and draping over the arm of the guy called Charlie. It was mink, and the long dress she wore underneath the mink was velvet and it clung to her hips and tits, and it was clear to Jocelyn that she wasn't wearing a fuckin' thing under it.

"This here's Charlie," shouted Bongo to the room at large. "He's from—where the fuck you from, Charlie?" Paris, Charlie said, with an uneasy smile. Bongo pounded him on the back. "Charlie's a big television producer— from Paris—an' maybe he's gonna pay us Nomads five hundred dollars so's he can spend a couple of days with us and show the whole fuckin' world how we live." Then he turned from Charlie to focus on the chick. "Now, pussy, what's your name?" The white chick smiled. She said her name was Irene, and Bongo grabbed her. "This here's Irene—Charlie's cunt," he said by way of introduction to Big Mama.

The whiteys coming put a crimp in the party. The crowd didn't know what to make of them, especially the chick, who began wandering around the clubhouse with Charlie in tow. Then the stereo began playing "Didn't I Blow Your Mind This Time?" and she started to dance by herself. The Frenchman just stood there with her mink coat over his arm and watched, while she swayed her hips and pawed the air with long white arms, which, bathed in the purple lights, were a weird shade of violet. Holy shit, Jocelyn muttered to herself, she's sure beggin' for a gang fuck . . .

Every time it looked as though one of the dudes might dance with her, Snake or Big Mama would freeze him with a look. Bongo was too far gone to see what was happening. He squatted on the floor by Big Mama's boots, his chin sagging on his chest. Just then Sugar and the Storm Trooper came out of the Sex Room, and the blonde danced right into him and, without missing a beat, folded her long arms around his neck and stood swaying against him. Sugar hesitated, not knowing what to do, but then she stepped back and the two of them started moving away from her. The Storm Trooper, whose name was Sword, slapped both hands on the whitey's ass and kept them there. Then, as they swayed past Jocelyn and Joey, he raised one hand, dipped it down the front of her dress, and came up with her bare breast. She said nothing, just kept dancing, or tried to—all she could do now was stand there and rub herself against him, because Sword was standing still, holding her breast in his hand and looking around the room, grinning.

Her friend Charlie didn't know what to do. He made a move as though to go and maybe throw her coat over her, but he looked round the room and changed his mind. The blond chick arched her back as though she wanted Sword to grab her other breast too. And it was then that King Cobra made his move, coming up from behind and pulling the dress down off her shoulders, until it hung around her hips. Sword let go of her, and she turned around and wrapped her arms about King Cobra's neck. All the sisters, including Savage Rose, moved back from the center of the room and stood, watching, taking care not to block Big Mama's view. If Bongo had been awake instead of lying at her feet, snoring, Big Mama might have made them stop. But the sight of the two whiteys—the intruders—had intimidated her. She had lost control, and now she decided to just sit there and let it play.

King Cobra had his arm around the blonde's naked waist, and with his free hand he snapped his fingers in the direction of the Sex Room. The two Skulls who had beat up on Stay High busted into the Sex Room and chased out the dudes and chicks who were inside finessing. One of them, a Latin Diplomat, came out pulling up his jeans, and he tripped and fell, his genitals exposed, as King Cobra walked the whitey past him and into the room, slamming the door behind them.

No one moved. No one spoke. Charlie, the Frenchman, stood in a corner with his eyes closed. Slowly then, the prezes of each of The Compound gangs—the Mongols, Seven Immortals, Latin Diplomats, Storm Troopers; all except Bongo, who was still on the floor, snoring—began queuing up outside the Sex Room. The sisters turned their backs to the door, and after a moment some of them began to dance with each other. Sword and some of the other dudes drifted out of the clubhouse and into the hallway, where they settled on the stairs, drinking and smoking. When the stereo played "Julia," everybody's favorite Spanish song, Joey and Jocelyn started dancing and so did Savage Rose and Sugar. Big Mama poked Bongo with the tip of her cane, but he was dead drunk, the only prez who wasn't going to get a piece of that white ass. The whiteys were there because of him, and now every prez was gonna pluck the white chicken except Bongo. He was too pissed to get his share. For the first time since the party began, Big Mama smiled.

Buckwheat stood in the kitchen, still extending his bare forearm, while Emma Williams yanked the belt out of his trousers and wrapped it around his arm. He looked, and the sight of his vein, thick and knotted, filled him with pleasure, as did the sight of the spoon, bottle cap, swab of cotton, and syringe. His heart was pounding so fiercely now that Buckwheat began to rock back and forth in an attempt to forget it, because he was sure it would soon explode inside his chest. "Stand still," she ordered him, and he obeyed—at once—biting his lips to stop from shouting for joy as she took the syringe and shot the H into his vein.

"Now you ain't floppin' here," he heard her saying. "No way you stayin' here. You gotta go." But he didn't care. It didn't matter. Nothing mattered now. He felt just fine.

By now the party had begun to pall for Joey and Jocelyn. The last prez was in the Sex Room finessing with the whitey, while the rest of them lay around the room now, half out of their skulls. Joey and Jocelyn sat on a mattress, sharing a joint and growing moody together. The two whiteys had gotten the party off the track. And furthermore, Joey was beginning to wonder if maybe it was Jocelyn's age that was getting in the way of the fun lately. She studied her out of the corner of her eye, and it was as though Jocelyn read her thoughts, for she turned on her and said, "What're you starin' at, bitch?" Joey got up, took her coat off the mattress, and said, "Why, nothin', George. Nothin' at all." Then she walked out of the clubhouse and down the stairs. As she picked her way through the Gestapo, who were now lazing on the stairs, one of them put his hand up under her skirt. "I'll buy her from you for a pack of cigarettes," another dude said, grinning up at her, but Joey kept on moving. As she turned around the landing, she heard the second dude say to a third: "Got a pack of cigarettes?"

Stepping out into the courtyard, who did she see standing there in the shadows but Buckwheat. She ran over to him, her clogs slapping the pavement, and gave him a kiss on the cheek. "Why ain't you upstairs?" she said. "What's a Nomad doin' if he's not at a Nomad party? Big Mama's come home from the hospital . . ."

Buckwheat staggered back against the building and shut his eyes. His nose was running. Oh, oh, thought Joey. "They tossed me out last month," he said. "Beat me up bad an' tossed me out . . ."

"Well, Buckwheat baby, you better not let them find you hangin' round down here, then. They got the Gestapo up there on the stairs gettin' high, an' they'd like nothin' better than to kick ass tonight. Anyways, you best not try to sleep over there in Nomad Park, less you got an ice pick ready to chop yourself off the bench when you wake up. If you wake up. It's freezin', Buckwheat. Don't you feel it?"

No, he didn't feel it. But Joey felt it, clear through her coat and skirt. She gave Buckwheat another peck on the cheek and took off down the stoop and around the corner. It was almost three-thirty—there was still time to get over to Hunts Point and work the trucks.

Buckwheat straightened up and started moving across the courtyard. When he got to the center he swayed, turned around, and headed back toward the building where the party noise was coming from. But it seemed to him that it was taking him an awfully long time to get there. He stopped, squinted, and thought he saw somebody he knew coming out of the building. He tried to get it all in focus, but he just couldn't manage it. No sense in moving, anyway, because it sounded as though whoever it was was moving toward him. *"Hey you! Junkie!"*

Joey hadn't gone more than a couple of blocks when she decided to go back and get Buckwheat. He could sleep on the sofa in her place. She wheeled around and ran back as fast as her three-inch-high clogs would permit. Music was still blaring out of The Compound, and she was just starting up the stoop when she saw Buckwheat lying on his back in the courtyard. She ran over to him. He was bleeding from his head. He looked up at her and said in an eerily calm voice, "Get help. Don't move me." Joey started in the direction of The Compound and then, thinking better of it, raced out of the courtyard and down the steps. A couple of blocks away she ran into Harry's Bar and shouted that a guy had just been hurt bad. By the time a phone call had been put through to the precinct house and Joey had run back to The Compound, some of the crowd from inside had collected around Buckwheat, who was lying very still, tears trickling down his cheeks. Joey knelt beside him, took his hand in hers, and held it until the cops came. Then she rode to the hospital in the ambulance, and she stayed there until he died, six hours later, from the bullet lodged in his head. Joey was the only one able or willing to give a statement of any kind to the police, and she hadn't seen anything, really.

No one apparently knew exactly what had happened to Buckwheat. It was rumored that one of the Savage Nomads had shot him, but no one ever came to trial. It was generally agreed that Buckwheat had made a big mistake coming around The Compound after he'd been tossed out. How come he didn't know better? Nobody likes a junkie.

It was almost noon when Buckwheat died, and at that hour The Compound was quiet. The gangs inside had broken the night and were still sleeping. Only a few of them were aware of who had gotten iced down there in the courtyard; most of them heard about it for the first time when they woke up. And by that time Black Bongo and his dogs were crossing the courtyard, past where Buckwheat had lain dying only hours earlier, and taking up the position on the top step of the stoop. Big Mama was home. Life in The Compound was back to normal.

Three days later, Big Mama was with Bongo on the stoop when Buckwheat's funeral cortege rolled by. His family had chosen the special Ortiz hearse outfitted with a loudspeaker, so that before you saw the hearse you heard the Spanish hymns being played on the record player inside. Ed O'Rourke and Vito Moles were parked outside The Compound, and they saw Bongo and Big Mama suddenly grow silent; at the sight of the cream-colored hearse, Big Mama made the sign of the cross.

8.
The Murder of the Transvestite

Members of street gangs are constantly putting their manhood to the test. They inflict monstrous physical punishment without hesitation, and accept it without flinching. That's being a Big Man. They take a girl with or without her consent. Big Man. And they take enormous pride in their ability to talk convincingly—to rap—and thereby earn respect. Another sure sign of being a Big Man. Under the circumstances, then, one might think that this street-gang machismo would pose a threat to a homosexual's survival in the ghetto. But that's not so. Street gangs usually have a live-and-let-live attitude toward the homosexuals of their ghetto—perhaps because they see them as a fragmented minority, even more alienated from the mainstream of society than they are. And without their manhood to protect them.

Interestingly, a sizable proportion of the homosexuals in the gang-infested ghetto of the South Bronx are transvestites. Adopting feminine first names and concealing their gender beneath wigs and dresses, they make a seductive appeal for protection. And while their company certainly isn't sought by the street gangs, they are tolerated and sometimes protected by them. The only unpardonable act is when a "faggot" carries the pretense of being a woman too far and causes a man to lose face. On his way home from the Welcome Home Big Mama party George (Jocelyn) Barnes made that mistake, and it proved to be fatal.

Nobody in The Compound had ever seen him as George, in the suit and tie he wore when he periodically played it straight and took a nine-to-five job. Certainly nobody at the Hunts Point market had ever laid eyes on George Barnes, the clerk. The workaday routine would last until one morning the alarm clock would ring, and the Jocelyn in him would turn it off, roll over, and go back to sleep. When he awoke, he would put on Jocelyn's Diana Ross wig, flashy earrings, and high heels and resume the gay life. Jocelyn had been arrested three times in six months for soliciting the truckers at Hunts Point, but no matter. The joy of "being" a woman was worth it. Furthermore, it paid. Sometimes Jocelyn came home with as many as six five-dollar bills tucked into her padded bra.

The Welcome Home Big Mama party had been evil, real evil. And now it was too late to go work Hunts Point. *Shit*. And even if it wasn't too late, no sense in going when you're feeling down. You have to feel foxy to score. But who wouldn't feel down if, coming out of a party—a lousy one at that—you step out into a courtyard and find a cop standing guard over a mess of blood and some crazy chalk marks to show how the body lay before it was scooped up and taken away?

—What happened, officer?

—A kid was murdered here, miss, a couple of hours ago.

And *Miss* Jocelyn had hurried down that stoop and fast away from that fuckin' Compound. And now here she was, still hurrying down the street, with the wind at her back and no place to go but home. Alone.

Barnes knew Jocelyn looked nothing short of sensational

in the new red dress and the almost-new white fur jacket. Well, all right, a fake fur jacket. A *fun* fur. And still she was going home alone. *Shit.*

Barnes also knew Jocelyn and her moods, and at this very minute she was heading for gloom. Gloom because she was going home alone. Gloom because when she got into that cold bed—alone—she sure as hell was going to dream about that caked blood and those chalk marks. Gloom because a whip of wind had just lashed her buttocks and reminded her of how nice it was when, between tricks down at Hunts Point, you warmed yourself by the fire the old watchman kept going. And she missed Lovelace, Crystal, and the other girls, who were probably doing that very thing this very minute.

Then, just as Jocelyn was about to slam her handbag against a brick wall to let off some of the steam building up inside her, Barnes heard the unmistakable sounds of a party spilling down from somewhere upstairs in one of a row of tenements he was passing, and Jocelyn made him stop. She stood and let the sounds of the music and laughter spill over her like so much golden sunshine before looking up to see exactly where all that happiness was coming from. Nobody on Hoe Avenue ever went to bed, that was her guess, for damn if every apartment in the building didn't have lights on. But one of them up on the third floor had plenty of shadows flashing by the windows. That was it!

Jocelyn ran up the stoop and into the vestibule, where she proceeded to run a comb through her wig and spray herself with perfume. She figured she'd probably know some of the dudes up there on the third floor, but what if she didn't? No sweat. There was always room for a girl in a tight red dress and reeking of a musky perfume.

She climbed the stairs to the third floor and went down the hall to the apartment where the party noises were coming from. The door there was wide open, as if to say:

Girl, you come right on in here now and make us happy! So Jocelyn stepped inside without a moment's hesitation, and she proved to be right: They were eager to greet a foxy girl flashing a big, juicy smile.

Jocelyn went into the bedroom, flung her white fur jacket across the bed, and came back into the living room, where the action was. Within fifteen minutes she had danced with a dozen dudes. Some she recognized as members of a new gang called the Vultures. Others, mostly younger, were Black Spades. And still others were complete strangers to her. New talent. She liked that best of all.

One of the Spades she had never laid eyes on before—a big kid built like a fuckin' football player—really liked her and wouldn't let anybody else dance with her. He held her close and kept brushing his lips across her cheek. And damn if Jocelyn couldn't feel him grow stiff. Then, right there in the middle of the room, he suddenly reached under her dress and shoved his hands between her legs. She tried to squeeze her thighs together, but too late. Holy shit! The kid pulled his hand away and, with one motion, ripped the front of her dress clear down to the waist. "Faggot!" It wasn't so much an accusation as a battle cry. And when he turned around to flag the attention of the other dudes above the din of the music, Jocelyn pulled away from him, leaving part of her dress clutched in his fist, and bolted out of the room. By the time she was swinging around the banister on the second floor, with the thunder of feet directly overhead, it was George Barnes, the mousy little file clerk, who was fleeing for his life. He had not only left his white fur jacket upstairs; he'd left Jocelyn, too.

Despite the high-heeled pumps he was wearing, Barnes made it out to the sidewalk without tripping. But by then a dozen or more dudes were charging down the stoop after him, shouting. He could hear windows being pulled up along both sides of Hoe Avenue. He had run perhaps twenty feet when he was struck from behind with a garbage can. The impact was tremendous, and he fell. But just as he was about to hit the pavement, he was grabbed and pulled upright. The big football-player kid had him on the left, and a tall, skinny kid had him on the right, and together they began yanking him from side to side. Barnes looked from one grinning face to the other, and then up, where he saw the curious faces leaning out of windows, staring down at him. Then he felt a pair of hands reach under his dress and pull his drawers down around his knees, and from the sound of the laughter coming from behind him he was sure there had to be at least twenty dudes running around him now like Indians around a covered wagon. Suddenly the two kids, who had been yanking him so hard that he felt his arms were going to be torn clear out of their sockets, let go. He was free. He couldn't believe it. They were going to let him go. They'd just been trying to scare him, that was all.

Barnes got ready to run, but found that he couldn't. The elastic of his drawers had him hobbled, and he pitched forward, landing hard on his hands and knees. He no sooner hit the pavement than someone kicked him in the back. He collapsed, one of his big, heavy earrings crushed against his cheek, and didn't dare move. Maybe, just maybe, one of those faces sticking out one of those windows had called the cops and any minute now he'd hear a siren and the sound of those dudes streaking down the street and away from him.

Instead, he felt a jumble of hands all over his body, clutching and pulling at him. His dress was thrown up, and he felt the cold air bite into the bare flesh of his buttocks. Then feet began kicking him, and hands were spreading his buttocks until he felt that he was being split apart. *Gimme the broom . . . Gimme the broom,* he heard somebody shout, and then it was the rattle of a garbage can being overturned, its lid sent clattering into the gutter. From somewhere he heard a dog bark, and a woman's voice said, "No, no— don't do that!" Then came the pain, the excruciating pain as the broom handle was shoved up into him, tearing into him with such a fury that it brought him up on his elbows. He arched his back, opened his mouth wide, and screamed. It was a pitiful, hideous cry that sent some of the faces reeling back inside their apartments, with their hands clapped over their ears. And before it was completely free of his throat, the tall, skinny kid, who had him by the arm only a minute before, ran around in front of him and dropped a garbage can down on top of him. As it smashed his face down against the cold pavement and he felt pain stabbing at him from both ends, he was certain that he was dying.

He didn't know how long he lay there. He must have passed out. But now he was conscious again, struggling for breath. His wig was askew, and from force of habit he raised his hand in a vain attempt to straighten it.

Margie Santiago, leaning out of her bedroom window on the third floor across the street, couldn't believe her eyes when she saw him move. She had been so sure that he was dead. But now he was getting up, staggering over toward a parked car, and leaning against it. She watched as the youths encircled him again, shouting, "Faggot! Faggot!" In apartments above her, below her, and across the street, people leaned out of their windows and watched too, hor- rified, as one of the gang ran up and kicked him in the groin. As he doubled over, groaning, another one pushed forward to punch him in the face, knocking him to the pavement. Margie Santiago gripped the windowsill with both hands and yelled, "You've done enough! You've done enough!" Others around her were shouting too, but it made no difference. The gang was on him again, kicking and stomping. One of them picked up the bloody broom handle and began to whack him across the legs with it. "Stop it!" she yelled, and an old man in a fourth-floor apartment directly across the street slammed his window shut and buried his face in his hands.

George Barnes had the sensation of feeling his body swell up around him. It was as though he was shrinking inside this mass of flesh that was being attacked on all sides, and any moment now the balloonlike flesh, which was growing fatter with each blow, each kick, would explode and he would be free. He could barely see now, both eyes were so cruelly swollen. And he began to feel himself slipping away, losing consciousness again, as the kicking, stomping, and shouting assumed a grotesque kind of rhythm. Then, from somewhere in the distance, he was being pulled back to consciousness. Again, it was a jumble of hands on his body, this time prodding, twisting, turning him. Finally he was flipped over, and he felt the cold air sting both sides of his swollen face when, suddenly, the skirt of his dress bubbled in the air and then descended over him like a veil. Hands grabbed hold of his testicles, and he felt the blade of a knife begin to saw away at him.

Only minutes before the police arrived, the youths had dispersed, as the shouting from the tenements on both sides of the street had become a veritable roar of protest. Amazingly, George Barnes was still alive. He died seven hours later in Jacobi Hospital.

Fifteen-year-old Rudy Rodriguez was coming down Hoe Avenue, on his way home after a date with his girl, when Barnes's attackers ran past him, almost knocking him over. Detectives asked him if he thought he could identify any of them, but he said no, they'd been running too fast and there were too many of them. Still, some of the people who had been watching from their windows would later maintain that they were certain he had arrived on the scene while the attack was taking place. Exactly one year later, the same Rudy Rodriguez would be one of several youths involved in another brutal murder on the same street.

Despite the number of people who had been witnesses to the murder of George Barnes, few of them believed they could identify his attackers. *There were so many of them, you see—maybe fifteen blacks and about five or six Hispanics darting in and out, punching and kicking—and I'm up in the window looking down and, well, their faces weren't clear from up there.* But all the witnesses were in total agreement on one point: This attack was the most gruesome they had ever seen.

Detectives from the Eighth Homicide Squad talked to the teenaged girl whose party George Barnes had come to uninvited. She said she hadn't recognized "the girl in the red dress," but then, she said, she didn't know more than half of the guys at her party, either.

"My daughter gives a party, and before you know it, these gangs bust in and take over," her mother explained. Both the mother and daughter said that they couldn't identify any of them. All they knew was that there was trouble all of a sudden, and then maybe a couple of dozen of them ran out of the apartment. They were fairly certain the blacks were members of the Black Spades. As for the Hispanics, they didn't know what gang, if any, they belonged to.

Herman Mandelbaum told police that he and his wife had lived on Hoe Avenue for over twenty years. Twenty-five, she corrected him, adding that it used to be a very decent neighborhood full of hard-working, respectable people. They said they had seen some ghastly things happen down there in the street, but never anything so terrible as what they'd seen from their bedroom window that morning. Mandelbaum said that at one point he had had to shut the window and hide his face in his hands, it was so sick-making. And he had been in World War II and seen men die.

When Margie Santiago spoke to the detectives, her voice was hoarse. "I shouted so much at those animals who were killing that poor man." Could she identify any of them? She asked the detectives to follow her into the bedroom. "Now you look out," she said, standing at the window. "See? Three stories up, and I'm looking down, and with everything moving so fast and half the time my eyes full of tears—I don't know if I could identify anybody. But I'll do anything I can to help. Maybe, just maybe I can recognize one or two. But I don't know . . ."

Herman Mandelbaum phoned the Eighth Homicide Squad the next day and asked that someone meet him at a neighborhood laundromat. When the two detectives arrived, Mandelbaum, who said he feared gang retaliation if he was seen talking to the law again, told them that he thought they should know that a woman had been walking her dog when the attack started. "My wife and I woke up when we heard so much laughter down there in the street—imagine, *laughter*—and we looked out and we saw this woman, and she was trying to stop one of those savages from hitting that poor man with a garbage can." And a few minutes later, when eight or nine of them were stomping Barnes, Mandelbaum said, the woman sicced her dog on one of them and the dog bit him. He said he didn't know the woman's name, but he gave the detectives a good description of her and the dog.

"Yes, my dog bit the guy," said Aurora Fields, who, it turned out, lived in the tenement next door to the one where the party had been held. "He jumped up and bit him on the stomach. Then the guy took the garbage can and tried to kill my dog. So I grabbed my pet and ran in the house and called the police. I was so upset, I don't think I gave my name." The black-and-white spotted mongrel lay at her feet until she snapped her fingers, and then it stood up and let her open its jaws. "You see, he's got strong, sharp teeth. It must've hurt." Did she think she could identify some of the youths who had attacked George Barnes? Yes, and furthermore she suggested that the detectives visit her neighbor across the hall. "A nice-looking girl, but she keeps bad company. I know because she was coming home with a guy who is big with one of the gangs around here, and she must've seen something, because from my window I seen her and him come down the street while it was happening."

Aurora Fields was correct on both counts. Anna Robes was very nice-looking and she apparently did keep bad company. Her date that evening had been Shaft, a leader of the Vultures gang, which had its clubhouse in the basement of a tenement on Hoe Avenue. They'd been to a party, she said, and sure, they'd seen some of it. "I see one black guy pull the faggot's head up and hold it, and then another black guy, he kick him in the face with his boot. I don't stay around. I say good-bye to Shaft and I run upstairs."

Meanwhile, Detectives O'Rourke and Moles were parked across the street from The Compound, and gang members drifted out to come and sit in the back seat of their car and talk about the murder of "the faggot." The street talk was that Shaft had seen most of it and, in fact, had custody of the knife used to mutilate Jocelyn.

The door to the clubhouse of the Vultures was locked, and Wolf Man, the building superintendent and a member of the gang as well, said nobody had been around for a couple of days. He opened the door and led O'Rourke and Moles through the three sparsely furnished rooms. "I don't know nothin' about no murder," Wolf Man said, locking the door again. "I got my own troubles." Which he did. Wolf Man was about to be indicted for the murder of his infant son. "Tell you what," he said, "soon's I see Shaft I'll tell him you wanna talk to him."

O'Rourke and Moles attended funeral services for George

Barnes in Brooklyn, where his sister and brother lived. Both were intelligent, soft-spoken individuals who made no apologies for their unfortunate brother. The sister, with whose family he spent the holidays each year, told the detectives that until now her children hadn't been aware of what she called "their uncle's private life." But she said that that didn't mean they loved him any the less now. "George was always so very kind." She said that when he came to visit he always dressed neatly and was a perfect gentleman. His brother, a tall, slender man, took Vito Moles aside and told him that he hoped the people responsible for the crime would be caught and punished. "I am not a vengeful person," he said, "but what they did to George was savage. That's why we couldn't have the casket open. Even with both eyes closed, you could still see the terror in his face." He turned around and looked at the small gathering of people sitting on the little straight-backed chairs, waiting for the preacher to begin the service. "Some of these people went to school with us. They'd only see George at holiday time, when he came over to celebrate with his family, but now they've come to pay their respects. They've seen the newspapers . . . they know how he died . . . but they don't hold it against my brother. They're good Christians."

O'Rourke and Moles stood in the rear of the funeral chapel during the short service. The preacher, who had never seen George Barnes in life, called him "a child of God" who had gone home to his maker. And when the sermon was concluded, a pretty woman who had attended grade school with George Barnes and was a close friend of his sister's got up, walked over to the casket, and began to sing a spiritual in a lovely mezzo-soprano voice. She sang softly, as though crooning to a child.

> "Goin' home, goin' home
> I'm a-goin' home . . .

Quiet-like . . . some still day
I'm jes' goin' home.
It's not far, jes' close by,
Through an open door . . .
Work all done, care laid by,
Goin' to fear no more.
Mother's there expecting me,
Father's waitin' too . . .
Lots o' folks gathered there,
All the friends I knew.
Home, home . . . I'm goin' home!"

Three days later, the two detectives found Shaft sitting alone in the clubhouse, drinking beer. "Murder? I didn't see this murder you're talkin' about. I didn't tell nobody I see this murder. First I heard about it was from the radio. You speak to Wolf Man. I hear he was to a party over there on Hoe that night—same party the fag been to—and maybe he saw the whole fuckin' thing. You speak to him."

Wolf Man swore that he'd been working at his regular job as a porter at the movie house over on Southern Boulevard. "I got my own troubles." But a check with the theater manager showed that Wolf Man hadn't been to work that night. Confronted with that information, Wolf Man changed his story. He'd forgotten—he'd been playing bingo that night with his in-laws, from six till three the next morning. O'Rourke and Moles visited the family, and they said that Wolf Man had indeed been with them that night, and the man of the house went to a closet and produced a bingo board as proof of his family's dedication to the game.

The next day the ticket taker at the movie house where Wolf Man worked called the Eighth Homicide Squad to report an incident he thought probably had something to do with "the fag murder over there on Hoe." He said that some members of the Black Spades had come into the theater the afternoon after the murder as he was sitting, reading a newspaper, in the lobby. One of the kids snatched the paper out of his hand. What's goin' on? he asked the kid, grabbing the paper back. "I think I killed a guy last night. I fucked him up bad. I cut his dick off." Then, he said, the kid went inside and took a seat. About fifteen minutes later another Black Spade came into the lobby and said to him: "I fucked up a guy last night. Fucked him up pretty bad. He could be dead." He said he asked him exactly what had happened, and the kid told him that the Spades had been at a party and one of them "snatched the faggot's pocketbook an' she started hittin' him and a fight broke out."

Based on the descriptions and the street names furnished by the ticket taker, Gang Intelligence was able to identify two of the Black Spades gang, and they were taken into custody for questioning. They denied having any knowledge of the murder, other than what they'd heard on the radio and on the street. Their mug shots were shown to the Hoe Avenue residents who had watched the crime taking place, but not one of them could be sure that these two youths were among the gang who had attacked George Barnes. As a result, the two Black Spades were released.

Sitting on seats ripped out of the cars abandoned in the Hunts Point market area, warming themselves around the fire the night watchman kept going in the fifty-five-gallon drum, the prostitutes talked to O'Rourke and Moles about their friend Jocelyn. They all agreed that she was nice, maybe the nicest of the gays who worked the truck line. "They oughta find out the bastard who iced her and shoot 'em dead on the spot," said a short, fat black girl who admired Jocelyn's good taste in clothes. "She never dressed like some drag queens do. She dressed like a movie star." The prostitutes said that none of the gays had been working the truck line since the murder, and suggested that the detectives go to some of the social clubs where Jocelyn, Joey the fag, Lovelace, and some of the other gays hung out. "They got a real underground goin'. Maybe they know something that'll help. That's if they'll talk. They're *real* scared."

O'Rourke and Moles spent the next evening visiting the four social clubs along Southern Boulevard that catered to the gay trade. Dismal-looking on the outside, they were just as dismal inside, with long, gloomy bars, rainbow-hued jukeboxes, and the inevitable pool table dominating the center of the dimly lit rooms.

"That is from when the El Albanico was a straight place," explained Lovelace, a reedy, black six-footer wearing a shoulder-length blond wig and silver dress, pointing to the pool table with one long, silver-polished fingernail. "But you can't take it out, it's too expensive. Anyway, maybe it gives the place atmosphere. Oh, but Jocelyn hated it. *Hated it!* She wanted everything glamorous and sexy. That's why we were all so depressed when we heard that they buried her in a suit and tie. She had such *beautiful* clothes. She shoulda been buried in her wig and a dress. When I go, I want to go lookin' just the way I do right now. I want to wear a long dress with a wide skirt, so's they can drape one side of it over the lid of the casket. Lupe Velez or one of them movie stars who killed herself way back there, she got buried like that, I'm told, and I never forgot that. I want glamor right to the end, the bitter end."

Lovelace said she hadn't been working the truck line since the murder. "Not that I'm scared or superstitious or anything, but not Joey or me or Crystal have worked Hunts Point since. We figure it's the least we can do in memory of Jocelyn. Next week it'll be different, but this week we're stayin' away. Right now it wouldn't be the same without Jocelyn. Y'know, the girls over there are O.K., but it's us queens give it class. The girls are kinda pushy. But we never push, or fight with one another. Jocelyn, Joey, Crystal, and me, we'd link arms and parade past the trucks, smilin' and jokin'. We worked together, and we always knew whose turn it was to turn the next trick. We never took advantage."

But Lovelace was reluctant to discuss the murder. "I didn't sleep for two whole nights afterward." The two detectives treated her to several cans of beer, and she began to relax. "Does your hair look as good in the daylight as it does in this light here?" she suddenly asked O'Rourke. "Because if it does, I'm gettin' me a strawberry-blond wig next. Platinum's too harsh in the daylight. That's another thing I admired about Jocelyn. She stuck to black wigs. Never anything showy. I get kinda showy sometimes." Then Lovelace burst into tears. She peeled off her spiky lashes, dropped them into her handbag, and dabbed at her eyes. She was ready to talk.

"That party Jocelyn busted was full of Black Spades—but I guess you know that. Some of them are crazier than the bunch you got over in The Compound. Now Jocelyn could go to The Compound and everything was O.K. But you don't go off the street to a Black Spade party and expect to come out O.K. Not with the Spades no how. The ones in their twenties, they not so bad, but the ones in their teens are still tryin' to prove they're big men. I hear trouble started when one of 'em came on with Jocelyn. Name's T.N.T. Now I don't say he iced her or even helped, but the trouble started with him an' Jocelyn."

Meanwhile, rumors filtering out of The Compound said that the Spades were blistering under the pressure of the murder investigation. "They already have two cases of rape pressing on 'em, so's they don't need more hassle," said one of the Mongols to O'Rourke and Moles as he slumped in the back seat of their car.

T.N.T. was brought in for questioning, and he maintained his innocence. Sure, he was at the party on Hoe

Avenue that night, but so were a lot of other dudes, "includin' some from the Vultures. Why you pickin' on us Spades? 'Cause we black?" Maybe he'd danced with the fag in the red dress and maybe he hadn't. "I was high, man." Had he been out on the sidewalk during the attack? "No way, man. I was havin' too good a time upstairs at the party."

Hoe Avenue residents were shown mug shots of some of the Black Spades—T.N.T. among them—and this time Aurora Fields, the woman with the dog, said she recognized four of them as being part of the gang that had attacked George Barnes. "The one my dog bit isn't here, though," she said with obvious disappointment. T.N.T. was not one of the four she identified.

Within the week—almost two months after the murder —the first arrest was made. The Preacher, a seventeen-year-old said to be a member of the Black Spades' Gestapo Squad, was picked up in a cafeteria, brought to the precinct house, and booked. Within the next two weeks three more members of the gang were arrested.

Some members of the gangs in The Compound told O'Rourke and Moles that street talk had it that if The Preacher were indicted for manslaughter, he would arrange to have T.N.T. iced. "The Preacher's sure it was T.N.T. who dropped the dime on him," confided Bricktop. "And T.N.T. ain't gonna stand still. No way. He think he knows where it was you got to him, and that faggot Lovelace better watch out 'cause he gonna come down on her hard."

Meantime, Margie Santiago reported receiving a series of phone calls threatening her life if she talked to the law again. Herman Mandelbaum and his wife closed their apartment and went to visit relatives in Long Island City. Aurora Fields, afraid that her dog might be killed, gave it to a cousin in Harlem "until this thing is over and done with."

A few days later the Gang Intelligence Unit received a

phone call from Lovelace. Ed O'Rourke told her that he had difficulty understanding her. "It must be a lousy connection."

"Ain't no lousy connection," replied Lovelace, trying to articulate more clearly, "it's my mouth. My fuckin' mouth's the size of my knee, and my knee's size of my fuckin' head. You and your partner come over here an' see me. I'm scared."

Lovelace's mother, as short and round as Lovelace was long and lank, opened the door and indicated a room down the long, narrow hallway, where Lovelace, wearing a service-able-looking bathrobe, sat on the edge of a big bed strewn with stuffed animals, beneath a ceiling studded with silver stars of assorted sizes.

"They stole my wig," she said, running a hand across her cap of grizzled hair. "Ripped it clear off my head after they knocked the shit outa me." She said she hadn't gotten a good look at her attackers. She thought there were five or six of them. Little motherfuckers. "There wasn't one even came up to my shoulder. Eleven or twelve years old, no more. I was comin' down Southern Boulevard from El Albanico and they popped outa some doorway just as I was passin' by and they got me across the back of the legs with a broom handle. Soon's I fell and got a look at that fuckin' broom, I thought right away of Jocelyn. They wasn't gonna shove that thing up me, so's I started yellin', and that's when one of the little fucks kicked me right in the mouth. Then they started stompin', and I kept right on yellin' an' they got scared and took off—with my wig stuck on top of that fuckin' broom handle."

Lovelace opened her mouth as wide as her swollen lips would allow and tapped one of her two front teeth. "I was holdin' this tooth in my hand when they took off. The kick knocked it clear outa my head, but I shoved it back

into my gum and damn if it didn't stick." Then Lovelace
pulled the bathrobe away from her legs, revealing a knee
swollen to three times its normal size. "I got no doubt in
my mind that T.N.T. set me up. He gonna try an' kill me if
The Preacher don't get him first."

The Preacher was indicted for manslaughter, and T.N.T.
promptly disappeared from the South Bronx. "I hear he's
gone south," said Bricktop. Two of the three Black Spades
were indicted along with The Preacher, but in a matter of
weeks charges were dismissed against both of them for lack
of evidence. One, in fact, had been hospitalized at the time
George Barnes was murdered. Since Aurora Fields, who had
identified him as one of the attackers, was the only one of
the Hoe Avenue witnesses to have positively identified any of
the gang members, the state's case was seriously weakened.
The Preacher pleaded guilty to a robbery charge that had
been hanging over his head and was sentenced to a jail term
for that crime. Then the remaining defendant pleaded
guilty to a charge of assault and was sentenced to a prison
term of four years.

Lovelace, Joey the fag, and Crystal began visiting George
Barnes's grave the first Sunday of every month. Jocelyn had
liked white flowers, said Lovelace, "so we put daisies or
tulips or whatever's white on her grave. Once we brung
white lilacs. I never seen white lilacs before. They're really
beautiful." But eventually they stopped the monthly pil-
grimage to the cemetery.

"It's not that we forgot Jocelyn," explained Lovelace,
who by this time had her strawberry-blond wig. "No way
we forget her. But . . . well, it's over an' that's it. If they'd
caught the dudes who iced her, then it'd be different. But
those guys are still out there—livin', fuckin', just like before.
It's all so unreal. So's it better we forget what happened.

Otherwise, us gays would have to move away. And man, bad as it is, this is home. We feel safe here just so long as we remember what happened to Jocelyn an' we don't make the same kinda mistake."

9.
The Rape of "Virgin Uno"

Every gang in The Compound had its graffiti expert, and the walls outside the clubhouse exploded with samples of his cunning. The street name of each member was included in among the giant jungle flowers, eye-popping circles and triangles, and arrows with flaming tails. The graffiti shared something else in common: an obsession with "Virgin Uno." It might be expressed with just those two words topped with a halo, or it might be something more elaborate—a crude drawing of a small vagina with a huge penis pointing to it, and a caption reading "Number Uno will be gotten!"

The virginity of fourteen-year-old Laverne Knight, "Virgin Uno," was a challenge to every gang in The Compound. Some of the Compound wives had gone to school with her. She was on friendly terms with the Peacemakers, whose clubhouse was just around the corner from where she lived. She was small, pretty—and streetwise. So how come she was still a virgin? In the South Bronx, where many a fourteen-year-old is an unwed mother, Laverne Knight's virginity seemed unnatural, and there were repeated boasts of a plot to kidnap her and bring her into The Compound—where she had never been—and gang-bang her. The Mongols had recently deserted their top-floor apartment because it was so messed up, what with broken pipes and smashed windows. She could be carried up there, to neutral turf, so no one gang could claim the distinction of having raped "Virgin Uno" in its clubhouse. Her rape would be a communal enterprise.

One night one of the dudes went over to the tenement where she lived with her mother and six brothers and sisters and with a Magic Marker drew on the wall above the mailboxes in the vestibule a vagina and penis and then scrawled, "Number Uno will be gotten!" When Pigmeat, prez of the Peacemakers, heard about it, he decided then and there that it was a matter of pride that his gang should kidnap her. "Virgin Uno" lived on their turf. She belonged to the Peacemakers. If anybody was going to have her, it was going to be a Peacemaker. And who was more deserving of the honor than Pigmeat himself?

An all-black gang, the Peacemakers was among the first to emerge in the South Bronx in the early seventies. As the gang grew in size, so did its file in the offices of the Gang Intelligence Unit. In a period of just three weeks, in 1971, for example, police of the Forty-first Precinct had confiscated from the Peacemakers a shopping bag containing several sawed-off shotguns and a dozen Molotov cocktails; investigated an incident in which members of the gang allegedly fired shots through the window of an apartment in a tenement across from their clubhouse; and arrested several Peacemakers, charging them with sexual abuse for having kicked and punched a girl in the vagina. More newsworthy was the charge of conspiracy to commit murder and aggravated harassment leveled against Pigmeat, who, early in 1973, had written a letter threatening the life of Police Commissioner Patrick Murphy if his cops didn't lay off the Peacemakers. "We got a arsenal with lots of M-15s and

M-16s," Pigmeat wrote in the letter. But when he was interrogated, Pigmeat allowed that he really had no complaints so far as the police were concerned; his primary interest was to get some publicity and television exposure for himself and his gang. "That's why I say right there in the letter that I want the cops to show what I wrote to the *Daily News* and Channel Seven *Eyewitness News*."

Pigmeat pleaded guilty to the charge of aggravated harassment, and he was sentenced to serve eight days on Rikers Island. So he spent Easter behind bars, and then he was back strutting the streets and wearing his colors.

A rangy black youth with a lot of spring in his step, Pigmeat wore genuine white mink stitched to the collar of his denim jacket. Everyone in his gang wore a fur collar, but only he wore mink. The remainder of the mink coat he had stolen hung in a closet in the gang's clubhouse, and just as soon as the collar on his jacket looked even faintly dingy, Pigmeat would rip it off, hack another hunk of fur from the coat, and have one of his wives sew it on the collar. Nothing was too good for the prez. And now it was time he had "Virgin Uno," before one of the gangs in The Compound got her. She was on his turf, right? He had been up to her place more times than he could count. Her mother, Miss Mary Catharine, had even given him a birthday party once. The time had come for him to repay the hospitality. Tomorrow—at the stroke of midnight—he would have Laverne Knight.

After dinner the next evening, Laverne and her older sister, Tacie, visited a girl friend a few blocks away. They each drank a glass of wine, they watched some television, and at about eleven o'clock they walked home. Miss Mary Catharine had been sick with fever practically the whole week, and now she was thirsting for some fruit juice. She sent Laverne to the grocer a block away, and she returned with a bottle of grape juice. After putting it in the refrigerator, she stole out of the apartment and went downstairs and sat on the stoop. When Miss Mary Catharine was sick, her children were apt to take advantage, which they wouldn't dare when she was well—she was a strict mother. But tomorrow was Saturday—no school—and it was a warm May evening, so Laverne decided to get real tired before she went upstairs to bed.

She was sitting on the stoop for no more than five minutes when Harlow the Albino came running down the street toward her, shouting, "Your sister's being raped! Your sister's being raped!" Laverne jumped to her feet and ran down the steps. Harlow turned around and started running back the way he had come, motioning for her to follow. She was almost up to him when he disappeared around the corner, and as soon as she turned that corner they pounced on her. Harlow clapped his hand across her mouth and with the other he grabbed her throat. Then, just before her head snapped back, Laverne saw Pork Chop bend over, and the next thing she knew she was being lifted off her feet.

They carried her down the alley and up four steps and into the clubhouse through a side door. Pigmeat was standing, arms folded, waiting for them in the center of a room lit only by two tiny red bulbs. Harlow and Pork Chop flung Laverne down on the sofa, which was situated beneath a boarded-up window, and they held her there while Pigmeat pulled off his trousers. She was screaming now and trying to bite them as they began tearing at her clothes. Their hands were all over her. First her body shirt was ripped off, and then somebody pulled the sneakers off her feet. Pork Chop lifted her legs, and he and Harlow began tugging on her dungarees. Suddenly Pigmeat was bending over her, and when his big hand grabbed the zipper she heard the cloth tear, and then all three of them were shredding her panties.

Harlow yanked off her training bra and began licking her breasts. Pork Chop inserted his finger inside her, and when she felt the teeth on her breast she screamed even louder. She was punched on the side of the neck, and she twisted her body around and tried to roll off the sofa, but Harlow and Pork Chop grabbed her. She heard Pigmeat ask: "What time is it?" "Almost twelve." Then Pigmeat was mounting her and, ludicrously, she was aware for the first time of music playing somewhere in the apartment.

Pigmeat was riding her now, and Harlow and Pork Chop were shouting for him to "Fuck her!" "Fuck her good!" The next moment she felt her body tearing wide open and the weight of Pigmeat crushing her. The pain was excruciating. She felt as though her mind was fleeing her body and flying around the room, batting its wings against the four walls. Finally Pigmeat was lifting off her and saying, "You no fuckin' virgin any more."

At the precise moment when Laverne Knight was being carried into the Peacemakers' clubhouse, her ten-year-old brother, Alexander, was coming down the stoop of their tenement. Miss Mary Catharine had drunk some grape juice and gone back to sleep, and he had tiptoed out of the apartment. He walked to the corner, where he ran into his friend Pete. Suddenly a neighborhood kid ran up to him and told him that Laverne was being hurt. "The Peacemakers, they got her!" Alexander and his friend raced down the street and through the front door of the clubhouse. The front room was empty, and they rushed toward the back room. They flung the door open, and inside there were a dozen or more dudes and chicks dancing to a record player. A few of them turned to look at the two boys, but no one made a move toward them. Just then Alexander heard a girl scream, and he slammed the door shut and ran to a room on the left, where the scream had come from. The door there was slightly ajar, but there was a crowbar on the other side, and it took the full weight of the boys shoving against the door to finally open it.

Pigmeat was pushing himself off Laverne when her brother burst into the room. "Get the hell off my sister!" Alexander shouted, and although he was skinny and small for his age, Pigmeat didn't stop to challenge him. The kid looked fierce, and he might have a knife. Instead, he snatched his trousers off the floor and ran out of the room, with Pork Chop and Harlow right behind him. Laverne grabbed her brother's arm and pulled herself up to a sitting position. Pete took off his jacket and put it around her shoulders, while Alexander grabbed her dungarees from the floor and handed them to her. Laverne shifted her weight to the edge of the sofa and managed to pull the dungarees up above her knees. With her brother's help she struggled to her feet, and it was then that Alexander saw the blood trickling down the inside of her thigh. With his arm around her waist, she pulled the dungarees on. Then she saw the torn body shirt almost hidden beneath one of the sofa cushions and she retrieved it. Alexander had her sneakers in his hand, ready to hand them to her, when suddenly she ran from the room and out the side door into the alley, with the torn body shirt over her arm and Pete's jacket flapping from her shoulders. The two boys pursued her down the alley, around the corner, and up the street.

Irma Jenkins, the superintendent of the building in which Miss Mary Catharine and her children lived, was standing in the vestibule by the mailboxes when she saw Laverne running up the stoop toward her. The boy's jacket was still around her shoulders, but it hung open, exposing her breasts. She had one hand pressed to her face, while with the other she was attempting to hold up the torn, bloodstained dungarees. "My God, what happened to you?" Irma Jenkins said as Laverne ran past her into the building and up the first flight of stairs.

Miss Mary Catharine was asleep when her daughter burst into her bedroom. "Ma, they raped me! They raped me!" Laverne hollered, flinging herself face down across the bed. Her mother lay there for a second, trying to make sense out of what was happening. "They raped me! Pigmeat raped me!"

Miss Mary Catharine sat up and saw the tangle of frightened children standing in the doorway. "You—you get!" she said, waving them away. Although Laverne was lying across her legs, sobbing and screaming, she managed to get out of the bed, reach up, and pull the cord that hung from the overhead light. Laverne twisted around and buried her face in her mother's nightgown. "No! Don't turn on the light! *Please.*" Miss Mary Catharine managed to pry her loose and get her to her feet. "Oh, my God!" she said at the sight of her daughter. The boy's jacket lay at the foot of the bed, and Laverne was holding the torn, bloodstained dungarees together with both her hands. There were long scratches on her neck, and teeth marks on her breasts.

"Now wait a minute . . . wait," Miss Mary Catharine said. "You tell me again who raped you."

Laverne squeezed her eyes closed and shouted, "Pigmeat! He raped me!"

Her mother folded her in her arms, and they fairly stumbled over to the bed together. They sat there for several minutes, the blood still trickling down the inside of Laverne's leg and the dungarees now in a tangle around her ankles.

Irma Jenkins stood at the front door, which Laverne had left open when she ran inside. Alexander stood there, still holding his sister's sneakers in his hand, encircled by his younger brothers and sisters, who were crying. "My sister's been raped," he said to her, and then he too started to cry. Irma Jenkins looked past the children and saw Miss Mary Catharine cross from the bedroom into the bathroom with her arms around Laverne.

With her mother's help, Laverne stepped into the tub and stood there while it began to fill up with hot water. Miss Mary Catharine handed her a bar of soap, and Laverne began to slowly wash the blood from the inside of her leg. Then Miss Mary Catharine left her daughter and went back across the narrow hallway to her bedroom, where she telephoned the police. Her voice was surprisingly calm. "I need an ambulance," she said, holding the phone very close to her mouth, "because my daughter's been raped." She gave her name and address, then put the telephone down and went back to the bathroom and helped Laverne out of the tub.

"Ma, look," Laverne said, pointing to the blood still rolling down her leg. Miss Mary Catharine moved toward her, but Laverne wiggled free and ran from the room and into the hall closet, where she sank to the floor. "I wanna die! I wanna die!" she started screaming, and Irma Jenkins stepped into the apartment, shutting the door behind her and herding Alexander and the other children into another room.

"Baby, it's going to be all right. All right. I promise you," said Miss Mary Catharine, kneeling by the closet door and caressing her daughter with her voice.

By the time the police arrived, Laverne had calmed down and put on one of her mother's housecoats. The policemen were very gentle with her, but in a few minutes she was sobbing again, and they told her mother to get her dressed and they would drive them to Jacobi Hospital. On the way out of the apartment Miss Mary Catharine disposed of Laverne's bloodied dungarees in a plastic garbage bag.

She stayed in the emergency room with Laverne while

the doctor examined her. He placed her on a table on her back, put her feet in stirrups, and examined her genitals. Then he wrote on his report: "Trauma caused to the hymen was done by a forceful and violent act." He asked Miss Mary Catharine to sign her consent for him to give Laverne shots for the prevention of gonorrhea and incubating syphilis. After that he gave her another shot to calm her down and make a good night's sleep possible. Before discharging Laverne, the doctor, a soft-spoken young man, told Miss Mary Catharine that if her daughter had any problems whatsoever she mustn't hesitate to bring her back to the hospital. When they returned to their apartment, she put Laverne to bed and sat beside her, holding her hand, until she was asleep.

Late the next afternoon, her eight-year-old son, Gary, ran into the apartment with a gash on his cheek. She picked up the terrified little boy and ran into the bathroom with him, washed the cut, and applied iodine to it. Gary said that on his way home from school a teenager had thrown a pop bottle in his face, saying, "That's for your sister." Miss Mary Catharine took him to the emergency room at Jacobi Hospital, and it required two stitches to close the gash on his cheek.

Back from the hospital, she was upstairs, leaning on the windowsill in her living room and looking out, when she heard her name called from the street. She looked down and saw Harlow the Albino standing on the stoop, looking up at her. "Hey, Miss Mary Catharine," he said, "next time your kid'll get worse. You go to the court about Laverne and we gonna bust his fuckin' head. We mess up your whole fuckin' family."

Laverne stayed home from school that week and never left the house. At night she slept in the room with her mother. The next week, when Miss Mary Catharine decided it was time for her daughter to return to class, she had to help her dress. Laverne clung to her outside the school and pleaded with her not to make her go inside. "I don't feel like goin' to school any more, Ma," she cried. "I don't wanna face up to it." But her mother insisted, and she finally went inside.

That afternoon Miss Mary Catharine leaned both elbows on the windowsill in her living room and watched for her children to come home from school. Laverne came last— some thirty minutes after the others—and when she got upstairs to the apartment she ran into the bathroom and locked the door. When she finally came out, her eyes were red and swollen. The other kids, she said, all knew about what had happened to her. They were pointing at her and laughing because she was no longer a virgin. "I can't keep up with it any more," she said over and over again. Miss Mary Catharine told her that soon everybody would forget all about what had happened and things would be back to normal, although she really didn't believe it herself. She wanted to see Pigmeat, Harlow, and Pork Chop punished, and she didn't intend to be frightened off taking action against them.

On her way home from school one day the following week, Harlow and Pork Chop dragged Laverne into the vestibule of an abandoned tenement. Pigmeat was there waiting for her, and he had a big belt in his hand. He shoved her up against the wall and then spun her around so that her back was to him. "Hold her," he ordered, and Harlow and Pork Chop grabbed her wrists. Pigmeat began to whip her back. She sagged forward, with her cheek pressing up against one of the ripped-out mailboxes. When Pigmeat finished whipping her they let go of her, and she stayed there, leaning up against the wall, until she heard the sounds of their feet going down the stoop. Then Pigmeat was coming back up the stoop and poking his face into the vestibule.

"You better not go to court, bitch—or we gonna fuck up your whole fuckin' family. Know what I mean, bitch?" Laverne shook her head, and this time they left and didn't come back.

The next day it was Alexander's turn. Harlow and Pork Chop pulled him into an abandoned building, knocked him down, and beat him across the legs with a bicycle chain.

That evening, together with Pigmeat, they stormed up the steps to Miss Mary Catharine's third-floor apartment and beat on her door with pipes. She herded Laverne and the rest of the children into her bedroom and called the police. By the time the squad car arrived, there was no sign of them. But Irma Jenkins said that on their way out of the building the three gang members had accosted her in the hallway and told her they were going to burn the building.

Laverne and the rest of the children stayed home from school the next day, and that afternoon Miss Mary Catharine received a call from the precinct telling her that Harlow had been arrested. Ten days later, Pigmeat was picked up by the police. Three weeks after that, Pork Chop, who had been sleeping in abandoned buildings since Pigmeat's arrest, was apprehended on a tip from an informer living in The Compound. "Virgin Uno" had been deflowered. And Pigmeat had done it. Everybody in The Compound wanted to see him get his.

A friend of Miss Mary Catharine's moved into her apartment with her, since she was too afraid now to live alone with her children. Since the arrests she had been finding threatening notes in her mailbox, and her phone rang in the early hours of the morning—but when she would pick up the phone, she'd always hear a click on the other end. She decided that she would feel much safer with a man in the house. Then one morning "Uncle" Arthur went to the store for her, and the next thing she knew, he was in critical condition in Jacobi Hospital with stab wounds in his chest and back. He had been attacked by a gang of unidentified youths.

Three days later, when her other children were in school, Miss Mary Catharine and Laverne, who had not gone back to school since her whipping, went to the grocer. Coming back with her arms full of groceries, Miss Mary Catharine looked up and saw smoke pouring out of the windows of her apartment. When the blaze was finally under control, firemen found five empty plastic containers on the floor of the kitchen. Gasoline had been poured in the living room and lit with a match. The apartment was no longer habitable.

On the first day of the trial of Pigmeat, Pork Chop, and Harlow the Albino, every seat in the courtroom was occupied. And every day thereafter, for the duration of the trial, groups left The Compound for the courthouse. The wives were particularly fascinated by the proceedings. Rape wasn't all that uncommon in the world of the street gangs, but rarely did a rape case come to trial. Usually the victim and her family were too fearful to go to court.

Each day anywhere from fifteen to twenty Peacemakers sat in the courtroom, wearing their colors and glaring at the jurors and prosecution witnesses. Graffiti in the courthouse's public phone booth and lavatories became commonplace. *Free Pigmeat. Virgin Uno is a whore.*

"Ladies and gentlemen, when we have finished with Mademoiselle Laverne Knight on the stand, you won't even have to go out and consider a verdict," promised one of the defense attorneys to the jury at the onset of the trial. "You can sit right there and do your thing. She is a low-life. We are going to prove it, and if I can quote Shakespeare again, 'Take her to a nunnery'—and as soon as possible."

Miss Mary Catharine took the witness stand and recalled

when her daughter burst into her room half naked. "Her whole body was a mess, and she was completely hysterical," she testified. The defense attorney asked if she was a welfare recipient. With considerable dignity Miss Mary Catharine said that she was. Why had she entertained Pigmeat in her home if, as she said, she disapproved of him? She replied that she felt that if he and his gang were going to know Laverne on the street, then she wanted to be able to feel that she knew them, too.

Laverne relived the night of the rape. In a quiet, sometimes almost inaudible voice, she said, "They was all grabbin' on my clothes. I was biting back, screaming and everything." One of the defense attorneys asked her about her father, who was living apart from the family. Laverne said that she saw a lot of him. Did she have a stepfather who had been living with her mother? She said she did. "Does he share the same bedroom with you?" the attorney asked, and Laverne burst into tears. A recess was called.

Back on the witness stand, Laverne was asked if she knew a girl by the name of Lila Howard. She did. Was Lila Howard her lover? "What?" said Laverne, sounding as though she hadn't heard correctly. Then: "No—no, I'm not no freak!" Subsequent questioning suggested that Laverne had been deflowered by the finger of Lila Howard, who was described as "a butch type."

Next, Alexander Knight took the stand to describe how he had found his sister nude on the sofa in the clubhouse of the Peacemakers. Ten-year-old Alexander was so small that it was impossible for members of the jury to see his face, so the witness chair was taken out of the box and put down on the floor.

In their summations to the jury, the defense attorneys voiced different theories as to what they believed had happened to Laverne Knight. "I don't think that that girl was deflowered by a finger," one said, suggesting that Laverne had been injured during intercourse with a boy friend and it was to protect him that she concocted a story of rape. "She had intercourse and she was scared to tell her mother. She was looking for something to help her boy friend . . . and it wasn't her first act of intercourse, either."

The other defense attorney favored the theory that Laverne had been injured by her lesbian lover and concluded: "Now, you saw that little girl cry, but did you see any tears coming from her eyes when she started crying? You were there. You saw her. I heard sounds like boo-hoo. Did you *see* any tears? I associate crying with some wetness in one's eyes. I watched. We have a girl that cried with no tears—strange—she has never seen Bette Davis. You see a girl that I would call a young harlot take the stand and accuse these three boys of raping her. Maybe they never looked at her. Maybe they didn't want to look at the tramp of the block. Could be. Boys also have pride, like men. You don't go to a house of prostitution looking for a wife, do you?"

The jury found Pigmeat, Pork Chop, and Harlow the Albino guilty as charged, and they were sentenced to terms of from five to fifteen years. The Peacemakers are still active as a gang. They have a new president and a new clubhouse. But membership is half what it was when Pigmeat ran the gang, and no one wears fur on his jacket any more. And, perhaps because now they're smaller in number, they've been experimenting with a more forceful-sounding and certainly a more apt name. From time to time they've been calling themselves the Savage Makers or the Outlaw Makers.

Miss Mary Catharine and her family have moved out of the South Bronx.

10.
The Hired Killers

By the spring of 1973, gas and electricity had been turned off inside The Compound. Conditions there were deplorable. Some of the gangs living on the top floors were finding it practically impossible to reach their clubhouses because of smashed or missing stairs. The Mongols moved out, and were soon followed by the Latin Diplomats, who had also maintained a storefront clubhouse in the neighborhood. And as soon as the Imperial Bullies heard of the empty space, they came around, hoping to be asked to move in.

The Imperial Bullies regarded the gangs in The Compound as the *elite*. The gangs in The Compound, on the other hand, regarded the Imperial Bullies as small change —an ambitious but dumb bunch of blacks. And although he was a West Indian black himself, Black Bongo felt no bond with a gang that had a prez called Snoopy, and played basketball. "Guys who play basketball—how tough can they be?" Furthermore, no gang in The Compound would tolerate an all-black gang—even a cool one—sharing their communal turf. Where a Puerto Rican gang might sometimes have a small number of black members, usually of

Puerto Rican origin, blacks were usually regarded as outsiders, tolerated but not encouraged to mix. Consequently, they formed their own gangs, of which the Black Pearls, 1 k Assassins, and Peacemakers were the most powerful. Compared to them, the Imperial Bullies were of little consequence.

With The Compound off limits to them, they had to content themselves with hanging around Nomad Park, rapping with the gangs there and basking in reflected glory. The Bullies, snorted Bongo, were "gonna fuck themselves up, you wait an' see." And they proved him right. When they did it, however, early one April morning during the second year of The Compound, it was far from The Compound and far from the South Bronx. They did it in Harlem, which to the gangs in the South Bronx was as remote as another planet . . .

By the time Detective Harry Buxton of the Homicide Assault Squad arrived at the scene of the crime, the long, narrow alleyway where it had occurred about an hour earlier, at two forty-five A.M., was already swarming with police. Buxton, a tall, husky black man, inspected the blood-splattered brick wall to the left of the rear entrance leading into the Harlem housing project. Then he turned around, and his eyes followed the trail of blood up along the ramp that tilted away from the alleyway and emptied out onto West 133rd Street. From there the by-now-sticky blood continued across the street, stopping at the curb. It was here, according to eyewitnesses living in the project, that the assailants had hefted the man's bleeding body into a black car and driven off. From reports just received at the Twenty-fourth Precinct, what was assumed to be the same black car had arrived, minutes later, at the pier at the foot of West 132nd Street, where two men—one of them an extraordinarily tall, lean black man who fit the description of one of the men who had put the victim inside the car

—had thrown a man's inert body into the Hudson River and then sped away. After some cursory conversation with the two policemen, one of whom gave him a man's blue hat with a pompom on top that was believed to belong to one of the assailants, Buxton walked back up the ramp, got into his car, and headed for the pier, where the Harbor Patrol had begun a grappling operation for the body.

Police lined the pier and watched, shuffling their feet and swinging their arms to ward off the damp cool of the early April morning, while the T-bar grapple dragged the bottom of the river. Detective Buxton was directed to Joseph Massad and Bert Glynn, two Transit Authority workers who had been sitting in the front of a TA bus parked in the city parking area adjacent to the river, drinking coffee, when the black car drove up with its lights out.

Glynn told the detective that at the sight of the black car Massad had said jokingly, "There's a body for the river." Glynn said he left the bus then and started walking toward the car, from which two men had just gotten out. As he came closer, he saw the men reach down behind the front seat and pull something out. A man's body. The taller of the two men had the feet and, said Glynn, "They're swinging it a couple of times . . . about three times . . . and out with it into the water." At which point Massad, still inside the bus, heard the splash, and then Glynn shouting to him, "They're throwing out a body!" Massad jumped out of the bus in time, he said, to see a very tall man get back into the car, which sped away in the direction of West 131st Street. At that hour, far away from street lights, neither Glynn nor Massad could see the faces of the two men clearly enough to describe them. But they agreed that the tall man was at least six feet four and "looked black." As the car sped away from the pier, they rushed back into the bus, where Glynn used the telephone radio to call the police.

Both men now got into Detective Buxton's car and toured the blocks near the waterfront, on the chance that they might sight the black car abandoned somewhere. When they returned to the pier, the grappling operation was still going on. Buxton parked his car, and he and the two men stood and watched the water churning. They were still there when, shortly after six o'clock, the T-bar grapple came up with the body of a black man hooked by the feet. Harry Buxton had lost count of the number of murdered bodies he had seen during his seventeen years on the force, but this was one of the grisliest sights. The man, slender and of medium height, whose body was now being swung onto the deck of the Harbor Patrol's boat, had been severely cut about the face and head and stabbed repeatedly, and where a knife had cut into his abdomen a loop of intestine was hanging out, protruding through the wound.

Walking back to his car a few minutes later, Buxton spied a knife lying in a pool of water near a fence. He took a handkerchief out of his back pocket, bent down, and retrieved the knife, which would eventually be identified as the one that had cut into the body of Henry Lee Kirkwood as he sat slumped against the brick wall in the alleyway at the back of the housing project, pleading for his life.

Mrs. Palmira Melendez lived in apartment 2C in the project located at 95 Old Broadway. At about two forty-five that morning, she said, she was sitting in a corner of her living room, reading, when she heard voices from the alleyway below. "Chris, don't kill me, I didn't do nothing to you," a man's voice pleaded. "Please don't kill me." She put down her book and got up, and as she walked toward the window she heard another man's voice say, "Kill him. Kill him."

Alarmed, she turned around and hurried across the room to the bed where her daughter Dora was sleeping with her husband, Ray, and their two children. She shook her daughter awake and told her what she had just heard. Dora reached over and grabbed her husband's shoulder. "Somebody is getting killed—getting murdered," she cried. Ray Carillo, a police officer assigned to the 102nd Precinct, jumped up, grabbed his gun, which was on a chair by the bed, and ran to the kitchen window in time to see two men dragging a third man's body up the ramp toward the street. Carillo put his head out the window and shouted, "Stop. Police!" The men dropped the body, ran out into the street, and took off in opposite directions. But a moment later one of them, a very tall black man wearing dark clothes and carrying a pipe, returned and resumed dragging the body up the ramp and across the street to where a black car was parked. By now another of Mrs. Melendez's daughters had been awakened from her sleep in the apartment's one bedroom, and she came into the kitchen. While her brother-in-law was struggling into his clothes, she stood on a chair and, looking out the window, watched a second man get out of the parked car and help the tall black man put the body inside. At this point Ray Carillo, who had dashed downstairs, gun in hand, arrived in the alleyway—in time to see the car pull away and speed west. Meanwhile, upstairs his wife was dialing the police emergency number to report that she thought a murder had just been committed.

At noon Harry Buxton went to the Medical Examiner's office, where the body fished out of the river six hours earlier was officially identified as that of thirty-two-year-old Henry Lee Kirkwood by Dorothy Moses, his common-law wife, who had reported him missing since two o'clock that morning. A young, pretty, soft-spoken woman, she was visibly shaken, and Kirkwood's brother, Jimmy Lee, stood with his arm around her shoulders. Buxton asked if either of them knew a man named Chris. Both said no. Then, a moment later, when they were about to leave, Jimmy Lee Kirkwood came to Buxton and said, "Dorothy would like to talk to you."

Buxton sat down beside her. Avoiding his eyes, she told him that yes, she did know a man named Chris. He was very tall and young. He lived in Harlem somewhere around Old Broadway, and he had called Henry early that morning and invited him to come down to his place. Dorothy said she'd taken the call on the kitchen phone, and Henry had picked it up on the bedroom extension. Before she hung up, she said, she heard the man she knew only as Chris say to him: "C'mon down. I have your money," and Henry replied that he'd be there in fifteen minutes. Usually, Dorothy told Buxton, her man would have taken a gun with him, but he knew Chris and he didn't intend to stop off any place else. He figured he wouldn't need his gun.

Dorothy Moses said she had seen Chris on several occasions. Henry had often visited his apartment, but when she was with him, she said, she had always waited outside in the car. She had seen Chris the previous evening at about midnight, when, after visiting with her mother, she and Henry had driven over to where Chris lived. They were just pulling up in front of the project as Chris was getting into a black car with two other men. Henry blew his horn, and Chris turned around and came over to talk to him. Henry got out of his car, but Dorothy said she remained inside, with her little daughter beside her on the back seat and their infant son asleep on her lap. Henry and Chris went across the street, and from what she could observe, they seemed to be arguing. When Henry returned, he said that Chris was treating him like a fool. He told her that he felt Chris was "trying to shoot him through the grease." It was her impression, she told Buxton, that Chris owed Henry about $1,500. He'd called Chris several times about this money, which she said had something to do with a drug transaction Chris had handled for Henry, a narcotics dealer who did all of his business on Eighth Avenue between 127th and 128th Streets.

When Henry, who had left at two o'clock that morning to meet Chris, hadn't returned by three-thirty, Dorothy phoned Chris's number; his mother answered and told her that neither Chris nor her man was there. About twenty-five minutes later Chris phoned Dorothy and asked for Henry, saying that he hadn't showed up. "When he comes in," he told her, "tell him I still have his money for him and he should come and pick it up."

Back at the precinct house, Buxton filled out the papers detailing the facts he knew so far in the murder case of Henry Lee Kirkwood. He mentioned to Detective Paul Gravina that he was looking for a black man named Chris who stood about six four or six five. "I know a Chris . . . Chris Ellis," said Gravina. "I even have a picture of him in the files. I locked him up for robbery. He might still be in jail or he might be out."

A records check revealed that Christopher Ellis, aged twenty-five, was in fact on parole, and a call to the State Parole Office on West Fortieth Street further revealed that he was to report there that very day.

Sitting behind the desk in his windowless cubicle, Frank Hawkins told Buxton and Detective Carlo Marino that Ellis, who'd been under his supervision since February, hadn't reported in so far that day. It was now four o'clock, and the parole officer had had no word from him. It wasn't like Chris to miss. Buxton and Marino decided to sit and wait, on the chance that he still might put in an appearance. Buxton, armed with a photograph of Ellis, questioned Hawkins about the absent parolee. He was, in Hawkins's opinion, a fairly sharp individual and what he would call a nice dresser.

Around five o'clock Buxton decided to drive to Ellis's apartment and wait there to see if he came in. Marino remained behind in Hawkins's office. Downstairs, as Buxton was about to step out of the elevator into the lobby, he found himself face to face with Chris Ellis, who had been standing there waiting for an elevator to take him upstairs to report to Frank Hawkins.

"Hi, Chris!" said Buxton. "We've been waiting for you." Ellis showed no surprise and offered no resistance. Hawkins and Marino were no where near so cool when they looked up and saw Chris Ellis, followed by Buxton, enter the tiny office.

"I think I'm in a little trouble" was the first thing Ellis said. When Hawkins asked him why, he replied: "I heard somebody was mugged and stabbed behind my building and somebody told me that the guy was calling my name." Buxton frisked him for weapons, and when Ellis had sat down beside Hawkins's desk he was advised of his rights. Ellis indicated that he understood, and he answered yes when he was asked if he was willing to talk to the detectives without an attorney being present. Recalling the next three hours spent there with Chris Ellis, Buxton says: "He was all set to baloney us right out of our socks. The kind of person who thinks he can talk his way out of anything. He had a story all prepared."

After putting an old Edison-model dictaphone at their disposal, Frank Hawkins left the two detectives alone with Ellis. Using a question-and-answer technique, they got the following story from him:

Ellis admitted he had owed Henry Lee Kirkwood some money, and said that he feared for his life. Kirkwood, he said, was a gangster who dealt in drugs and had a reputation for violence. He knew for a fact that "Pop," as he sometimes called Kirkwood, had set a kid named Richard on fire about two weeks before by pouring lighter fluid on

his feet and igniting them with a match. He knew he had
actually killed another fellow. He said a man like that had
a lot of enemies, and he theorized that his murder was probably been a crime of revenge. Sure, he'd had an appoint-
ment with Kirkwood that morning, but he, Chris, hadn't
appeared. Anyway, that morning he had heard noise downstairs in the alleyway and looked out the window and seen
a blue 225 Electra pull off just before police cars came
into the block from the other end. Later that morning he
went downstairs and saw a lot of blood on the ground. He
walked downtown to 125th Street and heard that whoever
it was who got killed was supposed to have cried out,
"Chris, help me, man, don't let them do this to me. Help!"
Chris said everybody was talking about it. He said it was
quite a big thing in the neighborhood and in the bars and
everybody was asking him why Kirkwood would have been
calling the name Chris. Personally, he felt that it was because he was the only Chris that Kirkwood knew lived on
that side of the street. And to make matters worse, he said
he heard a report on radio station WLIB that the police
were looking for a black man about twenty to twenty-five
years of age, and that was about his age. Anyway, he'd
stayed home, waiting to see if the police would come. But
he hadn't done anything.

It was at this point that Detective Marino interrupted
him. "Chris," he said, "I don't believe you. Why don't you
tell us what really happened? We know you were at the
scene. We know you were at the river."

Ellis promptly began another version.

Henry Lee Kirkwood had threatened him and his family,
and said he was coming down to settle with him. Chris
heard noise from the alley behind his building and went
downstairs. As he came out of the building he saw Kirkwood surrounded by some fellows, and one of them, a
Spanish dude—a lamebrain—told him to get the fuck back

inside. He hadn't recognized any of these dudes, but he did see a green Cougar parked in front of the project with a girl sitting behind the wheel. Later, he came back downstairs and saw Kirkwood sitting on the ground, motionless, and he walked past him and up the ramp and up the street . . .

Now Ellis had placed himself at the scene of the crime, but that was all. Again Marino accused him of lying, while Buxton took a more conciliatory tack. "Well, Carlo," he said to Marino, "just take it easy. Chris is probably a little nervous. He knows it's better if he gets it off his chest, and if you give me a chance then maybe we can find out the truth of the story."

Ellis took the bait and added the information that he had come out of his building with a knife in his hand and with the intention of helping "Pop." The dudes were kids. Four kids. And one of them hit "Pop" on the head with a pipe about six times and "Pop" had looked up at him and said, "Chris, why are you doing this to me?" It was then that the Spanish dude, the lamebrain, took his knife away from him, said Ellis.

Buxton told him that he found his story very difficult to accept, and so Ellis added a little more to it. He said he had gotten tired of listening to Kirkwood claiming that he was his best friend and why was he doing this to him . . . so he kicked him. Then he said to the dudes, "Kill him!"

After listening to more dialogue between the detectives, with Marino pretending to grow more and more angry and Buxton appearing to, very reluctantly, lose his patience, Ellis started still another version of his story. This time he portrayed himself as so fearful for his safety and that of his family that he confided in a friend that Kirkwood was coming downtown to hurt him; this friend, "Bugsy," took him to the Bronx to a "bull-dagger" to get a gun. This lesbian, whose name he didn't know, was in the clubhouse of a street gang, and she introduced them to a kid named Snoopy. They didn't have a gun, but Snoopy and three other kids said they would oblige him by coming downtown and catching Kirkwood in the alleyway before he could come upstairs and harm him.

It was now eight-thirty P.M., and Buxton decided to end the interrogation and go back uptown to the precinct house and get a written confession from Ellis in his own handwriting. He put handcuffs on him and took him downstairs in the elevator. In the lobby Frank Hawkins came up to them and said to Ellis, "Chris, you disappointed me." Ellis replied, "I'm sorry. I had to do it. He was threatening my life."

In the precinct house, Buxton brought Ellis into a private office, presented him with paper and pen, and asked him to write what he knew about the death of Henry Lee Kirkwood. Then he left the room. The following is the statement Chris Ellis wrote:

Well, to start with, I had been threatened by a one Henry Lee Kirkwood several times concerning some money connected with some narcotics he had given some other people. Now on the merits of his reputation alone as a gangster, I had to take him seriously for my own good . . . so I proceeded to obtain a firearm for my protection. I had no luck in obtaining one, so a friend of mine by the name of Jim Hynes, was to take me in the bronze [sic] to get one, but there wasn't any available, so a girl present introduced me to a young man by the name of Snoopy, and he told me that for twenty dollars he would have it taken care of. Snoopy, then got together three other fellows by the name of Dynamite, Robot, and Tito. I then informed them when he was coming back to get me, and they said they'd be there to meet him. We came down town and proceeded to wait for him in 133rd Street between Amsterdam and Broadway. Now before he showed up I went upstairs to a friend's apartment, and while up at this friend's apartment he Henry Kirkwood showed up, and I left my friend's apartment to go down to see what was going to happen. When I arrived down stairs, Henry Kirkwood was laying on the ground looking in my direction. He started calling my name, and it was bugging me, so I told the other fellows to raise up off him but they wouldn't, so I said then kill him, cause I really knew inside that I couldn't let him go now. I hit him with a pipe, I reall [sic] don't know how many times, but he was quiet now, just breathing hard. Now someone, or it could have been two of the guys I was with . . . were raising their arms in a stabbing motion, and I saw this as I looked back down at the group of them around him on the ground. It was now that a man in the building was making a lot of noise and everyone started walking up the ramp way . . . now someone yelled back to bring him along speaking of Henry Kirkwood, and I went back to get him. I dragged him to the car, speaking of was a black Buick Electra. Myself, Dynamite and Robot were in Henry Kirkwood's car along with the owner Henry, laying on the floor in the back. We went down to the river, and the fellow Robot who was part of the group was driving. At the waters edge we threw him in, but I didn't know he was stabbed to death at that time, but I'm sure now he was dead long before we threw him in.

Later that same evening, an assistant district attorney arrived at the precinct house accompanied by a court stenographer, and a twenty-six-page question-and-answer statement was taken from Chris Ellis. After that, Ellis—

addicted to a daily combination of heroin and cocaine—
was transported from the precinct house to a special
housing area for narcotics addicts on the ninth floor of
the Manhattan House of Detention, most often simply
called the Tombs.

It developed that the "Bugsy" who had taken Chris Ellis
to the Bronx in search of a gun was twenty-five-year-old
Jim Hynes, whose name and phone number Buxton had
found in Ellis's address book. He lived in the Bronx but
had formerly lived in the project at 95 Old Broadway. He
had served one year in prison as a convicted narcotics
dealer.

Hynes readily admitted taking his friend to the Bronx to
see a butch by the name of Debra. He didn't know her last
name, and he was equally vague about the names of the
four kids who'd come downtown with Chris to intercept
Henry Lee Kirkwood. Hynes said he'd never laid eyes on
them before, but one was—he thought—called Tito. Their
clubhouse was somewhere on Prospect Avenue, but he
didn't know the exact address. As for Kirkwood, he'd seen
him the night before his murder . . .

Chris, whom he'd known since they were kids, had
phoned him and said C'mon down. When he arrived, he
said, there was another dude there by the name of Max,
whom he didn't know, and the three of them just sat around
rapping. Then, at some point, Chris asked him where he
could get a gun. "I just took it for granted he was having
some kind of trouble." Hynes said he told him that he
might be able to get one up in the South Bronx.

Shortly before midnight all three left the apartment, and
Max was about to drive Hynes back to the Bronx when
Henry Lee Kirkwood drove up in his blue 225 Electra and
blew his horn to get Chris's attention. Then he jumped out
of his car and called, "Chris, wait up!" A woman was

sitting in the back seat with two small children, and one of them, the smaller, was sitting on her lap. Chris walked across the street, and although Hynes said he couldn't hear what they were saying, from the looks of things it seemed that Kirkwood "was arguing with Chris, like that."

When Chris walked back to Max's El Dorado he was boiling. "The motherfucker must think I'm some sort of punk," he said. Then, turning to Hynes: "O.K., man. Which way we go? How do we get up in the Bronx?"

Jim Hynes told Buxton that he took Chris to a tenement building on Prospect Avenue, where "a certain gang in my area stay here . . . like it was a clubhouse, you could say. I took him up there. That was the only place I know I could get a gun." Max stayed downstairs in the El Dorado and Hynes escorted Chris upstairs. The butch who came to the door said she didn't have a gun, but she might be able to get one the next morning. Chris insisted he had to have one right away. Max joined them then, and all three men went into the apartment, Hynes disappearing into a back room because "a sister I used to go with was back there." Chris and Max stayed in the living room, where several gang members were lounging around. Debra, the butch, introduced Chris to one of the kids as "a friend of Bugsy's downtown. He's having some static. So he wants you all to go downtown and straighten it out for him." Hynes said he had come back into the living room just as the kids were starting to get their artillery together: pipes, chains, knives. As he understood it, they were going to hurt Henry Lee Kirkwood—"hurt him bad." He figured the kids left the apartment with Chris and Max a little after two A.M. He stayed behind, drinking wine with Diane and her sister Bessie, who'd been his girl once upon a time.

Chris and the four kids returned at about four o'clock. Hynes recalled that "The kids were, you know, jumping up and down like it was a big thing, you know, like it was really happening." But Chris seemed very upset. "Fucking kids, man, they crazy, man," he had said to him. "They really fucked everything up. I told them what to do on my way down there, you know, how I wanted him fucked up, and they down there taking him off . . . robbing him instead of doing what I told them to do. I told them what the fuck you all doing? I want you all to fuck him up." According to Hynes, Chris told him that he had hit Kirkwood with a pipe and then "the kids just got started . . . like got their courage or something."

The next day, Hynes said, he came down to 95 Old Broadway and went with Chris to a neighborhood jewelry store. Chris brought with him a man's ring that had the initials *HK* set in diamonds. Chris told him that he'd taken the ring from one of the gang members. He instructed the jeweler to reset the diamonds to read his initials.

The job now was to find those kids. Harry Buxton contacted the Gang Intelligence unit stationed in the Bronx. All they had to go on was that the kids belonged to a gang with a clubhouse somewhere on Prospect Avenue and one of them was known as Tito. Now, for the first time since they had joined Gang Intelligence, Detectives O'Rourke and Moles wouldn't be concentrating on the gangs in The Compound, the layout of which they knew as well as those of their own homes. Instead they concentrated on the Fortieth Precinct, while three other teams worked other parts of the Bronx. It wasn't going to be easy trying to net four Puerto Rican teenagers with no known distinguishing physical characteristics in a forty-square-mile area with a heavy concentration of Puerto Rican families.

Meanwhile, Buxton began searching for Debra. He combed the area around Prospect Avenue, talking to anyone he felt might help. One day, while he was in conversation with a teenaged girl, a middle-aged woman standing nearby and listening came over to him and introduced herself as Debra's mother. She said her daughter hadn't been around lately and she had no idea of her whereabouts. But now at least Buxton had her full name: Debra Moore. A check of the files showed her to be twenty-one and an addict, with a history of one arrest for robbery. Her mug shot showed a slim-faced black girl with short hair that made her resemble a boy.

A few days later Buxton, cruising through Harlem in his car, sighted Debra standing on a street corner with one of her girl friends, whom he remembers as a "sweet-looking girl you'd think would make somebody a nice wife." Debra had let her hair grow, and despite her slim face, she was a husky girl. The men's trousers she wore did nothing to conceal her very ample hips.

Brought to the 100th Street precinct, she readily admitted that Chris Ellis had come to see her about a gun and that she had introduced him to members of the Imperial Bullies, of which she was a vice-president and head of the women's division. Debra seemed proud of her position in the gang. After all, few lesbians were admitted into gang circles. But she was a neighborhood girl who could be trusted not to let her lesbianism interfere with gang business. And she made it perfectly clear that introducing Chris Ellis around had been gang business—nothing more, nothing less. Talking freely now, she proceeded to give Buxton the names of the four members who had gone downtown to Harlem with Chris Ellis: Tito, Robot, Dynamite, and Snoopy, the gang's Supreme Commander. She said she didn't know any of their last names, only their street names. Satisfied that she had told him all she knew, Buxton transferred Debra Moore to the civil jail as a material witness.

About this time Officers O'Rourke and Moles were visiting The Compound, and while there they learned that the Imperial Bullies were scheduled to have a big meeting that evening at the Claremont Center, at 169th Street and Third Avenue. Both Tito and Snoopy would be at the meeting.

The Claremont Center was in the neighborhood of a project housing some seven thousand people, mostly black. The strategy was to take the members of this predominantly black gang by surprise and be off with them before the gang could organize and incite other youths in this generally hostile neighborhood.

At seven-forty P.M. four unmarked police cars carrying six Gang Intelligence officers and two Homicide detectives —one of them Harry Buxton—pulled up in front of the community center. The men raced into the building and downstairs to a large room in the basement, where thirty-five members of the Imperial Bullies had just started a meeting. O'Rourke and Moles had gotten a good description of Tito, and since there were only about three Hispanic youths at the meeting, he was easy to spot. As they collared him, someone in the group shouted, "Hey, Snoopy!" All eyes in the room turned toward a tall, cool-looking black youth with cropped hair. Tito and Snoopy were hustled up the stairs and out of the building, the whole operation taking no more than three minutes. On the ride downtown Snoopy remained silent, while Tito, a slightly built youth wearing a bush hat, said that his mother would be worried if he didn't come home. Tito, it turned out, was fifteen years old.

Two months had elapsed since the murder of Henry Lee Kirkwood, and two gang-member suspects were still missing: Dynamite and Robot. Gang Intelligence ferreted out a youth who said that he'd been arrested with Dynamite several months before. Arrest records showed Dynamite to be Cesar Velez, aged seventeen. His mug shot was copied and circulated among Gang Intelligence teams. Some two weeks later, Dynamite was seen in the company of fifteen other youths, members of the Undertakers and Black Knights gangs. A police car pulled up behind them, and Dynamite was promptly hustled into it and sped away.

Apprehending Robot was more difficult. At twenty-four, he was the oldest of the four and also one of the smartest and most articulate, as befit his role of the gang's spokesman. One day, tipped off that Robot had been seen at a popular store hangout in the South Bronx, Detective Buxton drove there and spotted him, but in the time it took to park the youth had disappeared.

Robot had been in trouble in the Virgin Islands before coming to settle in the Bronx, and a check was made with the police in St. Thomas to determine if perhaps he had gone back there. He had. Word was that he was living in St. Thomas with his grandmother and had a job as a night watchman with a protection agency. Detective Buxton and Tom Farrell, another black detective, were dispatched by the Bronx District Attorney to St. Thomas to arrest Robot and bring him back.

The islands were particularly sensitive at this time to the intrusion of law-enforcement officers from the mainland; white tourists had been shot and killed recently on a golf course on the neighboring island of St. Croix. So it was decided that, rather than arrest Robot at his grandmother's home, the detectives would apprehend him at his job, where the chance of a crowd gathering was less likely. All of this left Buxton and Farrell with a free afternoon to see the sights. They rented a car—a Toyota of the same color and year as Buxton's own car—and, in the company of a local policeman, they headed for the beach. Driving down a dirt road about a half mile from their destination, they couldn't believe their eyes. Approaching them on foot was Robot, heading for the main road, perhaps in hope of hitching a ride back to town. As their car passed him, he appeared to recognize the local policeman, and perhaps, Buxton says now, the green Toyota identical to his own car may have triggered the youth's memory of his narrow escape in the Bronx only a few weeks earlier. Buxton drove ahead a few feet and then spun the car around, but in those few minutes Robot had disappeared into the tall grass along the side of the road. They sped back to the main road and found the same people standing in line at the bus stop who had been there when they'd passed minutes earlier. Yet, upon being questioned, none could recall having seen a youth fitting Robot's description.

They drove directly to the police station in Christiansted, where they were told someone had just seen Robot standing outside the post office there. The three men got back into the green Toyota and drove to the post office, where they found him idly standing there by himself. "Hi, how you doing, Robot?" Buxton said to him as he stopped the car at the curb. Robot laughed and promptly got into the back seat. "I knew you'd get me," he said, almost good-naturedly.

The next morning—five months after the murder of Henry Lee Kirkwood—Detectives Buxton and Farrell flew back to the mainland with Robot, who, with the other three members of the Imperial Bullies, cooperated with the district attorney's office in the prosecution of *The People of the State of New York* v. *Christopher Ellis*.

Jim Hynes, Debra Moore, and the four youth gang members were the principal witnesses for the State. Piecing together their testimony, the murderous events of six months ago played out as follows:

When Bugsy (Jim Hynes) brought Chris Ellis to the Prospect Avenue address, he went directly to the apartment in the building where Debra Moore lived with her mother and sister. When he told her that his friend Chris wanted to buy a gun, she escorted them upstairs to club head-quarters on the tenth floor, where Snoopy answered the door. They went inside the apartment, where Snoopy's girl

Nebie and other gang members were sitting, and Debra told them that Bugsy's friend from downtown wanted to buy a gun. For what? She said she didn't know. Snoopy told Chris, "We ain't got none." Chris countered with "Do you want to make some money?" Snoopy showed interest, and Chris continued: "Well, all I want to do is beat up a motherfucker." Debra suggested Dynamite for the job, and Snoopy agreed to drive with Chris and Bugsy in Max's car and find Dynamite, who he thought was around a store hangout on Boston Post Road.

They found him there in the company of a kid known as Tito. Snoopy, very much the Supreme Commander, waved them over to the car. "Get in," he ordered, "a man want to talk to you." Dynamite promptly obeyed, just as he would obey other, more sinister orders very shortly. Tito got into the car, directly behind him. Driving back uptown, Chris, who was at the wheel, told them only that he wanted them to scare a fellow for him.

Back at club headquarters, however, he became more explicit. He spoke now about "knocking this brother off" who, he said, owed him money. In return for their cooperation they could have this dude's jewelry, money, keys, and car. "A car of the year—a deuce and a quarter." Furthermore, he said, Henry Lee Kirkwood had two guns in the glove compartment. As a final inducement, Chris offered them twenty dollars, and the kids agreed to do the job for him. They began rounding up their artillery: a pipe, chains, some double 07's (knives that open and close).

With Max at the wheel of the car, Chris and Snoopy beside him, and Dynamite, Robot, and Tito in the back seat, they drove downtown to 95 Old Broadway. En route, Chris Ellis reminded them: "Don't forget. Fuck up the dude. Make sure he don't get up."

While Max, Tito, and Robot waited across the street in the vestibule of a small apartment building, Chris took

Snoopy and Dynamite upstairs to his apartment on the eighth floor of the eighteen-story project. Hearing him come in, his mother called out to him from her bedroom. Chris assured her that everything was all right, and then he went into his room with Snoopy and Dynamite and closed the door. He began rummaging through his closet to find a weapon for Tito. He found a knife, which he handed to Dynamite. Then he went to the telephone in his room and called Henry Lee Kirkwood and asked him to come down at once. After that the three of them went downstairs, out the rear exit, and up the ramp that led out of the alleyway. They crossed the street to where Tito, Robot, and Max were waiting. At the sight of the knife, Tito wanted it, and he and Dynamite began an argument over it. Finally Dynamite surrendered it to Tito. Before returning across the street to lock the rear door leading into the project so that Henry Lee Kirkwood would be certain to be cornered by the gang, Chris admonished them to "Do it—you got to do it good, because if you let him come back he's going to get you."

Only minutes later, Henry Lee Kirkwood drove up and parked outside 95 Old Broadway. Max, who had seen him for the first time only a few hours earlier, recognized the car, and, turning to Dynamite, Robot, and Tito, he told them: "All right, all right, here you go." As Kirkwood started down the ramp toward the alleyway, the three youths raced across the street and down the ramp after him. Just as they reached the end of the ramp and were about to turn the corner, they encountered Kirkwood returning. He had just tried the door leading into the rear of the building and found it locked.

"Do you live in this building?" he said to Dynamite, who was standing closest to him. Dynamite replied that he didn't live in the building but had come to see a friend who lived there. Kirkwood said that the door was closed, and then, as he turned around in the direction of the door, Dynamite pulled out the pipe and struck him across the back of the neck. Falling to the ground, Kirkwood began to shout. Dynamite dropped the pipe and grabbed him around the neck, at the same time covering the man's mouth with his other hand. Kirkwood started to kick his legs convulsively, and Tito attempted to hold them down. Dynamite demanded the knife from Tito, and the younger boy, beginning to get scared, willingly handed it to him. Dynamite then pressed the knife against Kirkwood's throat, warning him to keep quiet. Kirkwood was now sitting on the ground with his back against the brick wall. Tito and Robot began to rob him of his wallet, watch, ring, and keys. "Take everything I've got but please don't kill me," Kirkwood managed to gasp, the knife still pressed against his throat.

Suddenly the back door to 95 Old Broadway burst open and Chris Ellis appeared in the alleyway. At the sight of him, Tito panicked. He raced up the ramp and disappeared, with Robot at his heels.

Henry Lee Kirkwood looked up at Ellis and said, "Chris, why are you doing this to me?" Chris didn't answer, and Kirkwood became more terrified. "Chris, Chris," he said, "please don't kill me. Chris, I'm your best friend. Don't kill me." Chris Ellis bent down and picked up the pipe Dynamite had dropped. Holding it in his fist, he turned to Dynamite and ordered: "Kill him. Kill him." Then he clubbed Kirkwood on the head with the pipe again and again. After which he stepped back and watched as Dynamite started to stab Kirkwood in the chest and stomach with the knife.

A woman yelled from a window on the second floor, "Leave the man alone or I'll call the cops!" By this time Tito was standing at the door of Henry Lee Kirkwood's car, attempting to open it with the keys he had taken from the man. But his hand was shaking and he couldn't operate the keys properly. Robot snatched them from him and opened the car door. In the distance they could hear Kirkwood pleading to Chris Ellis to spare him. Robot stood with his hand on the open door of the car and for a moment he felt certain he was going to vomit.

Stabbed five times and bleeding profusely from both the knife wounds and the beating with the pipe, Henry Lee Kirkwood was still breathing faintly. Chris Ellis asked Dynamite to help him drag the man out to the sidewalk. Together they began to drag him up the ramp. Suddenly a man's voice from a window shouted, "Stop. Police!" Dynamite immediately dropped his hold on the body and ran up the ramp and down the street. Chris hesitated for a split second and then raced up the ramp after him. On the sidewalk he waved to Dynamite to come back, and then together they returned to where Kirkwood lay bleeding. They proceeded to drag him out to the sidewalk, across the street, and into the car, where Robot was now sitting behind the wheel. Snoopy, who had been waiting in the vestibule across from the project—and had seen Tito and Robot open the door to the car, and heard Kirkwood's cries from the alleyway—in his own words, "shot up the hill and ran back as Max was about to take off in his car." Tito leaped into Max's car too, and the three of them drove back in the direction of the clubhouse.

Robot got out of Kirkwood's car and helped Chris and Dynamite pick up his body and stuff it behind the front seat. Then, with Robot driving, they headed for the pier at the foot of 132nd Street. Robot gripped the wheel of the car to keep his hands from trembling. Meanwhile, Chris sat beside him, wiping the knife free of bloodstains.

Robot parked at the pier and sat behind the wheel as Dynamite and Chris proceeded to lift the body out of the car. Dynamite discovered a Boy Scout hatchet under the back of the front seat, where the body of Kirkwood had been stuffed. As they started to pull him from the car, Kirkwood moaned softly, and Dynamite whacked him on the neck with the hatchet. Then he peeled Kirkwood's blue leather coat off him and threw it into the back seat.

The two men carried the body to the edge of the pier, swung it three times, and sent it plunging into the water. They heard the two Transit Authority workers shouting and jumped back into the car and drove away. By now Robot was too nervous to drive, and Chris ordered him to park and let him drive, which he did. They drove directly back to club headquarters on Prospect Avenue.

Dynamite gave the hatchet to Debra Moore. The blue leather coat he presented to Tito, who, noticing blood on it, proceeded to wipe it clean with a rag provided by Debra. "Baby," Chris said to Debra, "get me a rag for my face, and stuff." And while he wiped the blood of Henry Lee Kirkwood from his face, hands, and arms, Debra Moore knelt down and wiped away the blood that had begun to cake on his suede shoes.

No longer nervous but almost jubilant now, Robot ran downstairs to the street with a pile of rags, and with the help of Debra's sister Bessie and two small neighborhood boys, he began to clean the Buick Electra 225. After that he took a short ride in what he now regarded as his car. Debra, who had gone downstairs to see the car, came back upstairs to find Chris Ellis complaining. "Why you put them crazy fucking kids on me? I had to do it myself."

Ironically, during the course of the trial it appeared that no one knew what happened to the money Chris Ellis had promised the four gang members. Snoopy testified that Chris gave him twenty dollars only after he and Dynamite had refused his offer of drugs instead of cash. Debra, said Snoopy, had wanted the money, but he refused to give it to her, telling her that she hadn't done anything to earn it and he was going to divide it between Robot, Dynamite,

Tito, and himself. But Debra, under oath, testified that Chris had given her twenty-five dollars before driving downtown to kill Henry Lee Kirkwood, and that after he and the four kids had left she'd gone out into the street and used it to buy heroin, which she shared in the bedroom of the clubhouse with Jim Hynes. Her story seemed more believable, while Snoopy's assertion that Chris had given him the money appeared to be more in keeping with his very strong wish to portray himself as the gang's leader. The testimony of Chris Ellis regarding the money only added to the confusion. "Hynes gave twenty dollars to Snoopy," he testified. Then: "On second thought, maybe I gave it to Hynes to give to Snoopy . . . or maybe I gave it to Snoopy myself."

Throughout the three-week trial, Chris Ellis remained in character. That is, he acted as though he thought it possible he might still be able to talk himself to freedom. At the start of the trial he demanded that he be permitted to act as his own counsel and have his court-appointed attorney simply serve as his legal adviser. He steadfastly maintained that at the time he was taken into custody at the parole office, Detective Buxton had not advised him of his rights, and furthermore, he'd been suffering withdrawal symptoms, which was why he agreed to write a confession to a crime which he now swore had been arranged by Jim Hynes. Buxton, he said, had promised he'd be taken care of if he made a confession. Anyway, it was really his friend Bugsy, he said, who owed Henry Lee Kirkwood the money, and he thought the Imperial Bullies was probably the group for whom Hynes had obtained the narcotics for which he owed Kirkwood. Ellis also testified that when he came out of his project building to discover the gang members robbing Kirkwood and heard him pleading for his life, he told them to quiet him down because "I hate to be put on display or made a spectacle of." He said he found the youths "very boisterous, and actually ill contained." He admitted that he had hit Henry Lee Kirkwood once with the pipe, but when he swung the pipe "the motion was actually to counteract all the other motions that were going on around me. It was like being caught up in, you know, a whirlwind, just everything started rolling, one thing just led to another, and another and another."

Conspicuous in the courtroom during most of the trial was a friend of Ellis's, a Westchester matron, who had often put her Cadillac at his disposal. When it was discovered that she had gone to the jewelry shop in the Bronx where he had left Henry Kirkwood's ring to have the initials changed and retrieved the ring, she was about to be served with a subpoena. Hearing this, she bolted from the courtroom and was never seen again.

In his summation to the jury the assistant district attorney noted that he could, if he wanted to, harangue the jurors with what he called "the society of gangs" and their need for peer acceptance. He could, if he wanted to, tell them of the horror of drugs the gangs profess to have and also of their complete inability to deal with the problem rationally. He said the only way they knew to deal with the problem was to resort to violence. "So they go on this chivalrous campaign of ripping off and beating up drug addicts. That is the only way they know how to do it. I could go on and read social books on this forever, about the poverty in which they live and the lure of money. I could go all over that at great length, but I'm not going to. I have never said these are good citizens. They are not. They are terrible, pretty much evil kids. But that is not the point." He said he was not there to vouchsafe for the character of Dynamite and Robot and Tito and Snoopy. "I don't offer them to you as paragons of society," he continued. "Sure, it would be great if someone in the apartment in the Bronx—a nice person—had overheard Chris Ellis talk about the plan to kill the deceased. Sure, it would be great if we had a bishop who decided to follow this car downtown and drove after Max's car, and happened to walk in the alleyway and saw Tito taking the ring and the watch off the man. Saw Robot there, saw Dynamite stab him and saw the defendant hit him with the pipe after the deceased was pleading for his life. But the People don't go around, ladies and gentlemen, picking and choosing our witnesses. You get the witnesses where the criminal action is, and the criminal action is where the defendant is, and the people he chose to surround himself with."

The jury found Chris Ellis guilty of murder, and he was sentenced to prison for twenty-five years to life.

Of the four gang members, Dynamite, who pleaded guilty to the crime of manslaughter in the first degree, received the stiffest sentence: imprisonment for a term not to exceed ten years.

Robot pleaded guilty to robbery in the first degree and was given a prison sentence not to exceed four years.

Tito, a juvenile with no prior arrest record, was sent by Family Court to a juvenile detention center. As this chapter is being written, he's living at home in the South Bronx with his parents and brothers and sisters, but they seldom see him. His older brother says that Tito has gotten himself a woman. His brother, meanwhile, is trying to get Tito into the drug rehabilitation program at Phoenix House.

Snoopy, the Supreme Commander of the Imperial Bullies, entered a plea of guilty to the crime of conspiracy to commit murder and was sentenced to a term in Elmira Reformatory not to exceed three years. But since, like the others, he was already serving his sentence at the time of Chris Ellis's trial, he was back on the streets by the summer of the next year. One night he was shot three times in the chest by another black youth during a fight over a girl. He died on the sidewalk.

Debra Moore gave birth to a child at about that time, and her present whereabouts are unknown.

The Imperial Bullies are no longer active as a gang. Bongo was right—the Bullies had done themselves in.

11.
Operation Extortion

One night in the summer of 1973, all gang members were banished from The Compound at the command of their leaders. While Gestapo Squads stood guard on the staircases, the leaders met in a room in one of the five buildings, squatted there around the light of a candle stolen that day from a *botanica,* and discussed a plan to assassinate Snake, prez of the Savage Skulls.

Officers O'Rourke and Moles knew him well. They had watched Snake, a tar-shack kid from the hills of Puerto Rico, grow from a skinny, glue-sniffing ten-year-old to his present status as leader of a gang too big and proud to ever abandon its own clubhouse and share The Compound. With a record of rape, sodomy, and assault, and recently indicted for his alleged part in a murder, Snake was about to be released on bail. And it was how that bail money had been raised by his gang that precipitated this summit meeting.

Extorting money from local merchants wasn't anything new—all the gangs did it from time to time—but the Skulls hadn't been cool about it. The motherfuckers had actually signed a contract with each of the storekeepers they were ripping off. And now the district attorney was making noise. His office had set up a special phone number to hear complaints from the merchants—and guaranteed them police protection. The Skulls could cause big trouble for everybody. The shootings of Black Bongo and Big Mama on the stoop of The Compound and the murder of Buckwheat in the courtyard last January were trouble enough. The Compound had been swarming with cops. The gangs didn't want to tangle with the D.A.'s office all because of the Skulls. Now Snake was about to be sprung on bail. Better if he was iced before he could cause more trouble. Still, there wasn't a leader among them that night who wasn't aware that killing him might result in a bloodbath that could wipe out their own gangs. The Skulls, after all, had four hundred members in the South Bronx, and two hundred more in other boroughs. And Snake was their supreme leader. It wasn't going to be an easy decision to make.

This summit meeting and the events which led up to it illustrate how the street gangs of the seventies often operate in many ways as the gangs of organized crime did in the 1920s, before the Mafia adopted more sophisticated methods . . .

A few months back, during the subway ride to Brooklyn, Snake had regaled his brothers with stories of Farouk. A brain. A true revolutionary spirit! They had been in the same block at the adolescent center on Rikers Island, where there was always a brother to pass on a pamphlet to you so's you could read it, copy it word for word on a piece of paper, and memorize its teachings. *The 11 points of liberation. The 5 points of genocide.* "Man, we'd have discussions that'd blow your mind!" The brothers had rarely seen Snake this *up.* And when he looked around and saw how quickly the subway car had emptied out since they had swaggered in wearing their colors, he fairly gloated.

As the train lurched toward Brooklyn, where few of the twenty-five dudes with him had ever been before, Snake impressed upon them the significance of this trip outside their turf. They were going to Williamsburg to hammer out an alliance with Farouk's gang, the Satan's Souls. The Souls combined with the Brooklyn division of the Skulls, Snake said, would make the Skulls the rulers of every dude and chick in Brooklyn. The brothers exulted at the thought of so much power. And to be handpicked by their prez for such a trip gave a man plenty of prestige. So when Bones started to unscrew the light bulbs in the car and toss them on the floor, where they exploded, they wanted to kick his ass. Why couldn't that motherfucker be a big man for once? But Snake was feeling so expansive that he paid no attention to Bones. And Bones must have known he wouldn't, otherwise he would've kept his seat. You didn't mess with Snake. Ask Cartoon, who was sitting beside him now, a bandana hiding the fresh scar put there last week when Snake, high on beer and wine, tried to carve his initials into his forehead with a penknife. So Bones kept on unscrewing the hot bulbs with his bare hand until he got to the bulb hanging directly over the seat occupied by Snake. Wisely, he sat down then, and the two brothers on either side jabbed him with their elbows.

Snake was still telling them about Farouk: "He got two skinny braids—yeah, like a couple of worms—an' he combs them down like this . . ." Suddenly he reached over and snatched the bandana from around Cartoon's head. "Why you hidin' my art work?" he said, grinning. "You don't like my style?" He grabbed a fistful of Cartoon's hair, pulling his head back so that the overheated bulb shone in his face. Cartoon didn't dare even swallow. It sure looked like Snake was getting ready to be mean again.

"Hey, this is it—Broadway station. Door gonna close!" shouted Jelly Bean. Letting go of Cartoon, Snake jumped up and darted out of the car, the brothers at his heels.

Farouk and a dozen of the Satan's Souls were waiting for them outside a bodega directly across from the subway exit. The Skulls fanned out around Snake as he crossed against the traffic, which stopped at the sight of the Skulls wearing their colors, a detail that wasn't lost on the Souls, who were trying hard to match their cool. They were, after all, the Savage Skulls from the South Bronx. Everybody knew about them. They were the greatest.

When Snake made it to the sidewalk, Farouk stepped forward to slap palms with his brother. Then, with a snap of his fingers, he dispatched six of his gang inside the bodega, where they rifled the freezer of beer while the owner watched warily from behind the counter. That done, Snake and Farouk started down the street with their brothers walking in their shadows, their arms around each other's shoulders. Farouk stopped and slid up on the hood of a car parked beneath a street lamp, and Snake took his position on top of an upended garbage can. After depositing the beer on the sidewalk midway between the two leaders, the Souls slipped into the background along with the Skulls.

The meeting proceeded along prescribed lines. Snake, the supreme leader, dominated, but he paused now and then out of courtesy for Farouk, whose turf it was, allowing him to make a point. Drinking the beer and seeing the camaraderie that was building between the two leaders, the gangs started to relax. Suddenly one of the Souls stepped out of the shadows and moved hesitatingly toward his prez. He was a pale-faced dude with an Afro and eyeglasses, and he had to force himself to speak. "This is no good, man," he said. "This gonna hurt us. Do us Souls no good." He had a soft voice, and only those standing closest to Farouk could hear what he said. S.O.S., standing to the right of Farouk, looked from him to the dude and back again. With no word or sign from his leader, he jumped the dude, knocking him down with a punch in the face that shattered his eyeglasses. In a flash S.O.S. was on top of him, punching his face some more. Then he jumped up and watched as the dude attempted to get back on his feet. When he was on his knees and his hand had almost connected with his eyeglasses on the sidewalk, Farouk stuck his foot out and kicked them into the gutter. Still the dude who was called Papo struggled to stand up. That angered S.O.S., so he grabbed Papo by the hair and kicked him in the head.

"Don't hit me no more, S.O.S.!" Papo cried. "Don't hit me no more!" Farouk, a beer can in his fist, slid down off the hood of the car and planted himself in front of Papo, who was kneeling now, with his Afro tight in the fist of S.O.S. Farouk reached into his belt and pulled out a knife, a six-inch-long Bowie with a mean-looking curved handle. He took another swallow of beer and then tossed the can over his shoulder. It hit the fender of the car and bounced off, splattering beer as it rolled into the gutter, where one of the Souls, his attention riveted on Farouk and Papo, automatically ground it under his boot.

Moving so fast that no one saw more than a flash of the blade, Farouk bent over and jammed the knife into Papo's back, pulled it out, and then jammed it in again. The dude moaned, S.O.S. let go of his hair, and he fell face down on the concrete. Instinctively, both gangs moved in and formed a circle around him, while Farouk, holding the knife now dripping blood, remained in the center of the circle. From the perimeter, someone reached in and handed him another can of beer.

Snake stepped into the center of the circle now and began to methodically stomp Papo. Then the other Skulls started stomping him too, until one could hardly see Papo for the flying feet. Both gangs began to intermingle, moving in and out of the circle. One of the Souls reached out and touched Snake's arm. "Don't hurt him any more," he said, nodding toward Papo, who lay motionless on his stomach, the blood puddling around his head. "He's my friend." Snake looked at the Soul and said matter-of-factly: "Don't worry about it." But he didn't go back to stomping Papo.

One of the Skulls, called 8-Ball, a tall, skinny black, pushed his way to the front, unzipped his jeans, and began urinating on Papo. The stomping instantly stopped, and everyone watched, fascinated, as the stream of urine pounded down on his head and back. "He gotta die," 8-Ball said as he zipped up his jeans. The Skulls turned as one and looked at Snake. Cartoon, who was anxious to be noticed by him, pushed to the front and proceeded to pour the contents of his beer can on Papo. Then Bones, who somewhere along the way had picked up a discarded broom handle, used it to turn Papo over on his back. As the members of both gangs took up the chant "Die! Die! Die!" and resumed stomping, Bones gave Papo a couple of good whacks across the legs with the broom handle.

Papo's friend intervened again. "That's enough, man," he said to Snake. Turning then to include Farouk, his leader, who, like Snake, was now simply standing there watching, he said: "Enough. Look at the guy." Farouk was too high now to focus his eyes. He took another gulp of beer. But Snake's voice cut through the singsong chant: "Cut it!" The stomping ceased, and Bones sent his broom handle flying out into the gutter.

Snake started running up the street, his gang taking off after him. Farouk came miraculously alive then too, and ran in the opposite direction, hopping a fence and vanishing into the darkness behind a row of abandoned tenements. The Souls scattered in all directions as the sound of fire engines—almost as common a sound in Williamsburg as it is in the South Bronx—pounded the soft night air. Three children who had seen some of what was happening had pulled the fire alarm. When the engine pulled up there was already a little knot of people standing there, staring down at Papo's mangled body.

Minutes earlier, a squad car from the Ninetieth Precinct had intercepted Snake, Bones, and Cartoon as they ran down a street several blocks away. Snake hadn't been able to locate the subway station. He had no idea where the rest of his gang had gone to, but, considering what had happened back there, it was better that they split and reassemble back on their own turf. Meanwhile, he, Bones, and Cartoon had had the good sense to rip off their jackets with the skulls on the back and toss them into garbage cans. Panting but struggling to maintain his cool, Snake had told the cops that he and his friends had come to Brooklyn for a party and had gotten themselves lost. *Man, this sure is one crazy neighborhood. We wanna get back to the South Bronx, where we know where we're at.* Asked for their names, the three—surprisingly enough—gave their full Christian names. After patting them down for possible weapons and finding them clean, the police allowed them to go, which they did, moving slowly now, as though they weren't aching to get on that mother of a subway and back across the river while they still had the chance.

The children who had turned in the fire alarm weren't exactly witnesses to the murder. They had only seen some of the stomping. When they finally saw the dead body lying on the sidewalk, half the face caved in and the clothes stinking of stale beer and urine, the smallest of them got sick to his stomach. They didn't think they could identify anybody. They couldn't remember hearing any names. But, said the biggest of the three, some of the dudes wore jackets that looked real cool. They had skulls on the back.

The following afternoon Detective Warren Taylor of the

Ninetieth Precinct drove to the South Bronx. At the offices of the Gang Intelligence Unit, Vito Moles gave him mug shots of the hard-core members of the Savage Skulls gang. Taylor took them back to Williamsburg, and within twenty-four hours he was on the phone to Moles: 8-Ball had been positively identified by people who had been passing by during the murder, or had watched it happen from their windows. Several of these witnesses had picked out Bones as the tall, skinny black who had pissed on Papo. And one woman said that she was fairly certain that she had also seen him take a knife and stab Papo. None of the witnesses agreed on all the details of the crime—after all, there had been such a crush of kids around the body, at least half of them dressed exactly alike—but everyone who came to the Ninetieth Precinct had picked Farouk and S.O.S. from among the mug shots of Brooklyn street-gang members that Detective Taylor had shown them. Both were apprehended in a matter of hours.

Farouk insisted that he couldn't remember much of what had happened because he had been so high, but if somebody had iced that dude Papo, he sure was sorry. Papo had been a good brother. S.O.S. said that maybe he would have done more damage to Papo than he had but for the fact that the Skulls had crowded in and pushed him out of the way. He said he'd gotten in only a few punches, not enough to do any real damage. But before he was pushed out of the way, he said, he did remember a tall, skinny, black dude—one of the Skulls—saying that Papo had to die. But S.O.S. insisted that he didn't know who had iced Papo.

Detectives O'Rourke and Moles had a rough time locating Bones. They had gone to the clubhouse of the Savage Skulls in the basement of a tenement on Tiffany Street and found it deserted except for a couple of filthy mattresses and a pile of garbage in one corner, gathering roaches. For the next two days they cruised the South Bronx, on the lookout for any member of the gang. "It was uncanny," recalls O'Rourke. "It was like they'd disappeared off the face of the earth."

Bones was usually highly visible. He liked it that way, sporting clothes that featured such things as Nazi swastikas, flat-top felt hats, and lots of flashy jewelry. Frustrated, the detectives parked outside The Compound, hoping that one of the gang members wandering over to rap might know where Bones was hiding.

Her name was Cocoa Mouse—a tribute to her skin tone and her quiet voice—and at first she was very much on her guard. Sure, she knew about the murder over in Brooklyn. Everybody in The Compound knew about it. She sure hoped it wasn't going to mean Rikers Island again for Snake. He'd only been out a couple of weeks. The detectives assured her that Bones could help clear it for Snake if only they could find him. Cocoa Mouse bit her bottom lip and stared up at The Compound, at that moment ablaze with lights and exploding with the sound of bongo drums. "Well, maybe I know," she allowed, "but you gotta be sure he don't know I told you. Bones can be real mean sometimes." Once she had been promised that he'd never know who told them his whereabouts, she took her eyebrow pencil out of her pocket and printed an address on the back of the envelope Moles handed her. "Bones has got himself a chick and she's about ready to hatch most any day now," she said, giving back the envelope. "Her belly's out t'here," and she curved her arm about three feet beyond her middle. She said that Bones was staying with his woman at the address on the envelope. Cocoa Mouse didn't know her name. But she had hair that hung way down— and once again Cocoa Mouse illustrated, this time smacking her behind with the flat of her hand.

Parked across the street from the Dawson Street address

Cocoa Mouse had given them, O'Rourke and Moles observed an extremely pregnant girl sitting on the stoop of the tenement. And, as Cocoa Mouse had suggested, she was practically sitting on her glossy black hair. People entering and leaving the tenement seemed to take special care as they stepped around her. A few she rewarded with a wan smile. A pretty, quiet-looking girl, she didn't appear to be the type who usually associated with a violent kid like Bones. Suddenly, who but Bones should turn the corner, his arms full of groceries. The girl stood up and waved, seemingly overjoyed at the sight of him. The detectives watched as they went up the stoop together and disappeared inside the building. Then Moles got out of the car, went around the corner to a stationery store, and called Warren Taylor at the Ninetieth Precinct in Brooklyn.

When Taylor's car pulled up alongside theirs, the detectives filled him in on what they had observed. The Brooklyn detective parked his car, went inside the tenement, and a few minutes later came out with Bones in handcuffs. The girl leaned out a window on the third floor in time to see him bend down and disappear inside Taylor's car. Moles and O'Rourke waited a moment and then crossed over.

"What's happening?" O'Rourke asked, peering inside at Bones.

Bones lifted up his hands to show the cuffs. "They say I got something to do with a murder."

"Where are you taking him?" Moles asked Taylor.

"Brooklyn—Ninetieth Precinct."

O'Rourke interrupted. "We know Bones. Known him a long time," he said. "Before you take him to Brooklyn, why not bring him to the Forty-first? He'll be more relaxed there. Right, Bones?"

In the interview room at the Forty-first Precinct, O'Rourke made a point of "convincing" Taylor to take the cuffs off Bones, after which he left with Taylor, leaving Bones in the custody of Moles. Bones sat rubbing his wrists and looking genuinely bewildered. "Man, I don't know what this is all about," he said. "My woman's gonna have a baby by the end of the month. I got responsibilities. I'm clean."

O'Rourke returned alone, looking glum. "Bones," he said, "you're a loser. You're in big trouble now."

Bones's eyes widened. "What they say I do?"

"That you iced a dude over there in Brooklyn. A member of the Satan's Souls."

"I ain't never been to Brooklyn," said Bones, shaking his head.

"They've got witnesses who swear you were."

At that point Taylor, playing the heavy, burst into the room on cue. "Don't waste time, we've got our man," he barked, indicating Bones, who looked imploringly in the direction of Vito Moles.

"Nothing we can do to help unless you cooperate," Moles said. Bones pondered that. Then he looked from Moles to O'Rourke and back to Moles, evidently convinced now that of the two he was the more sympathetic. "Okay," he said, "I'll tell you where the Skulls are hidin'." They were in a secret clubhouse, with enough food, beer, and chicks to last them a month or more.

"Are they there now?" Moles asked.

"Yep, since the time of the murder," replied Bones. Now he looked less intimidated. "Before I tell you where, though, you gotta—you and Pelo Rojo," he said, nodding in the direction of O'Rourke, "you gotta protect me. They kill me if they find out I drop a dime."

Both detectives guaranteed him that he'd have protection, after which he proceeded to tell them all about the secret clubhouse in a basement apartment behind the E&B Supermarket on Southern Boulevard, twelve blocks south of

The Compound. Taylor left the room and phoned his precinct in Brooklyn. Moles gave Bones a cigarette, lit it for him, and then sat on the windowsill and took notes as Bones described in detail the physical layout of the clubhouse. When Bones finished, he sat there with his prominent Adam's apple bobbing up and down as he blew a series of perfect smoke rings.

"Who iced Papo?" suddenly asked O'Rourke, sitting across the room and out of Bones's line of vision.

"Farouk," he answered, without turning around. "Farouk, he iced him with a Bowie knife."

Two cars arrived from Brooklyn carrying a sergeant and five detectives armed with shotguns. One of the detectives got into Taylor's car and drove back to the Ninetieth Precinct with Bones, once again in handcuffs. Then, with O'Rourke and Moles leading the way, the two cars sped toward the secret clubhouse of the Savage Skulls.

Three men, including Moles, started toward the front door. Three more went around to the back, while O'Rourke and Taylor stationed themselves on either side of the escape hatch in the alley, which Bones had described: a small, high, chutelike window camouflaged by a square of cardboard taped across it. At the precise moment the three detectives were moving toward the front door, two gang members arrived. They were instantly collared and instructed to knock and identify themselves. As the door opened to admit them, the detectives pushed them inside and rushed into the room with their guns drawn.

The large, dimly lit room was separated from still another large room in the rear by curtains. In a dark corner, a youth jumped up, yanking at his trousers, leaving a naked girl on the cot. Moles passed into the back room, making his way through a tangle of stolen bicycles, and opened the door to the detectives stationed outside. When O'Rourke and Taylor came around from the alley, a head count was taken: ten boys and seven girls, with Snake, 8-Ball, and Cartoon among them. No weapons were found except for a couple of broken knives. No drugs, either. Meanwhile, in the front room, Moles found a cache containing literally pounds of paper, each a page of childlike script titled "Liberation Truths."

"That's mine, man. Don't mess with that, it's precious," said Snake, momentarily distracted from watching the girls, who were giving their names and addresses to the detectives before being permitted to leave.

En route to Brooklyn, Snake asked Moles if he would like to hear some of the "liberation truths" contained in the notes he had confiscated from the club hideaway. The detective said he would and handed some of the pages to Snake, who selected a few, calling attention to the fact that at the top of each he had noted that he wasn't writing from Rikers Island but "a concentration camp." Clearing his throat, he read:

> "*Five Points of Genocide*
> Point One. What's war if not Genocide?
> Point Two. What's birth control pills if not Genocide?
> Point Three. What's legal abortion if not Genocide?
> Point Four. What's heroin if not Genocide?
> Point Five. What's religion if not Genocide?"

He looked around the car at his brothers, who were listening intently, took a deep breath, and continued.

> "Point One. *War*. We have fought in the Civil War, Spanish-American War, World War I, World War II, Korean War, and actually we are fighting the Vietnam War (Indo-China). Out of all these wars we are the warriors and we are supposed to get equal opportuni-

ties in this so-called democratic system. We fought as second class citizens and we are still second class citizens. Our conditions in the slums (El Barrio) are worse than before, we are living like rats and yet we are still killing ourselves for these pigs.

"Point Two. *Birth control pills.* Don't you know, brothers, that the pills our women (sisters) are taking is being put there by the system. The only way they can destroy us is by finding a way to have control of our women, and that's what's happening out there in the so-called free world. They are destroying our future—which is our sons and daughters—by taking over the minds of our sisters. That's why we stated in the fifth point of the 13 points platform of the Young Lords Party that we want equality for women.

"Point Three. *Legal abortion.* As far as birth control pills are concerned, they aren't doing the job as these pigs thought. Now they got the new law out—'Legal Abortions'—and the first woman that died in the legal abortion was Carmen Rodriguez. As you notice they have experimented with our sisters first. Most of the women that are getting abortions are from 'poor families.' The proletarians—working class, lowest class families on the welfare, and so on. Most of these families are Spanish as well as black. Still in all our brothers are running away from reality.

"Point Four. *Heroin.* Who are the ones that fall victim of heroin if not us? Who is the one that's bringing in heroin if not the system which we live under? Heroin is exported from other countries . . . its flowers do not grow here. This country is so great and powerful that it can spend billions of dollars for space exploration, but she can't seem to stop the drug traffic. Most of the dope that comes here is sold in the slums —our communities—and that's supposed to be a coincidence. Most of the brothers and sisters in the penal institutions here in New York City and in every major city of the United States are being held for drug orientated crimes.

"Point Five. *Religion.* Religion is just another ideology like any other. Man has made gods. Religion have made gods as far as man knows. They haven't seen this mysterious god that people have been preaching about. The people that taught us to believe in a god are the very same people that have kept us in slavery.

Patria o Muerte."

When he finished reading, Snake handed the papers back to Moles and rode the rest of the way to Brooklyn in complete silence.

Waiting in the detention room at the Ninetieth Precinct, Snake and the other nine Skulls sat casually, showing no emotion. "All that fuckin' food gonna go to waste," complained Snake. Mindful of the promise to protect Bones, Moles said, "They're looking for one more guy—Bones." Snake grinned. "Sure as hell you ain't gonna find him hangin' around here in Brooklyn." Actually, at that moment Bones was locked in an office only a short distance down the hall. Moles bade the Skulls good-bye and left the precinct house, ostensibly in search of Bones.

Two hours later he and O'Rourke appeared in the cell block with Bones in tow. As they started to bring him past the cells containing Snake and the other Skulls, Bones muttered: "Make it look good, man. Otherwise I'm dead." O'Rourke cursed him loudly enough to be certain Snake heard. Then he shoved Bones into a cell and slammed it shut. "Blue-eyed motherfucker!" Bones yelled after him.

The next morning witnesses to the murder of Papo

viewed the ten suspects through a one-way mirror. They had identified Bones from his mug shot as the tall black who had urinated on Papo and decreed that he die, but now, seeing him in the flesh, they changed their minds. "It was the other black boy," said a young woman who had been walking on the opposite side of the street with her brother-in-law when the attack started. Her brother-in-law agreed. Bones and 8-Ball did look something alike. Bones was released, and 8-Ball, the only other black to make the trip to Brooklyn that night, was booked along with Snake and four other Skulls.

Within twenty-four hours Farouk had been taken into custody again, and this time he confessed that it was he who had stabbed Papo. He said he hadn't meant to ice him, but Papo's talking up that way—challenging his authority— had made him, the prez, lose face. "I got mad. I pulled out my knife—I had it in my belt over on this side," he said, patting his left hip, "and I stuck him with it. I know I stucked him more than once, but I was so excited I don't remember how many times." After the stabbing, he said, the Skulls kicked Papo and jumped on him. "I ran—jumped over a fence and hid behind some empty houses. I must've lost the knife."

News of Snake's arrest spread rapidly through the South Bronx. With their regular clubhouse under surveillance and their secret clubhouse no longer a secret, several of his most trusted lieutenants met outside Junior High School 133 early one Sunday morning, when they knew the area would be deserted. They concluded that the best way they could show loyalty to their leader was to raise the bail money demanded for his pretrial release. So they devised Operation Extortion, applying the techniques of organized crime as they understood them to a list of retail stores. And what better place to begin than the block on Southern Boulevard where they had their secret clubhouse?

Southern Boulevard, some seven miles long, threads its way through some of the seamiest neighborhoods in the Bronx, ending up at the gates of the Bronx Zoo. Stores along the route in the South Bronx are almost all owned and operated by Hispanics, and it is a common sight to see shoppers exiting from a bodega balancing a five-foot-long stalk of sugar cane on their shoulders and carrying brown paper bags brimming with everything from cold cuts and beer to nylons and aspirin. The jukeboxes of the many bars and the stereos of the record stores play almost constantly, but in no way seem to affect the concentration of the men sitting outside playing dominoes.

Mad Dog, a vice-president of the Skulls, assumed command. He made a list of the stores he considered ripest for a ripoff and went to work at once. Operation Extortion began with a band of Baby Skulls, boys of eight and nine, entering the jewelry store next to the E&B Supermarket. With sticks they shattered a glass showcase, telling the jeweler, "Don't call the police or we'll kill you." At precisely the same time the next afternoon, they were back along with older members of the gang—about twenty in all —and they stationed themselves on an iron fence directly across the street from the store. They made no move to enter, but simply sat across the street, staring, for what to the terrified jeweler seemed like an hour, although it probably was more like ten or fifteen minutes. "When this happened, I was frozen with fear," the jeweler, who had been in business at that location for twelve years, would say later to the police. "I knew that somebody was being held up every night. Terrible things were happening around there. I knew something big was going to happen."

And it did the next afternoon, when Mad Dog and two

of his lieutenants, wearing their colors, paid a visit to the store while the Baby Skulls took up their position once again on the iron fence across the street. Mad Dog, his hair in a braid that hung to his waist, stood absolutely silent, his back to the door, while his lieutenants wandered aimlessly around the store before disappearing into the tiny office in the rear. They emerged a few minutes later and stationed themselves on either side of Mad Dog. No words were spoken, and when they left the Baby Skulls remained in position across the street for another half-hour. The jeweler stood behind his counter, too frightened to move, even to answer the phone that was ringing in the office in the rear. When the Baby Skulls finally left, he rushed to the office and took a quick inventory. Not so much as a piece of paper had been disturbed.

The jeweler lived with his wife in an apartment above the store, and at about nine o'clock that evening there was a knock on the door. The middle-aged couple made no move to answer. Whoever it was out there began pounding on the door and rattling the knob, while at the same time someone on the sidewalk outside shouted, "Open the door! Open the door!" The jeweler and his wife stood in the center of the living room, paralyzed with fear. In a moment there was silence, and then the phone in their bedroom began to ring. Finally the man, panicky that someone on the street might see him cross the room, dropped to his knees and crawled into the bedroom. He picked up the phone, and a voice on the other end said, "Don't answer the door. They have guns," and promptly hung up.

Mad Dog came alone to the store the next afternoon. "I was lookin' for you the other day," he said, leaning across the counter. "I went to your house with a couple of my boys. I couldn't find you. I was gonna kill you." That said, he got down to business. He told the jeweler that some of his brothers were in jail and he wanted to get them released. He said that all the merchants on the block were going to help. From the jeweler he wanted two hundred dollars now and twenty-five dollars a week thereafter, without fail. In return, the Skulls would protect him and his store. "We wanna help you," Mad Dog assured him, patting his arm. "You're a nice guy, and we wanna make a paper which we want you t'put against the showcase and nobody is gonna bother you after this." Mad Dog pointed toward the back of the store. "Now I want you to type that paper."

He shoved the man into the office at the rear of the store and ordered him to sit down and start typing the following letter of agreement exactly as he dictated it:

> We the Presidents of the Savage Skulls
> PROMISE not to disturb the owner of
> this store, his friends, or any person working at
> the store.
> The Savage Skulls promise to help in any possi-
> ble way if trouble arises against us or our
> people.
> And we will protect him at all times.

Mad Dog signed the letter with his proper Christian name and gave it to the jeweler, after which he led the shaking man to the cash register in the front of the store and took two hundred dollars in cash from him.

The next day Operation Extortion was carried to the record store across the street. Hispanic music played constantly during store hours, and while some of the Baby Skulls danced on the sidewalk outside, others came into the store and began pulling records from the shelves and grinding them beneath their boots. Again it was "Don't call the police or we'll kill you." But, unlike the jeweler, the proprietor of this store didn't receive any visit or phone call to his home that night. Pleased with the ease with which he had extorted money from the jeweler, Mad Dog had decided he could afford to simplify Operation Extortion. So the next day, while the Baby Skulls stood at the curb staring into the store, he walked in and announced: "We're here for the money. Two hundred now and twenty-five a week from now on." The owner had only fifty dollars in the cash register, and Mad Dog took it, advising him that he would be back for the remainder the next day.

The next morning Mad Dog went to the jewelry store and made the owner type a copy of the letter of agreement he had with the Skulls. This duplicate was for the owner of the record store. On leaving, annoyed that the jeweler hadn't followed instructions and taped his copy of the letter on the front of his showcase, Mad Dog reached into the showcase and took with him an eighteen-karat-gold medal with a semiprecious stone valued at three hundred dollars.

The proprietor of the record store accepted the letter of agreement signed by Mad Dog and handed over one hundred and fifty dollars. "That's not two hundred dollars," Mad Dog said, tossing the cash back at him. When the man attempted to explain that he had already paid fifty dollars toward the two hundred, Mad Dog became furious and threatened to burn the store. The owner promptly gave him another fifty dollars.

That evening Mad Dog and his two lieutenants visited El Ganadero, one of the two bars on the block. The bartender, a former amateur boxer, refused to open the cash register. "Get out!" he said, waving them toward the door. Mad Dog reached into his pocket, took out a gun, and shot the bartender through the hand. Before fleeing from the bar, they said that they'd be back for two hundred dollars, and if they didn't get it they would kill him and burn the bar to the ground. The man was treated in the emergency room of Jacobi Hospital, where he said he'd been shot during an attempted robbery. The bullet had severed the tendons in his hand, and his fingers were permanently crippled.

The next evening Mad Dog and his lieutenants walked into the El Rancho Grande and reminded the manager there of what had happened to the bartender across the street. The frightened man took one hundred dollars out of the cash register and handed it to Mad Dog. The next day they returned for the other hundred, and he accepted the Skulls' letter of agreement. Within a few days the owner of El Ganadero did likewise.

For the next several days Mad Dog and his gang worked at top speed on both sides of the street. Before the week was out the Skulls had brought Operation Extortion to a bodega, a dry cleaner, and a meat market, as well as the jewelry store, record store, and two bars. Now the initial visit of the Baby Skulls as a prelude to the first visit of Mad Dog was canceled in favor of Molotov cocktails tossed into the stores. The owner of the jewelry store had been forced to type several more copies of the gang's letter of agreement, and had become so convinced that his store was going to be bombed or burned that he refused to leave it unattended; he put a mattress on the floor in the rear and slept there every night. When he had paid Mad Dog a total of seven hundred and fifty dollars, he was informed that the weekly payment was going to be raised from twenty-five dollars to fifty dollars.

Although none of the merchants on the block dared contact the local precinct, the epidemic of Molotov cocktails had become a matter of record—as were Mad Dog's repeated visits to the jewelry store. Curious, the police asked the jeweler if he was having any trouble, and he assured them that nothing was wrong. "I feared. I didn't want to tell them anything," he would say later. Eventually, however, when he was no longer able to meet Mad Dog's repeated demands for still larger sums of money, he confided to the police, and a plainclothesman was stationed in his office in the rear of the store. He was there the next time Mad Dog came to collect, and an arrest was made, but by this time enough money had been raised to spring Snake. He had been released on bail just twenty-four hours earlier, pending trial for his alleged part in the murder of Papo. A few days later the record store was firebombed, and the owner and his family promptly moved out of the state, leaving no forwarding address except with the police of the Forty-first Precinct.

The summit meeting in The Compound preceded Snake's release by only two days. By the time the gang leaders had blown out the solitary candle that symbolized the conclave, they had decided not to attempt to dispose of Snake. The risks were considered too great. He was too powerful. It was hoped that maybe a jury would find him guilty of the murder, and that way he would be finally taken out of circulation. It was quite possibly the first time in the history of street gangs that they left it to the courts to settle a score for them.

The murder case never came to trial, however. Farouk pleaded guilty to manslaughter and was sentenced to five years' imprisonment. S.O.S. and Snake pleaded guilty to assault second degree and received lighter sentences. 8-Ball never entered a plea; he died in prison of a heart attack shortly before his eighteenth birthday.

All the merchants from whom money had been extorted came forward to identify Mad Dog and four other members of the Savage Skulls. Bronx District Attorney Mario Merola would not identify the victims for the press.

The jeweler, the first victim of Operation Extortion, sold his business and, like the owner of the record store, moved out of the state. Fearful that he might still be tracked down by the Skulls, he moved a second time, though both men returned to testify at the extortion trial. Still fearing for his safety, the jeweler insisted on twenty-four-hour police protection while in the city. In court on the day the guilty verdict was read, the man broke down and cried.

While on Rikers Island awaiting trial, Mad Dog attemped to escape by swimming to the Bronx. He was found drowned under the Whitestone Bridge, his hip-length braid looking like a snake bobbing on the oily water of the river. The remaining four Skulls stood trial. All were found guilty.

12.
Mr. Popsicle

When fifteen-year-old Bobby (Mr. Popsicle) Dominguez escaped from the state training school in Otisville, New York, by simply walking into the woods that surrounded the property, he headed straight for home: The Compound. He expected that his gang would be happy to see him. He'd certainly be happy to see his brothers. But Mr. Popsicle, a very minor member of the Savage Nomads, was about to discover that, despite a street gang's protestations of brotherhood, a little brother was extremely expendable.

Hitchhiking just outside Monroe, New York, Popsicle told his fellow runaway, sixteen-year-old Perry Witlock, that if anybody asked his name he should say it was Hubert Simpson.

"Hubert who?"

"Simpson . . . Hubert Simpson. Black Bongo, he's our prez."

At about the time Popsicle and Perry were scrambling into the back seat of a car that would take them eleven miles nearer their goal, Black Bongo sat on the stoop of The Compound, flanked, as always, by his favorite companions, Big Mama and his two German shepherds. It was early in the summer of '73. Several months had passed since he and later Big Mama had been shot while sitting there. In the interim, the two-year-old Compound had really been "discovered" by the media. Writers and photographers were traveling to the South Bronx to see what was now often referred to as a phenomenon, an environmental scandal. On this extremely hot, sunny day, Black Bongo, barefooted, wearing a dirty undershirt and torn dungarees, was being interviewed—this time by a professor that Vito and Pelo Rojo had brought around, a paleface who stood on the sidewalk holding his tape recorder and looking up at the five battered-looking buildings, not one of which had so much as a sliver of glass left in any of its windows. Black Bongo turned and shouted at the kids who were standing around, watching and listening.

"I got no time for you brothers. This here is a professor and he want to know about me, Black Bongo. Get lost!" The kids scattered, as they always did when Bongo gave the order. Half of them belonged to the Mongols, the first gang to move into The Compound, and the first to move out. Still they hung around. It was home.

"Hey, man. C'mere!" shouted Bongo to one of them about to move across the street to Nomad Park. The kid shambled back toward the stoop and stood at attention. "You give him some money," Bongo said to the professor, a graying man from Pennsylvania who was in the South Bronx to do research on street-gang behavior. "He get me a bottle of wine." The professor put down his tape recorder, dug into his trouser pocket, and produced a five-dollar bill, which he placed in Bongo's outstretched hand. "Swiss Up and a pack of Kents," said Bongo, sticking the bill into the top of his motorcycle boot. The kid dutifully plucked it out and sprinted down the steps and across the street, after which Bongo turned the full wattage of his magnetic personality on the interviewer.

"My gang philosophy?" he said, a grin creasing his broad black face. "Hell, man, I don't have no gang philosophy. Only my personal philosophy. You want it?"

Big Mama stared as the professor moved the tape recorder closer to Bongo. "Black Bongo's philosophy," he said by way of announcement. "Peace, Prosperity, and Pussy."

When Mr. Popsicle and Perry Whitlock arrived at The Compound a couple of hours later, they walked across the rubbish-littered courtyard and upstairs to the Savage Nomads' clubhouse, where they found Stay Hard, vice-president and second in command, sitting on a windowsill and talking to a skinny black kid called Trouble Bubble. He nodded to Popsicle as casually as though it had been yesterday and not three months since he'd seen him last. Popsicle and Perry sat down on the sofa, taking care to avoid the cushion with the spring poking up through the ripped fabric.

"Bubble says Monk is causin' static," said Stay Hard, pulling on his moustache. "Hey, Shaft, you know Monk?" Shaft allowed as how he knew Monk. "You know where he's at?" asked Stay Hard. Shaft nodded. He liked to play it cool. At seventeen, he was a veteran gang member. Man, he'd been on heroin since he was thirteen. Now he was clean. And plenty cool.

"I don't know right now," he said, adding that he was about to go over to Junior High 133 to see his chick, Irma. Now that he was back home, Popsicle was eager to be noticed. "Well, there's a hooky set there," he said, addressing Shaft. "Monk might be there." Shaft looked across at Popsicle and Perry, sitting there on the fuckin' sofa like two little shitasses, and turned away. *A hooky set* over at 133. Big news. There were more dudes hangin' out in the schoolyard every day than there was in the whole fuckin' school.

Shaft stood up and started for the door. Just as he was about to step outside, he turned around and winked at Stay Hard.

Sure enough, the schoolyard was crowded. Shaft shouldered his way through, slapping palms with the dudes and winking at the chicks, but there was no sign of Irma. As he started toward the school building, he felt a hand on his shoulder, and turned around, and damn if it wasn't Stay Hard. So together they walked inside the school and past the guards, who, if they didn't actually make way for them, didn't get in their way, either.

Shaft and Stay Hard went into the cafeteria, Shaft walking between the tables looking for Monk, while Stay Hard stood waiting by the door. "Nope," said Shaft after he had covered the room, and then they went across the hall into a second cafeteria. Still no sign of Monk. Then Stay Hard left, and Shaft waited alone for Irma. When she came out of school a half-hour later, he pulled her over against the wall and, leaning with his palms flat against the wall on either side of her, told her what a swell time they were going to have that night at The Compound. A victory celebration. Victory? Never mind. Irma giggled. And although she didn't take her eyes off his face, she knew that she was being watched and envied by Rosa and Eppie, who'd give everything they had to be where she was at that moment.

Later at the clubhouse Shaft suggested to Stay Hard that they take the bus to Hunts Point Avenue and maybe they'd find Monk around there. "He used to live on Hunts Point," he said. So Stay Hard and he walked over to the bus, and damn if Popsicle and Davy didn't tag along after them. Not that there was anything wrong with Davy, but shit, man, he's only fourteen. And even though he's a warlord he still sometimes acts like what he once was—a Baby Nomad. Some of them kids never get cool.

The four of them walked up Hunts Point Avenue, Shaft and Stay Hard leading, with Popsicle and Davy keeping a respectful distance behind. Shaft spied a kid he knew and he said, "Ray, you know where Monk is at?" Ray, who wore an Indian band tied around his head, pointed to a pizzeria across the street and said he would go and get him. But as he started across the street, who should come walking out of the pizzeria but Monk. Shaft waved him over, and when Monk came Stay Hard said to him: "I wanna talk to you. Let's step in the hallway up the street." So, flanked by Shaft and Stay Hard, with Popsicle and Davy bringing up the rear, Monk walked up the street and through the vestibule and into the hallway of a red-brick tenement. But before Stay Hard had a chance to say anything, Sugar came downstairs in a new see-through blouse and a curly red wig. She leaned on the banister and batted her false eyelashes at them. "What's this," she said, "a family reunion?" "Sort of," replied Stay Hard, not bothering to look up at her, and with that Sugar continued down the stairs, buzzed Shaft on the cheek, and flounced through the vestibule and down the stoop, where Popsicle stood. Nobody had told him to stay outside; he just did out of force of habit. But if Perry had come with him instead of staying behind in The Compound, he'd have gone inside. That sure would have impressed Perry.

Although Shaft and Davy were inside, they couldn't hear what Stay Hard was saying to Monk. He was talking low and friendly-like. They didn't know what kind of static Monk was causing, but he was in big trouble, that was for sure. Otherwise Stay Hard wouldn't be out looking for him. Yeah, Monk was in big trouble.

"You wanna come back to The Compound so's we can talk?" Stay Hard asked Monk, loud enough so that Shaft and Davy could hear. Monk said O.K., and, once again flanked by Shaft and Stay Hard, with Popsicle and Davy a respectful distance behind, he walked up Hunts Point Avenue. Ray, the kid who had offered to go into the pizzeria and get him, watched the five of them disappear around the corner. He didn't know Monk so good, but he sure felt sorry for him. Those Savage Nomads were mean. Real mean. Monk was gonna get himself messed up but good.

"Sit down. Relax," Stay Hard said to Monk, pointing to the sofa with the spring poking up through the cushion. Monk sat down, and Stay Hard wasted no more time with pleasantries.

"Are you a DD?" he said, positioning himself directly in front of Monk. Stay Hard could have said "Dirty Dozen," but he preferred "DD"; it sounded dirtier that way.

Monk shook his head. "I used to be but I'm not no more. But I still go to their parties now and then." Popsicle and Davy sat on the arms of the sofa and stared down at Monk, while Shaft stood behind Stay Hard with both arms folded across his chest.

Stay Hard pretended to seriously consider Monk's reply. Then: "How come you go to their parties if you're not a member of their club?"

"Y'know. You pay a quarter and you go to the party," said Monk.

Again Stay Hard appeared very thoughtful. Then he put out his hand. "Let me see your belt," he said. Monk got up, took off the wide leather belt, and handed it to him and sat down. Stay Hard proceeded to fold the belt in half. "This belt," he said, "is gonna tell me if you're lyin' or not." He swung his hand, and the belt struck Monk across the mouth, splitting his lip. A stream of blood started trickling into his mouth, and he had no sooner tasted it than Stay

Hard struck him in the mouth again. Neither Popsicle nor Davy moved from where they sat on the arms of the sofa, although the second time Stay Hard swung the belt it passed only inches from Popsicle's thigh. Jesus, if only Perry was here. Where the fuck had he gone to?

Tossing the belt on the floor, Stay Hard began to beat Monk with his fists. Davy promptly stood up and started beating on him too. Popsicle felt a shiver of excitement rush through his body. Monk somehow managed to get to his feet, and at the sight of him standing there with blood pouring down his face, Popsicle leaped up and started to kick him in the legs. Only Shaft remained detached, standing with his back to the window. Popsicle's eyes fell upon a baseball bat on the floor behind the sofa, and he picked it up and struck Monk across the legs so hard that the bat broke in two. *"Mi madre! Mi madre!"* Monk cried, as Stay Hard and Davy both punched his head. Bending down, Popsicle retrieved the thicker part of the bat and hit Monk across the chest with it.

"Shaft! Shaft!" Monk sobbed. "Tell 'em I'm not a DD!"

Shaft, his arms still folded across his chest, answered him in his usual cool, even voice. "Monk," he said, "I can't do nothin'. I can tell them but they don't have to listen, because they're like staff over me." Which was half true, anyway. Stay Hard was vice-president, Davy the warlord. But as for Mr. Popsicle, Shaft would have liked to ice him on the spot. Stay Hard shouldn't have let him touch Monk, who now had fallen back on the sofa, his face puffing and bleeding.

When Stay Hard stopped beating on him, Popsicle and Davy stopped too, even though Popsicle had the bat poised to strike again. "Take him into the kitchen an' wash him up," Stay Hard ordered, and Shaft, unfolding his arms, went over to Monk and half carried him into the kitchen. He pulled up Monk's shirt and, grabbing hold of his T-shirt, ripped it off. Then, with Monk propped up against the wall, he poured cold water on the T-shirt and began, almost gently, wiping the blood off his face. He practically had him clean when Popsicle came into the kitchen and told him Stay Hard wanted to talk to him. Shaft tossed the bloody T-shirt into the sink and went back into the living room, where Stay Hard was sitting on the windowsill, looking very thoughtful.

"Man, we're gonna have to kill this guy," he said, looking past Shaft at Davy, who had gone back to sitting on the arm of the sofa.

"Why?"

Stay Hard looked up at him. "Listen," he said, making it all sound very reasonable, "the man knows you, and if we let him go he may go next to your family or go to the police."

Shaft knew that made sense, and yet . . .

Stay Hard sat there, waiting for his response. "Yeah, we might as well ice him," Shaft said, and once he had said it he felt better. Stay Hard stood up then, smacked him on the arm, and said, "Let's go!" Popsicle brought Monk back into the living room, his shirt hanging out of his trousers and blood trickling down from the cut on his upper lip. "Hey, I want your pants and shoes," said Davy. Without a word Monk sat down, removed his shoes, and then pulled off his trousers. Davy kicked off his shoes and slipped off his trousers, and they changed clothes while the others stood and waited. "Let's go, let's go," Stay Hard said impatiently, finally swinging his arm around Monk's shoulder and leading him out the door.

They couldn't ice him in the clubhouse; they were having a party there tonight. They'd take him into one of the other buildings and up to one of the empty apartments. Don't mess up their building with a party coming up. As they walked across the courtyard, Stay Hard with his arm around Monk and Shaft and Davy behind them, no one noticed that Popsicle wasn't still with them.

Trouble Bubble was on his bicycle, circling around the junk piled high in the center of the courtyard: the cardboard boxes, bottles, and the remnants of the doors that had been ripped off and airmailed out the windows. "Where you all goin'?" he shouted, staring at Monk. "Upstairs," Stay Hard answered, and then he stopped, removed his arm from around Monk, and went over and said something to Trouble Bubble. Then he came back, put his arm around Monk's shoulder once again, and steered him across the courtyard and up the stairs of the building next to the one where the Savage Nomads had staked their claim.

They walked up the stairs to the third floor, with Stay Hard kicking garbage out of their way as he went. There were plenty of empty apartments there, but he wanted to go up another flight. They literally had to scale the next flight of stairs, because half the staircase was missing. On the fourth floor every apartment was empty, with the doors off their hinges and lying on the floor outside. For no particular reason, Stay Hard chose apartment 4B.

Inside the apartment, he removed his arm from around Monk and ordered Shaft to tie him up. "Let's leave him here," he said, as though he actually meant it. Shaft shoved Monk into a corner by a steam pipe. Picking a blanket off the floor, he stretched it across the window. Finding a piece of electric cord, he said, "Let's hang the motherfucker." He didn't really mean it. It was just that he wanted to get it all over with as fast as possible. But he knew that Stay Hard and Davy were going to drag it out. Especially Davy, who was standing there staring at Monk and cracking his knuckles. Shaft shoved Monk back up against the steam pipe and proceeded to tie his hands behind his back with the electric cord. Then he stepped back and asked, "You want a cigarette?"

"No."

What the fuck was this dude thinking, anyway? Then Monk began shivering. He looked across at Stay Hard and asked, in an almost matter-of-fact voice, "Am I gonna die?"

Stay Hard didn't answer. Shaft found another blanket, and he put it around Monk's shoulders. "Am I gonna die?" Monk repeated, and this time his voice shook.

"No," said Stay Hard, "we're gonna leave you and then call the police and the ambulance t'cut you loose." He was smiling and walking toward Monk. Then he stopped, reached down, and pulled the blanket off one shoulder, while with his other hand he reached into his trouser pocket and took out a knife.

Davy immediately pulled out his knife too, its four-inch blade snapping out cold and silver. "The Lord giveth and the Nomad taketh away," he said, rushing toward Monk. Raising his arm, he sent the blade cutting deep into Monk's stomach. Monk groaned, staggering back against the steam pipe. Stay Hard inspected his stomach and said, "No blood. He's not bleeding." At that Davy stuck Monk again, and then Stay Hard jumped in and, with all his weight behind it, sent his knife into Monk's side. Monk groaned again and slid down the pipe to the floor, where he collapsed in a pool of blood.

"Gag him!" ordered Stay Hard. Shaft searched among the debris on the floor, found a pair of cotton shorts, ripped them, and made a gag. He knelt down, shoved it into Monk's mouth, and knotted it at the back of Monk's head.

When he stood up Trouble Bubble had come into the room, carrying three machetes, which he promptly stuck in the floor. At the sight of the machetes quivering there,

Stay Hard folded his knife and put it back in his trouser pocket. Picking up a machete, he spun around and hit Monk savagely across the head with the flat side of it. Trouble Bubble reached out as though to stop him. Stay Hard turned and swung the machete at him. The kid jumped back as the blade whizzed past his face.

"Don't touch me!" Stay Hard hollered. He looked as though he might be going to ice the kid. Trouble Bubble raised both hands high in the air. "What's the matter?" he said, panting. Shaft didn't move for fear that Stay Hard might swing at him too. But he spoke, taking care to keep his voice even and cool. "Calm down. Be cool. He didn't mean to touch you. He won't do it again." For a moment Stay Hard held the machete out as though he might swing at Trouble Bubble a second time. Then he turned around and resumed hitting Monk across the head with the flat side of it.

It made a sickening sound. So sickening, in fact, that Shaft thought he might throw up. "Don't smack him with it," he said, not so cool this time. "If you're gonna do something, cut him." And, like a robot gone wild, Stay Hard flipped the machete in his hand and cut Monk with it. Blood gushed through the gag in his mouth, and his head sagged onto his chest. Then Stay Hard cut him again in the neck and the leg.

It was as though he had been waiting to really see blood. Lots of it. And now he did as it poured down Monk's shirt and began moving across the floor, sticking in the cuts and crevices of the dry wood. Stay Hard watched it for a moment, and then he shoved the blood-stained machete under his shirt. Davy pulled another machete up out of the floor and put it under his shirt, while Shaft slid the third one inside his trousers. Then they filed out of the apartment, leaving Trouble Bubble standing there, staring fixedly at a stream of blood that was slowly heading straight for his feet. He had never seen that much blood before, and he couldn't bring himself to leave.

Down the four flights and across the courtyard they went, and then into the building next door and up to their clubhouse, where some of the brothers had just come in from the bodega, where they'd stolen a pile of fat candles to add to the candles they already had around the apartment. So they didn't have electricity. So what? They'd have a party by fuckin' candlelight.

Popsicle was in the kitchen, tracking down a cockroach, when Stay Hard entered. He took the machete out from under his shirt and ran water on it, sending the blood slithering down the blade into the sink and down the drain.

When Perry Witlock turned up for the party, Popsicle buttonholed him and told him how the Nomads had iced the DD. That dude, he said, was somewhere in The Compound turning stiff this minute. He gave Perry the impression that he had been there at the time of the killing. Then Popsicle took him into the kitchen and showed him the now-faint pink streaks in the sink. "Man, you shoulda seen the blood slippin' off that blade."

Within the hour the clubhouse was packed with brothers and their chicks. They danced to rock played on the transistor radio, and the air was sweet with the smell of grass. But the party really took off when Black Bongo and Big Mama came out of a back bedroom and joined them. The music seemed to grow louder, and the dancers moved faster. Bongo's electric-blue shirt was open down to the navel, displaying the pink scars of old knife wounds. Big Mama's hair stood out like a fan around her face, and from the crotch of her jeans a giant sequined butterfly spread its wings.

Popsicle sat between Perry and a chick named Minerva, a bottle of sweet wine in his fist. His eyes were riveted on

Bongo, who had just been handed a bottle. Standing there in the center of the room, the dancers spinning around him, he tipped the bottle and let a few drops spill on the floor in memory of missing brothers, dead or in jail. Everybody did that, of course, but when Black Bongo did it . . . well, it had class.

Stay Hard sidled up to Bongo, and they went over into a corner. Popsicle became aware that they were staring at him, and he felt elated. Back only a day and here he was at a party and it was like he had never been away. He tipped his head back and took a swig out of his bottle. When he brought his head down, Bongo was standing in front of him—so close, in fact, that Popsicle almost struck him in the thigh with the wine bottle.

"You been talkin' too much about what happened to Monk," he said. "You get the Nomads busted that way. C'mon, I wanna talk to you." He stepped back, and Popsicle stood up and walked in the direction of the bedroom to which Bongo was pointing. It seemed to Popsicle that now the music was less loud, and the dudes and their chicks were dancing in slow motion. As he approached the bedroom, a wicked kick in the small of his back sent him hurtling headfirst into the room. Just as he was about to fall across the mattress on the floor, Bongo grabbed him by the hair and twisted him around so that they were practically nose to nose. "I'm gonna fire you up for goin' round telling everybody that you killed a DD, because that's the way you can get the Nomads busted." Letting go of Popsicle's hair, he slammed him across the ear with his wine bottle. Bongo stood there and watched as the blood began to trickle between the fingers of the hand Popsicle held pressed against his ear. Then, bringing his head back, he tipped the bottle a few inches above his mouth and let the remainder of the wine pour down his throat. Wiping his mouth with the back of his big hand, he tossed the empty bottle down on the mattress.

"C'mere," he said to Popsicle, indicating a spot on the floor. Popsicle's head ached and his vision was blurred, but he did as he was told. When he was only inches from the spot, Bongo's fist came crashing into his face, and he was flung back against the wall. When the back of his head struck, the pain was so intense that he could see nothing but those daffy lights and rockets they draw in cartoon strips to suggest an explosion. "C'mere," he heard Bongo order, and he stepped forward only to stagger back against the wall again. "C'MERE!"

Popsicle blinked, but now there was blood in his eyes, and Bongo in his electric-blue shirt was nothing more than a blue blur bobbing on a red sea. Still, he did manage to stand up straight and take a few steps before he sank to his knees. Bongo was on him in a flash, kicking him in the chest with the toe of his motorcycle boot. Popsicle collapsed to the floor and lay there face down. Although he couldn't see anything now, he could still hear the music pounding and pounding from the other room, and he could feel the vibrations of the dancers' feet hitting the floor. He could hear, too, the sound of Bongo's feet walking to the bedroom door. Then more feet were rushing into the bedroom and they began kicking him. *Mother of Mercy!* Up and down they began jumping on him, each stomp crushing his face into the floor. Just before he lost consciousness, he could feel his face spreading wider and wider, until he thought that his whole head would surely explode.

Black Bongo and the other three Nomads who had stomped Popsicle into a state of unconsciousness now dragged him into the living room as the dudes and their chicks who had been standing in the doorway watching fanned out to make way for them. Dropping his hold on one of Popsicle's arms, Bongo went into the kitchen, untied one of his two German shepherds from the leg of the sink, and led it into the living room. "Sic him! Kill him!" he ordered the dog, pointing to Popsicle's inert body. The dog called Nomad promptly attacked, mauling Popsicle with its front paws as it dug its teeth into his chest, arms, and legs. Forming a semicircle, the crowd began chanting, "Sic him! Kill him!" above the sound of the rock still pounding from the radio.

Popsicle's head rolled from side to side, and blood was pouring from his ear. He was lying flat now, head up and facing the ceiling, his throat exposed. Suddenly, its nails tearing at Popsicle's shirt, Nomad went for his throat. Bongo lunged for the dog, commanding it to go back into the kitchen. The dog, paws and snout flecked with blood, slunk away. And at that point the party resumed, with the dudes and chicks dancing around Popsicle's body.

Perry Witlock sat on the sofa, a can of beer in his fist, staring down at Popsicle. What could he have done to help him, man? *Nothing.* They'd have killed him too, for sure. When the others had raced to the bedroom to watch Popsicle getting stomped, Perry hadn't moved. And the rock was playing so loud, he found that if he concentrated on the beat he almost couldn't hear the thumping sounds coming from the bedroom. Still, he wasn't ready for it when he looked up and saw Popsicle being dragged across the room by his hands and feet, his swollen head bumping along the floor. And when the dog started mauling and biting on him, Perry had shut his eyes, and he kept them shut until he heard the dancing start up again. Now he sat there getting drunk, because that was the only way he knew to stop himself from staring at Popsicle and then at the tips of Bongo's motorcycle boots, which were caked with matted hair and blood.

Somewhere along the way one of the chicks—a stringy

one with long, skinny legs—took some kind of fit. She fell
on the floor and thrashed around until somebody ran into
the kitchen and came back with a clothespin and put it on
her tongue. Then they picked her up and took her to the
hospital, and that more or less broke up the party. Just
before he passed out, Perry heard Bongo tell a couple of
the chicks to pick Popsicle up off the floor and put him on
the sofa. By this time Perry was lying on the floor, and he
looked across at Popsicle as he was being lifted up and
he looked dead, all right, but Perry figured he wasn't
because . . . well, they wouldn't bother like that with a
dead man, now would they? And Perry had heard Popsicle
making sounds—a sort of gasping noise—so he was certain that he was alive.

Perry woke up to find himself on the kitchen floor, and
through half-opened eyes he saw this big dude pushing
Popsicle off the sofa and then shoving a girl down on it
and crawling in beside her. Perry's head ached something
fierce, but he managed to stand up, and he began walking
aimlessly about the apartment, stepping over the bodies
sleeping on the floor or on mattresses or blankets spread
on the floor. When he had made it back into the living
room, Popsicle wasn't there. Perry went into the kitchen
and found him propped up in a chair, with Stay Hard
standing in front of him, hitting him in the chin with the
butt of a gun and commanding him to "Wake up!" Perry
turned around and, grabbing hold of the sink, threw up.
Then he went down the hall to a back bedroom, where
Bongo was squatting on a mattress, a can of beer in his
fist and Nomad at his feet. Bongo paid him no mind, and
so Perry went back to the kitchen, where he found Popsicle on the floor. His eyes were rolling around in his head,
and as Perry would testify later, "he was bringing this
green stuff up." Perry went back to the rear bedroom, and

this time Bongo looked up at him. Perry said, "Can we take Popsicle to the hospital?" "Yeah, go ahead," Bongo replied, sending his empty beer can rolling across the floor.

Perry found a couple of Nomads who were awake and willing to help him get Popsicle downstairs. He hailed a taxi, and they hoisted Popsicle into the back seat. Then Perry got in and, with his friend's grotesquely swollen head cradled in his lap, they rode to Jacobi Hospital.

Popsicle was wheeled into Emergency, and Perry lied and said that he had found his friend unconscious on the sidewalk outside The Compound. But it didn't take much prodding for a detective to discover that Perry had run away from Otisville, and within the next twenty-four hours he was on his way back there.

At about the time Perry Witlock was lying to the detective at Jacobi Hospital, police officer Robert Haber of the Forty-first Precinct found Monk's body lying face down just inside the entrance to apartment 4B in The Compound. Monk's hands were still tied behind his back, and a trail of blood led from the spot where the body was found to a steam pipe in the living room, where a blanket covered the window. A check of the victim's pockets produced a letter addressed to David Cintron, and for the next several hours it was believed that this was the body of David (Davy) Cintron.

Joan Dominguez, Popsicle's mother, who was a waitress, saw him in the hospital for the first time late that afternoon. Detectives O'Rourke and Moles drove her there— a pretty woman who sat silently between them in the front seat, fingering her rosary. Later, at the trial of Black Bongo, she would testify that her son "looked like a monster. His head all blown up and bandaged." He was unconscious, and he remained unconscious for three months. Then one morning he briefly regained consciousness. The hospital telephoned Joan Dominguez, and she rushed down, and she was certain that he recognized her. She tried to get him to say hello. But all he could do was stare at her, so she sat by his bed and held his hand. Two days later Mr. Popsicle died of contusions of the brain caused by the stomping that had smashed his brain against the inside of his skull.

Davy was the first to be apprehended, but since he was only fourteen he could not be tried in Criminal Court. He was sentenced to eighteen months in a training school. At the present time, he is awaiting trial for his alleged part in a grocery-store murder.

Shaft pleaded guilty to manslaughter in the first degree in the death of Monk, who died as a result of four stab wounds in his neck. Since this was his first offense, Shaft was put on probation.

Stay Hard stood trial for the murders of Monk and Mr. Popsicle. He was convicted of manslaughter in the first degree in both cases, and on each charge he was sentenced to a term of twenty-five years to life, the terms to run concurrently.

Hubert (Black Bongo) Simpson, looking neat and almost docile in the courtroom, often turning around to smile encouragingly at his mother, was convicted of manslaughter in the first degree in the death of Bobby (Mr. Popsicle) Dominguez. Shortly after he was sentenced, Big Mama vanished from the South Bronx. Rumor has it that she has a new man and has settled down.

Had Bongo and Big Mama remained in The Compound, it's highly likely that the gangs still there that summer would have hung on a little longer despite everything. Hadn't they stayed until then without heat, electricity, and water? But when the Ma and Pa of The Compound left, it was no longer home—simply a string of ravaged buildings.

13.
Dear Charmin...

The gangs began moving out of The Compound, floor by floor, over a period of some six months between the winter and summer of 1973. All utilities had long since been turned off. The top floors were abandoned first, because the stairs leading up to them were either broken or missing and it had become virtually impossible to reach the apartments there. Then, as the stairs leading up to the floor below would disintegrate, the gangs living there would move. This continued until finally the last gangs on the premises were occupying basement apartments, and when pipes burst and flooded the rooms with two feet of water, they moved too. So the exodus progressed from the top down, while the invasion of the five-building complex two years earlier by the street gangs had progressed from the bottom up—the earliest gangs took over basement apartments, forced lawful tenants on higher floors out, and then moved upstairs, leaving the basement for the gang that came next.

Not wanting to be traced to their new locations, the gangs usually stole away in the very early morning hours.

Ed O'Rourke and Vito Moles would inspect every room in each vacated apartment, hoping to find some clue as to where the gang had moved. Broken bicycles, hacked doors, chairs and tables, scorched mattresses lay in heaps in the courtyard, making entry into the buildings more a matter of climbing than walking. Inside the apartments shards of glass littered the floors and plumbing was either smashed or totally missing, sold for scrap by scavenging junkies and winos.

Late in August of 1973, the city claimed the five buildings. It took teams of sanitation workers four days just to clear away the mountain of rubble in the courtyard. The following letters, written from Rikers Island, were discovered by O'Rourke and Moles on a mattress beneath a mound of bottles and cans in the clubhouse of the Mongols . . .

Dear Charmin—I hope when you get this letter you are in the best of health both physical and mentally. Well Charmin, if you knew how I feel in here without a friend coming to see me. I'm mad now.
Well Charmin, I want you to know one thing I will always love you as a friend and no matter what happened with me and this case I will always remember you and Ramon as some beaitful friends. Well Charmin I'm running out of words so take care. Yours truly, *Pito*. PS Said hello to your mother and father & friends for me.

Dear Charmin—Hello again! Well I hope when you get this letter you are in the best of health. As for me I'm fine. I was hoping to be out by July but things did not work out as I want it. Well I finally made captain of the Kitchen in here. Oh yeah I'm going to tell you how to get here. You take the G train and the bus must say *to* Riker Island. The visiting hours are from 9 to 11 so come early. Well Charmin I'm running out of words so take care of yourself.

Love, *Pito*

Dear Charmin, Just a few lines to let you know how I'm doing. Charmin if anybody is Disrespectful you let me know so when I get out I take care of that for you. Charmin it took me a while to make up the two Poems I got for you. Since I know you are VIRGO I made one out to Virgo. Well Charmin, I want you to send me one of your pictures. Well I don't have much to say so take care and write me back soon. Yours truly, *Pito*. PS Send me your picture. Please you write back.

Dear Charmin,

Hi? And what's happening. I got your letter and it was nice to hear from you again. Well you know the Sitation I'm in. I hope to be out soon if that witness comes to court they might let me go home soon. Well you ask me something in the letter you wrote. You ask me if I got a kid well I do have one, and his name is Donny. He is five months old. My woman comes every Monday with the kid. Well I had a bad Easter it was bad in here the day took long and it was bad.

Well I'm writing to everybody I know and everybody is writing back to me.

Well you forgot to do me that favor. I told you to send me one of your pictures cause I want to see you sooner then you think.

Well you know I'm not the same person I used to be. I change a lot. My personality change and my

body (?) change. I'm not the same person anymore.
Well it's time to say Good-bye for Now! Yours truly,
Love
Pito
PS Write back S O O N and send me the pictures
please.
L. O. V. E.
A. L. W. A. Y. S.

Dear Charmin. Hi! I hope when you get this letter you
are feeling fine. Well Charmin I don't know how to
said this or write you but I'm going to Kill Myself.
I'm tired of being in jail and I think I'm going to stay
in here for ever So that's why I'm going to do this
Charmin. I'm very sorry for doing it, but I got no
choice. I think I'm going to be in here for life. Charmin I want to go home. But the only home I'm going
to is to hell or heaven. That the home I'll be going to.
I must do this horrid thing. I'm very sorry. Yours
truly, *Pito*

Peace Charmin—I'm very sorry for Not writing you
any sooner than this. Charmin tell your Mother and
Father I said hello. I be going back to court next
week. I shall start trial. When you see my cousin Hector tell him to write me.

Charmin I want you to send me some of your pictures. I know you not going to send it. But I see that
you send Ricky one. He was going to bring it to
court. He told me in the picture you was standing by
a cat. So I be waiting for your picture when you
write back. And I hope it won't keep you three weeks
to write me back. Write me back when you receive
this letter. And send the picture please. Charmin

tell everybody I said hello. And tell the Girls I said to write me and send me a picture of them.

Charmin if I do COP-out to those ten years I will go upstate and I will be home in 1982. But if I do good up there I will be home in 1978 or 1979, But I'm not thinking about copping out yet. I'm running out of words So take care of yourself.

Love Always
Justice Allah   Charmin Always Remember this
     Pinto   Someone Always thinks of some one
                OLD days
                OLD times
                OLD friends
                forever

Peace Charmin

I am sitting in my cell looking out the window on a cold night thinking and wondering when will I be home again. Now I'm going to court every day. I'm in trial now and if I blow trial I will get 25 years to life and I don't think I can handle that much behind bars. And wont know how your going to feel about that. Charmin tell Ramon that I found out who drop a dime on me tell him it was Mrs. Velez and this lady name Dominguez. Charmin to tell you the truth I think you fucking up out there. You are having those new girls around Hoe avenue calling you King Kong that what I heard from a Guy in here that lives around there. Im not going to tell you no names and I heard that you was in his house you him and Ramon and you and them were drinking and you got drunk and Ramon pull your pants down and you had sex in front of the Guy. I'm not getting out of line by talking to you like this or I don't know to believe him or not. To tell you the truth I don't believe him cause I only believe what I see. And if you did it is your life. You do what you want.

Charmin I want you to do me a favor tell the Guys and the girls if they don't write After all this time for them Not to consider me as a friend no more. Cause if they speak to me when I'm out there why can't they write me. The same goes for Hector. If he don't write me for him not to consider me as a cousin no more. Charmin tell your Mother and Father I said hello— Charmin I hope you not mad at me for telling you what I did. Remember I don't believe what they tell me unless I see it. O.K. (Smile) cause I'm not mad or anything like it. Charmin you know those new girls around Hoe avenue. Well if you want to ask them to write me I know I don't know them yet But I want to see what kind of girls they are. Tell Kenny to write me. Charmin I'm running out of words so take care. Love, *Pito*.

UNDER—stand

Charmin—I want you to sit down and understand why I'm a 5 percenter.* When our people was in slavery over 400 years ago they used to pray for that Mystery God up in heaven they pray so that they be taking out of slavery and it never happened, so they never knew that they were God's and Queens Because some of them were Deaf-Dumb and Blind. That's why

---

* A sect formed in the 1960s by a former member of the Black Muslims. It is their philosophy that 85 per cent of the world are cattle, 10 per cent are devils and false prophets who mislead the cattle, and the remaining 5 per cent are the true and honest teachers who will eventually lead the 85 per cent to freedom. The Five Percenters are very active in prisons, where they recruit new members from among black inmates.

I'm here as my Duty to teach the uncivilized to be civilized thats why I'm God of the Universe, father of Civilization. You know a woman has Understanding and all they must get the Wisdom and Knowledge of herself. And for them to have Knowledge and Wisdom is a form what they must learn to deal against the white man (Devil) and by having that they would know how to take the Devil off the face of the planet Earth cause the Black Man Duty to Deal and to Deal against others is never ended. And by taking the Black Woman away from the Black Man, the Black Man won't have love peace and happiness and without that the Black Man won't be able to get along with any other But his own kind. See Charmin, you have to Be able to keep up with Today's present. Don't you know that the white Man is taking away all the Black Man and Black Woman jobs. Why because he realises that the Black people are going up so fast the only way he can stop us is by taking away our Jobs and making the prices for food go up and the only way they can survive is by stealing. And by them doing that they will go to jail and when we are all in Jail its like putting us back in slavery and that's when he will take over the planet earth. And your Black Woman can avoid that by giving Respect and you will get that Respect by all. That is why I'm Justice Allah, God of the Universe Father of Civilization here to Deal against the White Man for hes the one that thought of our people to eat the wrong food and trying to keep our people from living out their true culture.

Yes he's the one I'm going to take off the face of the planet earth. Hes the one I deal against every day. Yes me. He brought me to another country and I myself swam 9,000 miles to get back to my own country.

Yes, he fool our people telling them they will receive more gold for their labor. But did they receive more gold for their labor? *NO.* The only reason he got them because they were Deaf Dumb and Blind at that time. Now that they are living out their true culture he is trying to keep us in Jail. Yes, he got me in here physically but not mentally. My Mind is still in the streets and I can deal with my physical body and my mind to. Charmin if you don't have the understanding to give this to Preston Armstrong and tell him to build on it for you so you can understand it.

Smile Cause I love you
Pito

Peace Justice Allah
P.S. Write Back Soon

"Peace Charmin"

I hope when you receive this letter it finds you in the very best of health and as for me I'm fine. My trial is going good. I think I'll be back home soon.

Oh yeah Red Fox was out here Friday. He came out here to give us a little show.

So who is left around the Block nobody? Everybody seems to be going places or moving away. Tell Mom and Pop I said Hello and I send my Love. Charmin I need something for my head if you know what I mean. See if you can send me some Acid some paper acid all you have to do is put it on the back of the envelope. You can put it right where you close it at. If you can do that alright. So take care of yourself.

Love
Pito

PS. I will stay sweet just for you. (SMILE)

Charmin,

I guess you heard about me all right. I am NOT coming home in the near future. The trial found me *Guilty.* I will be in jail from 15 years to LIFE. Like I said before, I don't think I can handle that much time behind bars. I dont want to see my kid any more. I ask my woman not to bring him to jail where his Father is like a slave. Charmin—I'm full of HATE and it hurts. I know I will KILL Myself and maybe thats the only way. I want to get out of this skin. If I can't go home then I want to die and go to heaven or Hell. But not jail. Charmin you are a good and true friend. I'll never forget you no matter what happens.

Yours truly,
Pito

OLD days
OLD times
OLD friends
forever

Epilogue

The Mongols, the first gang to move into The Compound, no longer exist. Nor do the Storm Troopers or the Latin Diplomats. The Seven Immortals disintegrated and then reemerged, with new leaders and a new name—the Brothers and Sisters of the Revolution—suggesting a new purpose. Of the five gangs who lived in The Compound, only the Savage Nomads are still functioning and viable. Since the imprisonment of Black Bongo, there have been three subsequent presidents; the first was deposed, and the second was killed in a fight in a social club. The Savage Nomads and the Savage Skulls are still the two most powerful and violent gangs in the South Bronx.

Ed O'Rourke and Vito Moles estimate that anywhere from 50 to 70 per cent of the gang leaders of the early seventies are now either dead or awaiting trial, charged with a serious crime, and at least 20 per cent of their gangs' membership are dead or in jail. The two detectives still maintain their close rapport with all the gangs in the forty-square-mile area that comprises the Bronx—which in 1976 became the first borough of New York City in which whites are a minority. But, ironically, as gang problems mount, the city's fiscal crisis has reduced the borough's Gang Intelligence Unit from its peak of nine men in 1973 to only two today: Ed O'Rourke and Vito Moles.

How much longer gangs such as the Savage Skulls and Savage Nomads will continue to use the South Bronx as their base is anybody's guess, for the South Bronx, with its blocks of abandoned, burnt-out buildings, is rapidly becoming an urban ghost town. It has been estimated that its reconstruction would cost a minimum of $3 billion. Robert Moses, the city's master builder in years past, considers it beyond rebuilding, and thinks it should be leveled to the ground. The action is moving now into the West Bronx, where conditions are as turbulent as they were in the South Bronx in the early seventies, when organized street gangs first surfaced, the Forty-first Precinct there became known as Fort Apache, and, as I noted in the beginning of this story, *The New York Times* called it "a jungle stalked by fear, seized by rage." The fear and rage are still there but must feed on something and the South Bronx has been depleted. Now the Forty-fourth Precinct in the West Bronx is being called Jungle Habitat . . . the Savage Nomads and Savage Skulls have each established a division there . . . and the turf is ripe for producing new gangs as well as nuturing these established ones.

And so the cycle continues, as it is doing now in every major American city coast to coast.